THE
GREAT PEARL ROBBERY
OF 1913

" Cammi " Grizard.

THE GREAT
PEARL ROBBERY
OF 1913

▲

A RECORD OF FACT

▼

BY

CHRISTMAS HUMPHREYS

M.A., L.LB. (Cantab) of the Inner Temple,
Barrister-at-Law

LONDON
WILLIAM HEINEMANN LTD.

First published 1929

Printed in Great Britain
at The Windmill Press, Kingswood
Surrey

CONTENTS

PART ONE: THE STORY

I " CAMMI " GRIZARD, A MASTER CRIMINAL   I

II HATTON GARDEN AND THE FAMOUS PEARLS   23

III STOLEN!   46

IV THE SEARCH   65

V AMATEUR DETECTIVES ON THE TRAIL   84

VI HOT ON THE SCENT   108

VII THE TRAP   128

VIII ARRESTED!   150

IX BOW STREET   167

PART TWO

X THE TRIAL   189

XI THE TRIAL (CONTINUED)   207

XII THE CASE FOR THE DEFENCE   229

XIII SUMMING UP AND VERDICT   255

XIV APPEAL AND EPILOGUE   279

LIST OF ILLUSTRATIONS

" CAMMI " GRIZARD   *Frontispiece*

PLAN OF HATTON GARDEN, SHOWING NO. 88, THE
GLOBE P. H., AND THE VIENNA RESTAURANT
(THE " FLEA-PIT ")   *pp* 30

THE LATE MR. MAX MAYER, THE OWNER OF THE
PEARLS   36

COPY OF THE REWARD BILL   56

CUTTING OF THE " DAILY CHRONICLE " OF JULY
18TH, 1913   68

A PHOTOGRAPH REDUCED IN SIZE OF THE £150,000
NECKLACE AND THE MATCHBOX   110

MR. SAMUEL BRANDSTATTER AND EX-SUPERINTEN-
DENT LEACH LEAVING BOW STREET POLICE
COURT   168

THE LATE SIR RICHARD MUIR, THE HON MR. JUSTICE
HUMPHREYS   180

THE UNBROKEN SEALS AT ONE END OF THE BOX   210

THE NINE FORGED SEALS AT THE OTHER END OF
THE BOX   210

THE " BACK SHEET " OF MR. JUSTICE HUMPHREYS'
BRIEF AT THE TRIAL   258

" JIM " LOCKETT, SIMON SILVERMAN AND LEISER
GUTWIRTH   288

PREFACE

As modern life gets more and more uninteresting,
fiction tends to supply the deficiencies of fact. Yet
the ancient saying to the proof of which this book is
dedicated is as true to-day as when the phrase was
first expressed. Truth is still stranger than fiction.
The market is satiated with " thrilling " fiction of all
kinds, and the point of saturation being reached, the
demand for a new form of entertainment brought
about the supply. First, we had numerous " famous,"
" notable " or " remarkable " trials, accurate records
of fact no doubt, but cast in legal as distinct from,
nay, as opposed to popular form. Only the keenest
" criminologists," whoever they may be, desire to
read through hundreds of pages of a shorthand
note. Secondly, by way of a much-needed set off
to this rigid form, appeared innumerable Memoirs
and Biographies of those who remembered cases
which at the time were *causes célèbres*. Such
reminiscences, however, only record the briefest outline of each story, and so the third variety was born.
This is the story of *soi-disant* " fact " which has,
however, on its way to the public passed through the
fertile imagination of its Editor, and is thus at the
best a story of fiction based on a record of fact.

The present writer, firm in his belief that interesting fact is more acceptable to certain minds than the
most " thrilling " fiction, presents herewith a fourth

suggestion as an experiment. The following pages are neither fiction, a dry reproduction of the shorthand note of a trial, nor highly coloured " fact," but an honest account of actual, and comparatively recent, happenings. In order to ensure the maximum of accuracy, the proofs of the book have been read and passed by representatives of those concerned. Mr. Justice Humphreys, who was Junior Treasury Counsel at the trial, has spoken in his Foreword to his knowledge of both facts and law; Mr. Percy Mayer, son of the owner of the famous necklace, has passed as substantially correct the pages which relate to pearls and the Hatton Garden trade; responsible officials in the General Post Office have read and corrected passages which deal with the conduct of their own officials, while all the facts obtained from the Police have been both soberly and carefully put down.

Needless to say, in spite of these efforts to maintain the highest accuracy, errors of detail will appear, and the writer can only apologise to those who knew the facts first hand for such discrepancies.

These pages also represent an effort to disprove the theory that the general public will not read descriptions of pure law. In this respect the book is a compromise between the need of accurately reporting the trial for the benefit of those who wish to file it among its kind, and of telling a readable story for the benefit of those who ask no more. At the same time I have tried, having faith in my contention, to present the technical aspects of the trial in popular form, presuming nothing of my readers save a willingness to be conducted into mental " pastures new."

Preface

The story as such will be found to contain all the ingredients of the best " detective-thriller " save the heroine who, fortunately, seldom figures in real life. The pursuit of criminals is generally complicated enough without the introduction of " feminine-interest " and " sex-appeal "!

We have, however, the most famous necklace in the world, of fabulous value, stolen by the greatest criminal organiser of his day in that home of wealth and mystery, Hatton Garden. The Police arrive and are duly baffled. Enter a young pair of amateur detectives in search of the £10,000 reward. They trace the necklace and the thieves and then invoke the Underwriters and their own detectives to their aid. Enter the disguised " buyer " of the stolen property specially brought from Paris for the purpose, whereupon a wholesale game of bluff and counter-bluff begins. The climax comes when the necklace, as a whole, is run to earth and Scotland Yard is let loose on the trail. Plots and counter-plots. Then the trap is prepared, but several times in vain. Finally . . . the story's ending which no fair reviewer would reveal, save to assure his readers that virtue is, in fact, triumphant and that the heroes once more win.

What more could the most fastidious desire?

One thing remains before the play begins, to render thanks where thanks are due.

They are due, and freely offered, to the Director of Public Prosecutions, Sir Archibald Bodkin, K.C.B., for the loan of the official papers of the trial. To Mr. Norman Kendal, Assistant Commissioner at Scotland Yard, for enabling me to assure myself of the accuracy of certain facts. To the Hon. Mr. Justice Humphreys for his Foreword and his valuable revision of the facts and law presented in this story. To Mr. M. B. Spanier for the valuable detail which his vivid memory has supplied. To Mr. Mayer, Superintendent Cornish, ex-Superintendent Leach and Mr. S. T. Felstead for their unfailing courtesy and help, and to others too innumerable to mention, but whose help is none the less appreciated to the full. Finally, to my wife for that painfully frank criticism which only such can give, and for untiring assistance in correcting proofs.

Which being said, I say: " Ring up the curtain "!

1, *Temple Gardens,*
  Temple, E.C.4.

July, 1929.

FOREWORD

By the Hon. Mr. Justice Humphreys

WHEN I was invited some years ago to take part in a debate upon the subject " Is Truth stranger than Fiction? ", I related the story of the loss and recovery of Max Mayer's pearls, as being at least as dramatic as anything to be found in fiction. Reading the story again in these pages, it seems to me to have lost nothing in the telling. Verbatim reports of criminal trials are dull things to read. A great part of the evidence consists in the proof of matters not in dispute while an effective cross-examination, to be appreciated, must in the majority of cases be heard and not merely read. For this reason I think the author of this book is to be congratulated upon his decision to tell his tale in " novel " form. The fascinating interest of the case lay, not in the trial of the accused men, but in the inconsistencies and apparent contradictions in the evidence as to when and where the crime was committed, and in the plotting and counter-plotting of the redoubtable Grizard on the one hand, and of Mr. Price and his assistants on the other. In one respect the Great Pearl Robbery was remarkably like a modern detective story, in that the official police had very little to do with the elucidation of the mystery.

What was to those engaged in the case the most remarkable because unexplained incident, remains apparently an unsolved enigma. What is the explanation of the throwing away of the match-box containing the necklace? Did the person, obviously an accomplice, who dropped the box intend merely to get rid of an embarrassing piece of loot, or was the intention that it should be picked by a confederate? If the latter alternative is preferred, why adopt such an odd method of transferring the stolen property? What advantage could be expected to accrue to the men who were already in custody from this method of disposing of the pearls? Their safe return to Max Mayer, easily accomplished through the post, might conceivably have been pleaded in mitigation of punishment, but the action of the person who dropped the match-box in the gutter, where the pearls might well have been broken by a passing vehicle, was then, and according to the author still remains, " one of those things that no feller can understand."

The legal argument which loomed largely in the actual trial was ingenious but unsound. Had the alternatives, larceny in England or larceny in France, been ordered by the Judge to be tried separately, the Prosecution would certainly have elected to put before the Jury in the first place those Counts of the Indictment which stated the facts as they believed them to be, namely those alleging the larceny to have taken place in England, and the verdict of the Jury shows that the result would have been the same. The suggestion, however, that the accused were embarrassed by the form of the Indictment was not one which stood much chance of success before a Judge of the great experience and profound common sense of Mr. Justice A. T. Lawrence.

The author has suggested to me that I should vouch for the accuracy of his facts and law. I can only say that I have not discovered any mis-statement of fact in the book, while, as to the law, it is notorious that learned Counsel know much more of this subject than any mere Judge.

TRAVERS HUMPHREYS.

PART ONE

THE STORY

CHAPTER I

" CAMMI " GRIZARD, A MASTER CRIMINAL

GREAT criminals are few and far between, but Joseph Grizard was unquestionably one of them. On the other hand, it is pointed out that he was not one of the greatest criminals, for the greatest are never caught. He is a clever man who manages for years to live upon the proceeds of his criminal propensities before being laid by the heels; he is cleverer who lives in such a way and dies an " honest " man, officially unknown to Scotland Yard, but he is cleverest of all whose depredations are so brilliantly conceived that none can call him criminal, in that no one knows his secret means of livelihood. How many of the latter live contentedly within our midst no Officer of Scotland Yard can say, and from the public point of view, the motto seems to apply: " Where ignorance is bliss, 'tis folly to be wise."

Of those who are known as criminals much is written and being written by self-styled " criminologists," whose knowledge of the subject ranges from just a little to nothing at all, but certain classifications of the genus " criminal " are matters of common sense. Clearly, there is a broad division between the professional and the occasional criminal,

I

the man who lives by crime and the man who looks upon it as an interesting and highly lucrative hobby to be practised over and above his honest work. Another division occurs between those whose crimes are frankly criminal, and whose only hope of freedom lies in not being caught, and those who live by forms of crime which need a fraudulent intent, and which can always be defended when the time comes by interminable explanations showing that their motives were unrivalled by the saints of old. For example, a " snatch thief " must rely upon his heels, but a fraudulent bankrupt can cloak his efforts in delightful casuistry, a cloak through which the penetrating eyes of English juries fortunately see without much difficulty.

All these classifications, however, have another in common, that when several men are working on the " job," some will follow and some will lead. It may be said at once that " Cammi," the " hero " of this story, if the unhappy life and painful death of a dangerous criminal can earn for him that title, was a professional criminal in the sense that his legitimate business was negligible, and he was one who always worked " behind the scenes." In addition he was a born leader, or rather organiser, of men.

This raises the question of intelligence. Popular fiction makes the criminal a man of brilliant though misguided intellect, of iron will and perfect self-control, to be stopped by nothing in achieving his nefarious end. The answer is that criminals are human beings, and as such differ as widely, but, as only those whose lives are spent in the machinery of human justice know, the average criminal is a man who has tried in vain to make an honest living, and has found in crime the obvious " way out." The intelligence of these, the failures in life's handicap, is naturally low, and their crimes are as elementary as their minds. But among them, often organising and controlling them, are those who are the buccaneers and highwaymen of old, men, and sometimes women, to whom the paths of honesty are unattractive compared with the swaggering, dangerous, glorious uncertainty of the " open road." Poor things! They speak of freedom from restraint, yet move with halters round their necks, and though in popular imagination they are rich for the asking and without the need of work, it is true, and not so strange, that the great majority of them die in miserable, uncared-for poverty.

Of late years the craving for stories about crime and the lives of by-gone criminals has done much harm, and yet is doing good. Slowly but surely the false, yet attractive mask of " glory " and " romance " is peeling off, and criminals are seen for what they are, a congregation of unhappy, miserable men, deserving more of sympathy and understanding than the scorn of the self-righteous or the adulation of foolish, feeble minds. Yet stories of crime and its unmasking will ever be popular, for, like the Mystery Dramas of the Middle Ages, they depict the age-long conflict between Right and Wrong and the final victory of all that human instinct tells one is the right.

Judged by such a standard the following tale is moral to a high degree. The villains steal the famous pearls, the " heroes of the ' Yard ' " are duly baffled, amateur assistance comes from unexpected quarters and, after plots and counter-plots galore, the villains are captured and the pearls restored, amidst the plaudits of the multitude, to the rejoicing owner. What more could the most fastidious desire?

Let us, then, turn to the villains of the piece, and first to the master-criminal.

Grizard was much more than a famous " fence," though exactly how much more will never be known. In the words of ex-Superintendent Leach, he was " essentially a putter-up," that is, an organiser of crimes which he carried out through carefully trained subordinates. The public little realise with what detailed care the more substantial burglaries and similar crimes are carried out. A man like Grizard is in the position of a theatrical producer. Having chosen his " scene " he has to " cast " the drama to be played, and he may have considerable difficulty in finding just the right men. Even as a certain individual wanted by a producer may be already engaged elsewhere, so may the " star " cracksman required for a delicate robbery be staying with His Majesty for a while—on Dartmoor. Months are sometimes spent in surveying the ground and mapping out the difficulties, and money has to be found to pay for men who may be staying weeks on end in a small hotel in the country while they are planning how to rob the local bank. Then perhaps transport has to be arranged as well as signals, decoys and the all-important " get-away." Finally, the means of " smashing " the booty is elaborately worked-out. Speed is everything, and the exact terms of division of the spoil and the price at which the " fence " will buy it from his trained subordinates is all prepared beforehand. If it be said that the part of the receiver is a cowardly one, the answer is that from the point of view of physical danger it is, but in crime as elsewhere brains will ever dominate mere brawn, and the " putter-up " is like a General on the battlefield, commanding operations which he cannot see. Moreover, as will be subsequently seen, it is one thing to buy for a seemingly small price the proceeds of a burglary, quite another to resell at a profit goods for which the Police of Europe are keenly on the watch.

However that may be, Grizard was no burglar, but in Leach's words, " essentially a putter-up," and Leach, if anyone, should know. Ex-Superintendent Alfred Leach knew " Cammi " as only a detective of long experience can know the principal criminals in his area. For ten years he was the Inspector in charge of the Hatton Garden division, in which the vast proportion of Cammi's " jobs " were planned. In 1908, however, his health broke down and he retired. He soon grew tired of doing nothing, and obtained occasional employment among Underwriters at Lloyd's as a private detective. Though working as a " freelance " detective, he worked mostly for the firm of Price and Gibbs, who called in his aid in the famous Pearl Robbery. Hence his appearance in these pages as a famous detective once more on the trail.

At the risk of wandering away from Grizard and his underlings, there is one story of this grand old man—he is now seventy-four—which must be placed on record.

The story will go down to history as the case of " arresting a Public House "! It was one autumn in the early 'nineties, and burglaries were rife all over London. Information in the hands of the Police made it almost certain that the actual burglars lived in, and brought their spoil to a certain neighbourhood, then in the charge of Mr. Leach. The rumour grew that the arch-receiver was a certain Harry Clarke, the licensee of a public-house in the City Road. Now burglars at the time in question were apt to work in cliques, dividing London into definite areas for their unlawful raids. Having left their loot at the public-house, they would return to their hunting-ground in pony-carts and on bicycles, which were the predecessors of the modern car for evading the police. It was difficult to watch the public-house without being recognised, so an informer was presented with an aged and unloaded revolver by Sergeant Leach and sent into the house with money to spend. He reported that the bar was a den of thieves, and described the men. To check his evidence a second informer was sent in, who described the self-same men, and included a certain unknown desperado who at times would murderously flourish a gun! Satisfied that the two men did not know one another, and yet gave the same particulars, the sergeant got to work.

One Sunday morning he watched the carts and bicycles go off, and returned that night with three of his men. " If anyone ' tumbles ' us," he said, " rush the pub. and lock the doors inside." After a while two women came out, and were followed by one of the officers. They seemed to recognise him and doubled back to cover. Leach and his men raced after them and into the bar, where a glorious " roughhouse " ensued. Women screamed and fainted, and

6

a rush was made for the doors. Clarke himself escaped by the roof and swam the canal to safety, while Leach, who entered as the aggressor, found himself behind the bar with an angry mob of well-known criminals out-numbering his men by four to one, " Charlie the Postman," " German Jack " and other delightful characters fiercely to the fore. With great presence of mind he addressed his audience. " Now, now," he said. " I came for Harry Clarke, not you, and I've lost him. Well, I must get him another time. Meanwhile let's have a drink and be friends again." Drinks were produced all round and the tension was correspondingly relaxed. When occasion offered Leach announced that he would see that the coast was clear of his men and let the others go. He left the building before any could say him nay, sent the first man he saw to Old Street Police Station for reinforcements, and within seven minutes had, as he said, " a regiment " of police on hand! Then, and far too late, the inmates of the bar appreciated how they had been fooled, as the public-house in its entirety was arrested by his men! The innocents were allowed to depart, the rest, consisting of eight burglars and the staff of the public-house, were removed to the nearest cells. On searching the premises, two van-loads of stolen property were found, while at the trial which followed no less than ninety-six cases of burglary were brought home to the men in the dock. Having heard the records of the men before him, the learned Judge wasted no time on speeches. " You're a mischievous lot of black-guards," he said. " Ten years . . . ten years . . . ten years . . . ! "

Ex-Superintendent Leach's son seems to have inherited his father's ability. For sheer cheek the following story is second to none. " Young Leach," as he will probably be always known, was out to arrest a receiver in a jeweller's shop in Goswell Road. On arriving there he detained the man he wanted, as also the man from whom he was purchasing some highly questionable jewellery. On the spur of the moment he made his men take the two of them into the little office at the back and keep them there. Taking the shopman's apron and placing it on himself, he took his place behind the counter and waited for flies to walk into his trap. They came. One after another, on that Saturday night, they arrived with their ill-gotten gains, and one by one the " new assistant " glanced at the property, arrested the astonished burglar and sent him handcuffed into the office to join the rest. Four were thus arrested, booty in hand, before a fifth, suspicious of the " assistant," gazed at him and then, in a flash, bolted for safety with a yell for all the neighbourhood: " My God, it's Leach!"

To return, however, to the subject of this story, Grizard was a London Jew, born in 1867. Of middle height and somewhat portly build, his impudence and swaggering self-assurance served to create a personality which dominated the smaller fry who hung about the " Garden," and turned them when required into willing, if not able, tools. To create the impression of settled opulence he invariably appeared with an enormous cigar beneath his blonde moustache or held in the diamond-studded hand with which he waved away objections to his flow of arrogance. More than once, while lounging among

8

his "customers" in the public-house outside which he was usually to be found, he noticed Leach among the crowd, and it was typical of the man that he at once acclaimed him as a trusted friend. "A cigar and a drink for Mr. Leach, please!" he would shout on seeing him, and the other's curt refusal in no way damped his self-esteem. He was always theatrical among his cronies and before the police, but he had at least one virtue rightly associated with the theatre —generosity. Not only would he help such friends as came to grief at the hands of Scotland Yard, when they returned from prison, but he would help their wives and children while they were away. Crime was to him a sporting pastime, and he never sought to seduce an honest man into his own nefarious ways. On the contrary, he more than once found honest work for those who were unable to find it for themselves.

Another of his virtues, rare among receivers, was unswerving loyalty to those who served him well. His word was his bond, and no one ever complained they were not paid what had been promised them. Presumably for this reason no one of his tools was ever persuaded to give their "Chief" away, though more than once considerable pressure was put upon men in custody to turn "King's Evidence" against the master criminal. The proof that crime was to him a sport lies in the fact that long after he was a comparatively wealthy man he preferred to continue "trading" rather than settle down. Again and again his less disreputable friends attempted to persuade him to "run straight," but all in vain.

His self-conceit was pitiful. He would enter a

public-house, announce in his noisy way that he had " just made £50," and call for drinks all round.

In the words of a well-known lapidary who has carried on his trade near Hatton Garden for twenty years, " his voice betrayed the man " and, as is usual with his type, he was impervious to the natural dislike which his boastful manner produced in the honest traders in his area. " Like so many criminals," said the same authority, " he was a great man with a twist in his character which made him prefer to go crooked where he might go straight." As was pointed out above, so long as the pirate element in man is uncontrolled, or, as modern psychologists would say, " unsublimated " into useful channels, so long will certain clever men run counter to the whole community, until restrained by force or banished from their midst.

But the boastful braggart of the " Garden " was a different man when seated with his chosen underlings in a common rendezvous. Here, the man of action became paramount, the cool, scheming brain which left no detail overlooked and knew the worth of everything. None but a very clever man could have carried on his trade beneath the eyes of the police and yet concealed from them the evidence upon which a conviction could be obtained. Scotland Yard is not given to superlatives, and the following summary of the man, contained in the police report prepared immediately after the arrest, not only betrays a grudging admiration for his cleverness, but crowns him king of the receivers' underworld.

" The prisoner Grizard is a well-known receiver, commonly called ' Cammie ' or ' Kemmi.' He is a diamond merchant by trade, but has no established business premises. He does undoubtedly do a little business, but the greater portion of his time is taken up by organising crimes, and buying and disposing of stolen property. Much has been heard of him during the past fifteen years as having been connected with many serious crimes. A large number of statements made by prisoners are in our possession showing that they have disposed of their property to him, but unfortunately we have been unable to prosecute him for lack of corroborative evidence.

" I have no hesitation whatever in saying that for a number of years past he has been the most notorious receiver of stolen property in this country."

His operations were therefore twofold, as an organiser of crime and as a receiver of the proceeds of the robberies. Two examples may be mentioned of crimes in which, though all unseen, he was the controlling brain.

The first was the case of two men, Higgins and Grimshaw, charged at the London Sessions for a brilliant jewel robbery at the Café Monico. Four years previous to the events of this story, in 1909, a French jewel dealer, by name Frederick Goldschmidt, arrived in London to do business in connection with his trade. He therefore had with him precious stones to the value of some £60,000. " Cammi " heard of this and at once put spies upon his track. He was followed and watched for weeks on end until his habits in connection with his precious burden were fully known. Needless to say, he gave the robber the minimum of opportunity, for he never let the bag of jewels leave his person by day or night.

11

Higgins and Grimshaw, however, two notorious thieves, noticed one occasion at least when the jeweller had to leave his bag unguarded—when he washed his hands. He was accordingly followed to the Café Monico, where he went to wash his hands. Having filled the basin he placed his precious bag beside it and reached out for the soap. A flash of an arm, a shoulder jerked against his to throw him off his balance, and the bag was gone. His rush from the room was " accidentally " barred by a confederate, and the " job " was done. A hue and cry was raised, and the thieves were duly caught—while " Cammi " was quietly examining the jewels upon his table at home.

The police knew perfectly well that Grizard was the " putter-up," but had no proof. Mr. Richard Muir, later Sir Richard Muir, appeared at the trial for the police, and worked untiringly in the hopes that one of the men would turn King's evidence against their hidden " Chief," but loyalty and kindliness will breed their like even in London's underworld, and both men preferred to go to penal servitude rather than give him away.

A little while later Muir made a second attempt to lay the elusive " Cammi " by the heels, but equally in vain. In this case the personal element was involved, for the victim was an old friend of Sir Richard's, Mr. Vaughan Morgan, son of Sir Walter Vaughan Morgan, the City Alderman. Mr. Morgan had a butler, Frank Ellis by name, at his house in Carlton House Terrace, who as a young man had entered his employ in 1904. In 1911 he left of his own accord and set up as a bookmaker in Regent

Street. Shortly before he left, his master asked him to find a footman for the household, and Ellis secured through an agency a man named Robinson. During the three weeks they were in the house together, Robinson had learnt to bet with Ellis, and continued to do so after Ellis had left. About this time the latter, to his great misfortune, got to know one William Bangham, a notorious jewel thief and a tool of Grizard's. In November, 1911, Ellis' premises were raided by the police, and he was subsequently heavily fined for offences against the law. As his business was going none too well, this fine was a serious blow, and the path of dishonesty invited him. He accordingly sent for Robinson the next time he was free and asked him to let him into the house one night in order that he might steal his master's jewellery. He explained that the question of the receiver was all arranged and other details planned. Robinson naturally demurred, but being a weakling finally fell to the other's blandishments. A night was chosen when the unfaithful servant was alone in the house with the maids, and at midnight Bangham and Ellis were let in. The two men opened the owner's drawers with a master key and found the keys of the safe, Robinson, cold with fright at his own treachery, keeping guard at the door. The safe was then unlocked and its contents swiftly valued. Bangham wanted to take the jewellery that night, but acceded to Robinson's request that it be left until more people were in the house, as under the circumstances the blame would certainly fall on the man who had been left in charge. Many meetings took place, " Cammi " always speaking through his underlings, and never appearing in person. On the night of Mr. Morgan's return, the burglary took place exactly as arranged. Drawers were forced and windows quietly broken to give the impression of a genuine burglary, while Robinson, a terribly apt pupil, went upstairs to collect from his master's dressing-room a further collection of valuables. Finally the two professionals, for so had Ellis become, went off, and Robinson retired to bed. In the morning the " burglary " was discovered by a maid, and Robinson, ironically, was instructed by his master to send for the police. Inspector Tappenden and Sergeant West arrived at once, and it is to their credit that they soon dismissed the burglary suggestion and began to inquire about the present and previous employees in the house. The description of Ellis so exactly tallied with the man who had been seen of late with Bangham and the still more famous Grizard that it was only a matter of time before his association with Robinson came to light and the game was up. Robinson, when arrested suddenly, confessed the whole of his delinquency, and after due consideration was discharged in order that he might incriminate his far more dangerous confederate.

At the trial, Muir did his best to implicate the " putter-up," and in spite of Alfred Tobin's violent protests for the defence that such association was irrelevant, proved beyond doubt that " Cammi " was the brains behind the robbery. He could, however, do no more, and when Ellis went to twenty-one months' hard labour he left his principal free.

Stories of " Cammi " might be multiplied indefinitely, but this volume is reserved for an account of his greatest exploit in the detail which it deserves. There is one story, however, which cannot be omitted, for it shows the consummate coolness of the man, and helps to explain why he was never arrested before.

It was after the clever robbery by Higgins, the Hatton Garden butcher, and Grimshaw, the ex-jockey, of Mr. Goldschmidt's jewellery, and " Cammi " was negotiating for the sale of the jewels so obtained. One night he invited three potential buyers to dinner at his house in Dalston, after which the necklace would be auctioned by the delighted criminal. Suddenly there came a ring at the front door bell and thunderous knocking on the door. The four men looked at one another. The maid answered the door, and from the the dining-room the strained ears of the diners heard the well-known voice of Chief Inspector Ward. As the door of the dining-room opened Grizard made a swift movement with his hand and sat back in his chair. The inspector apologised for his intrusion, but explained that he had a warrant to search the house for the stolen jewellery. Grizard, with equal courtesy, explained that Ward and his men were at liberty to do so, and the search began. Hour after hour the four conspirators sat silent under the scrutiny of one of the Inspector's men. Finally the men themselves were searched, and the officers, baffled in their hopes of finding evidence, retired disconsolate. At the time of their entry the dinner had got no further than the soup, which was green pea. Without a word " Cammi " drank up the tepid beverage and then removed from the bottom of it—the

15

diamond necklace, where it had lain all the time! The necklace was duly washed and the sale proceeded.

In the course of his career the great man must have handled tremendous sums of money. He had no bank account in his own name, but carried about on his person enormous sums in cash. There was hardly a robbery of any size in London in which he did not handle at least a proportion of the goods obtained, and he knew and was trusted by the biggest Continental dealers in stolen property. In this way jewels of enormous worth were sold for prices little short of market value, and when it is remembered that they had been bought by Grizard from the actual thieves for the proverbial song, it is not surprising that he died a wealthy man. It is true that his will was passed for probate at £47, but it is an open secret that his family proceeded to collect enormous sums of money, which were distributed in various safe deposits and the like in London and the provinces.

Grizard had a triple personality, but it is doubtful if he really enjoyed any one of them. Whether as the respectable family man in Dalston, with the clever head and " genteel " collar and tie, or as the boastful, swaggering salesman of the " Garden," or as the cool and brilliant organiser of other's robberies, he never lived outside the shadow of the watching, waiting police, and when he finally made his one mistake the hands of the law were all too ready to receive the man who had defied them so successfully.

We have said that Grizard worked through innumerable human instruments. The chief of these was James Lockett. Lockett was the burglar, a big,

16

powerful man, and one who succeeded in arousing at
least in Mr. Leach's breast a feeling of ungrudging
admiration. "Lockett, the lion-hearted—the man
who never knew fear," was his description, and the
ex-Superintendent knew his man.

A man of many aliases, his first conviction of any
consequence was at the Liverpool Assizes in 1906.
On that occasion he was concerned with three
associates bearing the picturesque names of " Shirtie
Bob," " Red Bob " and " Long Almond " in an
attempt to rob a jeweller's traveller of his stock.
They shadowed this man, Hutchinson, and gradually
learnt his ways. Finally, they scraped an acquaint-
ance with him under pretext of his weakness for a
bet, and learnt that he was shortly bound for Liverpool. They followed him to his hotel, and found that
he used to leave the jewellery locked up in his room,
taking the key of the room with him to the lounge
downstairs where he would write his business letters.

Lockett and " Long Almond " took the room next
door and perfected their plans. At the appointed
time " Shirtie," with his eye on the unsuspecting
Hutchinson, saw him finish his letters and leave the
hotel. From his position in the lounge he raised
his hat, and " Red Bob," who was in the street,
immediately raised his. Lockett and " Long
Almond," watching from their window, saw the
signal and knew that their man had gone. The
coast was clear, and they entered the traveller's
room. Fate was, however, against them. Hardly
had they got possession of the jewels when the door
opened and Hutchinson walked in. He had forgotten something and had suddenly returned. The

watchers outside had attempted to attract the burglars' attention to the traveller's change of plans, but they were busy in the room and all unheeding of the signals frantically given them. Lockett was standing with the jewels in his hands, so " innocent " explanations were out of place. He attempted to pass the astonished traveller, but the latter was a plucky defender of his master's property. In the words of Ex-Superintendent Leach, " the devil of a fight ensued," but finally, with considerable assistance, the two men were subdued. Lockett was sentenced to five years' penal servitude and " Long Almond," with a far worse record behind him, to ten.

Three and a half years later Lockett was released, but made little attempt to secure an honest livelihood. In the words of the police report: " It is said that he has an interest in a motor-car business at Finchley and a cinematograph palace at Hendon, which is believed to be true. He does not, however, spend much of his time in these concerns, and does no other work. During the winter of 1911 and 1912 there were a series of heavy burglaries at West End jewellers' establishments, and enquiries satisfied us beyond doubt that Lockett was the ringleader of a well-organised gang of daring criminals."

It is not difficult to imagine who received the proceeds of these robberies. On the other hand Inspector Ward, who drafted the report from which quotation is being made, seems to have exaggerated the organising ability of Lockett, who was really the able lieutenant of a clever " C.-in-C." No one, however, will quarrel with the report when he is described as " one of the most daring and expert criminals of his day," and the following words seem to show that he found it lucrative.

" The house at Golders Green where he lives is his own property, he having purchased it two and a half years ago with the proceeds of a heavy larceny in Birmingham. The house is well furnished and he owns a motor-car."

By way of illustrating the care with which these robberies are planned, and the fact that being planned to such perfection they must, when begun, be carried through, the following story may be told.

It was the day of the St. Leger, some thirty years ago, when " Jimmy " and " Red Bob " were youngsters at the game. Inspector Leach was standing in a scent shop in the " Garden " talking to the proprietor about the race. Across the road, the two young criminals had slipped into an all-but deserted office, whence the owner, a jeweller, had been neatly decoyed, when they saw the Inspector across the road. It was too late to go back, so they carried on " according to plan " with their enemy chatting away in sight of them! The wretched caretaker was duly chloroformed and bound, the safe wrenched open and the jewels pocketed. Blowing a kiss to their arch-enemy they slipped out with their booty and proceeded, in the language of our Transatlantic cousins, to " leak out of the landscape "! Leach, to his credit, tells the story against himself.

That Grizard and Lockett worked together as a dangerous combination of brains and executive ability is demonstrated by more than popular belief amongst the police and the criminal underworld, for the documents which record the police investigations at the time

include statements by officers who actually witnessed
meetings of these two men with each other and with
Silverman and Gutwirth months before this greatest
of their plans was materialised into action on July
16th, 1913.

For example, Grizard was observed at twelve noon
on the 11th of March of that year outside Henekey's
Wine House in High Holborn, where he waited aim-
lessly for half an hour. At 12.30 he set off in the
direction of St. Paul's Churchyard, where he waited
outside Short's Wine House until Lockett and two
men, whom the officer did not know, arrived. In the
words of the report: " They all stood together for a
few minutes, and subsequently entered and remained
there about an hour, then left. I followed them to
Oxford Circus, where after a consultation, they
parted. Lockett and a man unknown to me
went along Regent Street to Conduit Street,
where they loitered for about fifteen minutes outside Messrs. Austin and Williams, jewellers, and
afterwards rejoined the other two men. After a few
minutes' conversation Lockett, Grizard and the other
man went off in the direction of the Bank. I followed
the fourth man to Chapel Street, W."

The following day they were seen again, this time
at Charing Cross Station, where Lockett and Grizard
were seen in conversation with a third man. They
were kept under observation for three whole hours,
in the course of which they did nothing except have
light refreshment in a Lyons's Restaurant. They
parted at 5 p.m. What was their game? For whom
or what were they waiting? Or was the station
merely a convenient rendezvous for discussing

future " operations " on some inoffensive person's jewellery?

Apparently their conversation had something to do with the station, for on the following day the Austrian Jew already mentioned, Simon Silverman, was seen at the station with one of the men who had been seen with Lockett and Grizard on a previous occasion. The stranger, after a parting word from Silverman, left by the two o'clock train for Paris.

The purpose of these elaborate and mysterious movements has never been disclosed. Nor was Gutwirth the innocent diamond broker he would have the world believe. No man in the trade did business with " Cammi " in ignorance of his true identity, and on the 17th of May, just two months before the robbery, he was seen in the afternoon at the old Oxford Music Hall. The officer watching spoke to him and Gutwirth cheerfully admitted he was waiting for Grizard. For what purpose? To discuss the time of day?

Of the other two men who figured in the crime about to be unfolded, little need here be said. Both were Austrian Jews, and neither had been previously convicted in this country. Silverman had an office in Hatton Garden, where he traded as a diamond broker, and lived with his mother and sister at Bow. An associate of thieves, he was a friend of Lockett's and a tool of Grizard's. Those who knew him in Hatton Garden described him as a greasy, always smiling, little hunch-backed Jew. He was always apologetic and polite to everyone, too much so for the blunt and honest English mind, and none too popular. Perhaps such curious transactions as the following did not increase the respect of those who only knew him as an apparently honest man.

A certain firm of jewellers sold a ruby for £58. Nine months later Silverman, who had in some way got possession of it, offered it to another firm for £18. He seemed content with this sum, so it is left to the imagination to suggest the sum for which he must have bought it, and if a stone worth £58 is sold for a profit at £18, can it be come by honestly?

Leisir Gutwirth was an obvious foreigner, and in the opinion of those who knew him in Hatton Garden, the most unpleasant personality of the four. He was known to the police as a suspected receiver of stolen property, but his character comes out so well in the story about to be described that nothing need be said of it in advance. Unlike the finest type of criminal, he played for himself alone and could be trusted by none. It was a flaw in Grizard's judgment that he was ever chosen for the task he so disgracefully performed . . . but we anticipate.

CHAPTER II

HATTON GARDEN AND THE FAMOUS PEARLS

HATTON GARDEN, the centre of the London market for diamonds, pearls, and precious stones, is to the general public a land of mystery. The name by which it is known among the inhabitants of the area in which it lies, just north of Holborn Circus, betrays its history, for the " Garden " is indeed the one-time garden of the Bishops of Ely, belonging to their residence in Ely Place nearby. The rapacious Queen Elizabeth, however, of glorious fame, removed it from their possession on some trifling excuse, in order to give it to her favourite of the moment, one Kit Gratton, in consideration for his services upon some private mission of her own. Hatton Garden to-day, like the one-time Covent Garden, now of opera and vegetable fame, has long since passed into the hands of commerce, though the respective commodities on sale therein are as far apart as cabbages and pearls.

To the casual eye the " Garden " is a dull and unpretentious street of mid-Victorian houses, mostly converted into offices, with shops on the ground floor level. Certainly there is nothing to show that the somewhat depressing outer walls conceal a series of Aladdin's Caves, in which are to be found not only precious stones of every hue, but diamonds worth an Emperor's ransom and enormous pearls as large as

23

the marbles on a schoolroom floor. There is probably greater value of unmounted " stones " behind the walls of Hatton Garden than in any other street in London, but the number and size of the safes in which the jewels are kept, and the intricacy of the various burglar alarms is at least commensurate.

Exactly why this area should have become the acknowledged centre for the jewel trade has never been discovered, for though the history of the City of London shows how industries were localised for general convenience, Hatton Garden is much further West than any of the others, and dissociated from the home of the gold and silversmiths on the East side of St. Paul's. However that may be, this home of jewellery has kept up, though for a different reason, the practice of conducting a large proportion of its trade in the street itself, in preference to the offices and shops which line the length of it on either side. Just as the average old-established London market consists of provision shops and the like abutting upon a pavement, on the other side of which are a line of barrows which display precisely similar goods of a lower class, so the inhabitants of Hatton Garden are divided into those who trade in offices and those who are content with the open air. The personnel of the pavement, and of the restaurants and public houses which abound in the immediate neighbourhood, provides unique material for the student of his fellow men. Of every nationality, though Jews predominate, they have one thing, though often only one, in common, the fascination of the tiny articles in the handling of which they make their honest or dishonest livelihood. A stroll down the street on a

summer's morning will reveal a dozen little groups
of men on the edge of the pavement engaged apparently in casual conversation. Suddenly, however,
with a movement of the fingers, one of the group will
produce from a wallet, case, or even a twist of paper
an enormous sapphire, maybe, or a single unset
diamond, the value of which alone is far in excess
of its temporary owner's whole financial worth. If
manner of dress and general appearance is a guide
to occupation, one would expect these men to be
selling wares of extremely humble value, or at the
best engaged in securing orders for a valuable commodity. Certainly, one would never suspect them of
handling, in the apparently casual way so puzzling
to the stranger, a veritable fortune in a class of goods
which, for stability in value, is almost equivalent to
cash. Hard is the bargaining, and keen the examination of the stones produced, but even should the
passing stranger overhear an example of such bargaining, the chances are that the language used would be
Yiddish, German, Dutch or French—anything but
English! Yet the prices paid would shock the Bond
Street buyer from his opulent urbanity, for what is
bought in the Garden for a modest sum will appear
in the West End, set in a sovereign's worth of gold
or platinum, for a price out of all proportion to its
proper worth. Only when the innocent and unsuspecting buyer tries to sell his purchases does he
realise that the jeweller's motto, thanks in part to
the value of the stock he has to keep in hand, but
thanks in part to sheer rapacity, is: " Think of a price
and double it!" But though, in view of the tremendous value of the traders' wares, this pavement

bargaining seems highly dangerous, in fact it proves the truth of a maxim well known to the gang with whose adventures we are here concerned, that the safest place for handling precious things, whether information or a more tangible commodity, is in the midst of one's fellow men. Pearls and diamonds, the former especially, need daylight for a proper examination and appraising; hence these pavement sales are never conducted after dark, by which time the jewels have been safely returned to those who lent them, or to a hiding place which offers safety.

If the trading stock of the pavement vendor is out of all proportion to his intrinsic worth, the value of the stock in the inside offices is infinitely greater. Needless to say, the bulk of this is taken for the week-end to the nearest bank, but on a weekday night the prowling watchmen guard between them several millions pounds' worth of diamonds, pearls and made-up jewellery. Whether by accident or design, each set of offices consists of a suite of rooms, one within another, and a thief who attempted to " snatch and run " from the merchant's office would have to pass through a number of rooms inhabited by clerks and trusted members of the Corps of Commission-aires before he reached the outside door, only to find it bolted, if not locked as well!

We have said that the inhabitants of the " Garden " are divisible into street and office traders. A cross-classification would be into honest and dishonest traders, for the nature of the merchandise unfortunately has a fatal attraction to the crook, presumably by reason of its value, size and, if we may coin a word, disposability. The honest element, comprising almost every merchant of any standing, is in a way the most exclusive circle in the world. As in no other type of trade, the most complete and open confidence exists between the members of this inner circle, which has, however, no existence in a corporate capacity in the sense of a society or association of those concerned. All deals are based upon a mutual trust in the other's perfect honesty, and only when a newcomer to the community has shown himself to be completely trustworthy will he be granted the entrée to the carefully guarded ring. Once trusted, however, a man of little financial standing will be allowed to take away on approval or to show to an unnamed customer a quantity of jewels the value of which, if lost or stolen, he never could replace. The man to whom one would not lend £100, on the ground that he never would be able to repay it, is allowed to take away in his pocket, without security or even receipt, a necklace worth perhaps £10,000, but such a man will have been tested, proved and passed as trustworthy before he is given this implicit confidence.

In order to maintain this standard of confidence, the most elaborate precautions have to be taken to ensure that none of the jewels handled are stolen property, and none of the members of the inner circle will ever buy from a broker whom he does not know. If a member of the public tried to sell a valuable diamond in Hatton Garden he would find that none of the bigger merchants would do business with him until they had received and taken up his references, and the " dealer " who has " just arrived in London," and has no references, or has strangely enough forgotten to bring a card with him, or who has some other hackneyed excuse for failing to prove his *bona fides*, is promptly " shown the door."

But every community, however clean at the centre, has its fringe of blackguards at the edge, and these receivers of stolen property, as we shall see, enable jewel thieves to live. The subject of receiving will be considered in a later chapter, and it will suffice here to point out that the cleverest theft of jewels is useless unless the proceeds can be sooner or later converted into cash. But no reputable pearl or diamond merchant, as we have seen, will handle a stone or pearl from a man he does not know; hence the need and existence of innumerable " receivers," expert in their way in the valuation of such merchandise, who buy the proceeds of the robbery for a paltry sum in cash and sell at a later date, in many cases on the Continent, the best of the jewels in a now unrecognisable form. The habits of this class deserve a volume to themselves. Of half a dozen nationalities and speaking as many languages, some of them work alone in their nefarious trade; others work in gangs, but confine their larcenies and subsequent disposal of the stolen property to the London area, while the more clever and experienced not only employ, at excellent remuneration, a host of confederates of every kind, but are in touch in a swift and intimate way which makes detection difficult, with their " opposite numbers " on the Continent. Crime has become international more swiftly than the international organisation for its detection. At a time when the police forces of Europe were still strictly confined to their own area, and all co-operation between the various forces was fraught with jealousy, misunderstanding and delay, the criminal classes had learnt to take from those who were " working " a given Capital the proceeds of their robberies at an agreed scale of values, and dispose of it in cities many hundreds of miles away in a form which none would recognise. Nowadays, fortunately for the honest portion of the community, the international relationship between the various forces is improving year by year, as difficulties of language, methods of working and " red tape " are slowly cleared away.

It is obvious that only organised team-work on the part of the police can effectively combat organised team-work on the part of the criminal community, and the higher branches of the latter are unquestionably highly organised. Students of criminal psychology have discovered that one of the main factors in the formation of the most dangerous type of criminal is the thwarted desire for leadership, excitement and " romance," the latter word covering, apparently, melodramatic emotional stimulus. If this be so it is not surprising to find occasionally a first-class intellect being concentrated on a life of crime, and when a mind which, more fortunately directed, would have made its mark in any field of honest activity, is turned to criminal ends, it needs a body of men of collectively equal intellect to detect and punish the former's inroads on the quiet possession of the community at large.

As an example of such organisation turned to nefarious ends there is a geographical division of London not yet marked upon even the most expensive of our large-scale maps, which show the Parliamentary, parish, police, Local Government and other divisions, but not the definite areas presided over by a chief and many subordinate receivers of stolen property. We have seen how Cammi Grizard had a definite " beat " where he could always be found by those who were embarrassed with the spoils of their dishonesty, and other " areas " are equally well known. The inter-relation between the sites chosen by the chiefs of the receivers and the liquor trade would provide, were they to notice it, our friends who advocate the abolition of all alcoholic beverage with yet another arrow for their quiver of invective, for the site in nearly every instance, and needless to say they are all well known to the police, is outside a public house!

To this rule there are exceptions, one of them being " Duke's Place " on a Sunday morning. This unique market, situated in Houndsditch, in the East End of London, is a receiver's paradise, where jewellery is bought and sold on barrows as though it were so much grocery. Here in his time would " Cammi " be found, smoking his inevitable cigar, but never buying in person. His paid subordinates would do the haggling and arguing, and ultimately pay the bill. Grizard, his quick, shrewd eyes darting about among the array of glittering finery of such varied value, would indicate with a gesture the article he wished to buy, and his underling would set about its purchase for a sum which would produce a comfortable profit when the famous buyer ultimately sold in on the Continent.

It may be asked, and the question is reasonable, why, when so much sale and purchase is conducted

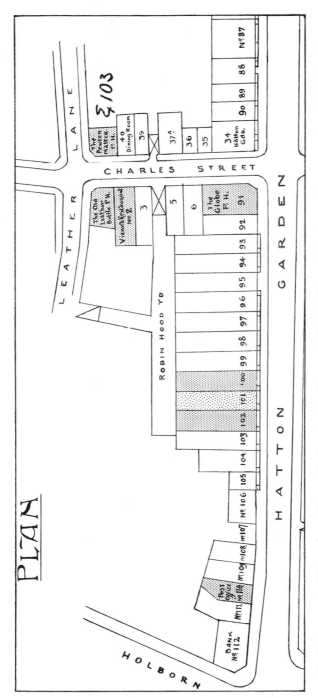

Ex. No. 103 at the Trial, a plan of Hatton Garden, showing No. 88, the Globe P. H., and the Vienna Restaurant, (the "flea-pit,"), which has since changed hands.

openly of goods which the most casual examination will show to have been stolen, are not those who handle it arrested for having it in their possession? The question is simple, but the manner of answer is more complicated. The possession, to be criminal, must have the additional qualification of " knowing it to have been stolen," and it is one thing to be morally convinced of the culprit's " *scienter* " or knowledge, quite another to prove that he acquired it dishonestly, that is, knowing the manner in which it was acquired, as distinguished from the ordinary way of trade. It is true that to combat this difficulty a legal rule has been introduced, whereby the fact of " recent possession " of stolen property places upon the possessor, under certain circumstances, the onus of proving that his possession was lawfully acquired, but this alone is hardly sufficient to convict him of the crime of " receiving." To add to the difficulty, in many cases the possession is no longer " recent," while in others it cannot be proved, as it must in law be proved, that the article is in fact stolen property.

On the other hand, there comes a time when all but the very greatest men, and they are happily rare, go a little too far and find themselves for a time, sometimes for a long time, in the hands of the police. There are those in Hatton Garden to-day who knew " Cammi " well, and wondered, as he paced his little " beat " outside the " Globe," why no one arrested him, for the trade which all knew that he carried on. The answer is that Grizard had sufficient brains not to be caught. Stolen property left his possession very soon after he purchased it, and such a man knows well how best to exploit the difficulties of the police in administering a legal system which seems designed to place all possible difficulties in the way of convicting anyone of crime!

The elaborate organisation of the receiving world, however, makes the task of tracing stolen jewels somewhat easier, for the police by long experience gradually acquire a knowledge of the channels through which property stolen by a certain gang will probably pass, and hence are often able to trace it to its whereabouts.

We have already introduced the members of the gang whose last and greatest exploit is about to be unfolded, but a word must be said of them in the setting in which they were usually to be found. Cammi, as already said, was usually to be found when " on duty " outside, or in the vicinity of " the Globe," with occasional excursions to the " Pewter Platter " (since demolished) and the " Old Leather Bottle," which is still going strong. Silverman had his office at 101, Hatton Garden, but it seems that Cammi seldom visited him, and Lockett frequented " the Garden " least of the four. He was the burglar, the effective instrument for acquiring other people's property, which his less daring but more wily confederates proceeded by devious means to convert into the gold which is the immediate object of most crimes. There remains Gutwirth, a real Hatton Garden habitué, who stands mid-way between the two divisions into which the merchants in the " Garden " are divided, for while not being a street trader he had no proper office of his own, but was allowed the use of a drawer in the desk of the proprietor of a restaurant then known as the Viennese Café. This restaurant was situated in Charles Street, which leads east and west out of Hatton Garden about halfway up, and westwards runs into Leather Lane. It still exists as a restaurant, but under another name, more topical if less euphonious, that of the Diamond Merchants' Restaurant. Here it was that Gutwirth was usually to be found, using the address for letters, telegrams and messages, and as a meeting place for members of the gang. That it was hardly a salubrious resort of the highest quality is shown by the nickname by which it was then known, the " Flea-Pit," and " jobs " were discussed and organised, and deals arranged across its narrow tables which the police—and writers of detective fiction—would give much to have overheard. In such a way would stolen property be handed to the first of a series of " fences " for a sum ludicrously out of proportion to its proper value, only to mount up in the course of its passage from hand to hand until, as we shall see later, the price at which it was presented back to the public was approximately its market price. Such are the members of the gang whose last adventure is about to be recorded, and such is the world in which they carried on their trade. Into such a world another type of human being entered day by day, conventional in his uniform of blue and red, and in the ordinary way an emblem of conventional security. This representative of orderly routine, the postman on his rounds, is seldom associated with violence in any form, and yet to the imaginative mind, as to at least one member of the police whose duties made him conversant with the Hatton Garden underworld, the

bulging sack upon the shoulder of this unarmed and
unguarded officer might well produce the remark:
" I wonder no one ' thugs ' and robs them every time
they set out on their rounds!" It is true that the
registered parcels are generally confided to the morning, that is daylight delivery, but all who pass the
postman on his rounds know perfectly well that his
bag contains a quantity of registered packets for the
merchants on his beat, and any one of those will
probably contain commodities of greater value than
the proceeds of the average burglary. However, it
is not for the writer to suggest and publish details
of (for England) a new form of crime!

To turn from the criminal fraternity and their
means of livelihood, actual and possible, to the
merchants whose magnitude of honest business draws
the dishonest element around them, to the discredit
of an ancient and honourable trade, one of the leading and most respected merchants in the " Garden "
was in 1913 Mr. Max Mayer, whose rise to fame in
the world of precious stones was as romantic as his
trade was vast.

Born in 1859, Mr. Mayer began his life, like
many others before and since, in the humblest way.
In the absence of capital he began trading with imitation jewellery, and by the use of his natural ability
and business acumen acquired sufficient capital and
experience to open business in genuine but non-
" precious " stones. Fortune was kind to him, and
he began trading in diamonds in addition to his far
less valuable commodities, gradually abandoning the
latter in favour of the former, until he definitely
took his place in that comparatively small circle of

international diamond merchants who are known among the trade throughout the world. As a diamond merchant he founded a large fortune at his offices in Hatton Garden, but some years previous to the date of the famous robbery he began to change his speciality from diamonds to pearls, saying by way of explanation that diamonds were gradually going out of fashion in favour of pearls, and he preferred to follow where fashion, and his fortune, led. By 1913 he had become as famous in the pearl trade as he had previously been in the world of diamonds, and an enormous sum would need to be considered in any attempt to estimate the value of the property which passed through his hands in a given year.

As he said to a reporter the day after the robbery: " I used to be mainly a diamond dealer, but during the last ten years the ' consumption ' of pearls has so greatly increased that this pearl branch of my business has become the most important. And I am very fond of pearls. The reason of their growth in popularity is that the taste of the class of people who buy valuable jewellery has improved. If rich *parvenus* wanted to make a display a few years ago they gave their women diamonds, but by the time a woman has adorned herself with £100,000 worth of diamonds she looks garish. She can, however, wear £200,000 of pearls and remain dignified and in good taste." With stock of such enormous value it is not surprising to learn that Mr. Mayer's office was " almost lined with safes." Allowing for the heated imagination of the reporter this certainly conveys a correct impression that very strong safes are used to house such merchandise, and the insurance, of which we shall deal later was naturally proportionate.

To pass from the general to the particular, Mr. Mayer was the proud possessor of a pearl necklace which was of such fabulous value, and was destined to play such a prominent part in the melodrama about to be unfolded, that it deserves description in detail. Mr. Mayer had bought it complete the previous October in Paris for the enormous sum of £123,000, confidently expecting to be able to sell it in London for at least £135,000, for which sum he insured it, but hoping to make a larger profit still by selling it for the then colossal figure of £150,000. Its ingredients were chosen and matched with consummate skill, and had taken scores of men over ten years to collect. Beginning with two or three flawless, enormous rosy-coloured pearls strung side by side on a piece of silk, this humble and yet exquisite nucleus had slowly gathered round itself others of equal perfection from all parts of the world. To quote from an article upon the Pearl Case, in the *Premier Magazine*, " slowly the wondrous thing had grown. It had taken years and years to perfect, thousands of pounds had been spent in its collection, the building up of the pearl necklace that should be *the* pearl necklace of the world. It had started with one magnificent pearl—flawless, of that live, rosy delicate tint which exceeds in beauty even the charm of woman's delicate rosy flesh, and possessed of that splendour of lustre known to jewellers as ' Orient.' If others could only be found of such beauty as to be worthy to be strung beside it, equally flawless, of similar tint, perfect in shape, fitly graduated in size, they would form an ornament

36

The late Mr. Max Mayer, the owner of the pearls.

[*Photo : Harrods*]

which might make the heart of an Empress throb with envy of possession. And so the work had gone on. In all parts of the world jewel dealers, pressed into its service, had been on the watch to find a pearl that might be worthy to be added to the wondrous ornament. Thousands had been submitted and rejected for one reason or another, but gradually the necklace had grown. A fruitful year would perhaps add six or seven to it; then would come a year of barrenness; then, from one end of the earth or the other would come three or four pearls to join the glorious band."

Exaggerated as this sounds, Mr. Mayer's son, who still carries on his father's business at his Hatton Garden office, states that it is substantially true. It may be that by way of frivolous comment one is reminded by the thought of one pearl beginning a necklace of Mark Twain's typical reply on being told that in order to be received in audience by the Tsar he must " Stand in a row ":—" Certainly, I love standing in a row, especially if I have other people to help me!" But that is neither here nor there.

The point is that by 1912 the necklace was complete, being then composed of sixty-one perfectly matched and graded pearls, joined with a diamond clasp, and when Mr. Mayer triumphantly returned with it from Paris, it only remained for him to find a woman whose neck would be worthy to be encircled with such a world-famed and unique display of artistry.

With regard to its cost it must be realised that three ingredients went to the building up of this enormous sum. In the first place each pearl was all

but perfect in itself, though none of course was
" flawless." Secondly, these sixty-one pearls, valuable in their aggregate but unrelated worth, became
of very much greater value as a row of perfectly
matched and graded pairs, which culminated in the
enormous centre pearl. In the same way a pair of
horses worth, for example, fifty guineas each, will
be worth as a perfectly matched, smooth working
pair, a great deal more than the hundred guineas
which they would fetch if separately sold. In the
case of this necklace, however, there was a third
factor, never disclosed at the time, that the nucleus
of pearls round which the necklace was built up came
from the Portuguese Royal Family, and this factor
of Royal ancestry, known only to a chosen few, made
the value of the necklace greater even than its ingredients seemed to justify. As a piece of jewellery,
however, apart from its historic interest, it was
unique, and when Mr. Mayer himself described it
as " one of the finest in existence," no one challenged
such an expert estimate. As will be seen from the
photograph which is reproduced on page 110, it was
by no means large in size, being in fact about twenty-
three inches long. Its colour, which no photograph
can reproduce, was one of its loveliest assets. Pearls
vary in colour more widely than the public realise.
As Mr. Mayer said to a *Daily Mirror* representative
a day or two after the robbery which deprived him
of this most beautiful of his possessions, " Pearls
vary so much in colour that necklaces can be matched
up to suit any kind of complexion. South American
women like yellowish pearls best, to suit their tawny
skins; English and German women, with their very

white skins, like the whitest pearls they can get. French women, who I think are the cleverest in their judgment, like pearls of a live, warm, rosy tint, like those of mine which are missing. I love that kind of pearl best, and think they look the most charming on a woman's neck. Often it takes years to match up pearls to make a necklace of the right colour throughout. If the pearls are large as well as well matched and good in colour the necklace becomes extremely valuable. I buy from India what are called ' series ' of pearls, a parcel being worth from £5,000 to £75,000. From these are sorted out gradually the pearls required to complete necklaces, which may take years." The necklace which was stolen was composed of pearls of a fine, warm, rosy tinge and averaged in weight from fifteen to fifty grains, its total weight being twelve hundred and fifty nine. The centre pearl, weighing 47 1/16 grains was almost unique, while the smallest of all was perfect of its kind. It is, therefore, not remarkable that Scotland Yard, less modest than the owner, should describe the necklace as " the finest in existence." In point of fact, Mr. Mayer, in the course of the subsequent trial at the Central Criminal Court (better known, from the street in which it is situate, as the " Old Bailey ") actually showed to counsel for the prosecution what he considered in some ways a finer necklace still, and this where he considered it safest and most effectively displayed, round his wife's neck! None the less, the combined effect of perfect pearls, perfectly matched, made the stolen necklace almost, if not quite, unique. Technical details of its various ingredients would only weary the general

reader, but a description of three of the finest, as
noted down by a young expert, Mr. Quadratstein,
who was destined to play no mean part in the recovery of the necklace and the capture of the
criminals, may be of interest, if only as illustrating
a peculiarity of the pearl trade which will be later
described. The notes read as follows:

1. 47 1/16 grains.
     Close to one hole white pointed inden-
        ture opposite small lump.
     2nd hole small cavity about 1/3 of
        circle.
     Slightly pique. Pink.
     ———

2. 39 grains—looks at first quite perfect.
     White point under first skin.
     Skin slightly hammer marked.
     Slightly brighter colour than first.
     ———

3. 33¼ grains. Yellower colour.
     Close to one hole very small circle.
     Very fine lustre.
     Under skin almost imperceptible white
        stripe.
     Hammer marked.

It will be seen that it is by the flaws that the pearl
is chiefly remembered and described, and this has an
important bearing on the larceny of such forms of
jewellery, for it must be realised that an expert will
remember stone for stone and pearl for pearl the
ingredients of such a necklace, even as dealers in

horses would remember seeing, much more having owned, a priceless thoroughbred. Mr. Mayer told a story of such feats of memory to the *Daily Chronicle* at the time. " There was a case in which pearls were offered to me for sale, and I remarked to the gentleman who brought them, ' I know the pearls very well —I sold them once.' He looked very much astonished. I was able to tell him that it was twenty-two years ago, and reference to my books confirmed this."

Mr. Spanier, a Parisian pearl merchant, now in business in London, from whom many of the details in this volume have been obtained, confirms this faculty possessed by members of the trade. He says that Mr. Mayer was once robbed of two pearls which he, Mr. Spanier, had sold to him. Mr. Mayer at once telephoned to Mr. Spanier in Paris to inform him of the loss. Four weeks later a man walked into the latter's office and offered him one of the pearls. Mr. Spanier at once recognised it, and confronted the man with the details of Mr. Mayer's loss. The man confessed to having stolen that pearl and another from Mr. Mayer's table in London, and later shot himself.

Another time Mr. Spanier was entertaining a Cuban gentleman at lunch when the latter showed him a pearl which he wished to sell. Mr. Spanier looked at it and replied: " I sold that fifteen years ago to a man called So-and-So." He was quite right —only it happened to be fourteen years ago!

It is no part of our story to consider imitation pearls, but it may be of interest to know that Mr. Mayer's already mentioned change of speciality, from diamonds to pearls, has not been affected by the modern vogue of imitation pearls, which range from perfect replicas of considerable value and workmanship to the mass production obtainable for a matter of pence. " On the contrary," said Mr. Spanier, when I asked for his opinion on the subject, " the best of the imitations act as missionaries for the genuine article." The average woman no sooner has a lovely imitation necklace than her one ambition becomes to make it " real." It is true that the public sometimes get cheated by being sold as genuine a pearl or string of pearls which are but clever forgeries, but as Mr. Spanier said, that is their own fault for going to second-rate firms. The best firms have a reputation to maintain.

Needless to say, such a priceless article as the completed necklace which we have described was heavily insured, and in fact is was covered by what is known at Lloyd's as a " floating " or Jeweller's Block Policy, a method of insurance peculiar to a trade in which a rapidly changing stock of enormous value not only passes from hand to hand in a seemingly casual way, but is frequently sent away to a prospective customer by post. It is obvious that the usual method of insurance, by which each article of more than a certain value is specifically mentioned with its value, would be quite inappropriate for such a purpose, for a jeweller's stock is changing every hour of the day. The principle of the Block Policy was therefore evolved to meet the difficulty. Like all such contracts it is one of " *uberrimae fidei*," of the utmost confidence and trust between the parties. The jeweller who is taking out the policy fills in a complicated form, in which he has to declare not only details of his stock at the moment, but his methods of business, the proportion of his goods which are sent by post or left in the hands of agents, the care which he takes of his stock by the use of safes, night watchmen, banking at the week-end, and the like, and in brief the utmost details of the way in which he carries on his trade. A policy is then affected on the average value of his stock, and in the event of any of its contents being lost or stolen he will recover the value of the stolen article. The policy in this case was to cover fire, burglary and loss in transit, but of course can be made to cover further risks, as agreed between the parties. The premium of the policy in question was 10/- per £100 of stock, with a rebate at the end of the year if no claim was made. On such a necklace alone the premium payable would thus be £1,012 10s. 0d., which is an enormous sum to pay per annum for a single article of stock, and is of interest as showing the sums in which these pearl and diamond merchants deal. On the other hand, in the event of loss, the underwriters as a whole would have to find the sum of £135,000 for Mr. Mayer, and no one syndicate would, of course, assume the responsibility for the full amount. The policy was in fact divided among a number of syndicates, each of which again is subdivided into many " names," and the heaviest single commitment was given in the Press as only £10,000.

Enormous sums are insured in this way, even bigger than the value of the necklace in this case. To quote from the *Daily Mirror* of July 18th: " At the Jewellers' Exhibition at the Agricultural Hall yesterday afternoon the *Daily Mirror* was shown an annual floating policy with more than two hundred signatures of underwriters on it, the risk accepted by each being specified. The total amount insured— by a Paris firm of pearl dealers—was £700,000."

A still more remarkable feature of this type of insurance, as proving the confidence which exists between the underwriters and the clients whose goods they agree to insure, is that not one of the " names " who signed the policy had ever seen the necklace which they were agreeing to " cover." Max Mayer had signed the request for the policy and stated certain particulars. They knew Max Mayer as a man of the highest integrity and were satisfied. As was said in the *Daily Chronicle* of the same date:

" Surprise is felt in circles other than those concerned that so large a sum should be insured without the underwriters ever seeing the goods. ' We cannot describe the necklace, for we have never seen it,' said a member of the firm, ' but we have known Mr. Max Mayer and done business with him for many years, and we should not think of doubting his word. Besides that, there are the assessors, whose business it is to decide what is the amount to be paid.' " Confidence between client and broker in these big jewel insurances is only established after the closest enquiry. References are required when business is first proposed, and the books of the would-be insurer must be open to inspection. Thus the amount paid for the goods and the person from whom they were purchased can be ascertained.

That such insurance was a clear necessity is shown by the number of thefts of a similar kind which had recently taken place. I quote from Inspector Ward's report to his superior officer. " In March, 1912, a packet of jewels valued at £2,300 was stolen in transit between Paris and London, and during this year two consignments of gold valued at £15,000 were stolen (between London and Egypt) and lead substituted. In January this year (1913) a parcel of pearls, value £1,300, was despatched from Paris to London, and on arrival it was found that the contents had been extracted and imitation seals substituted, and as recently as the month of June a parcel of jewels valued at £7,000 sent from Paris to London were never traced beyond the Paris Post Office." In another instance, which occurred only seven months previously, the Paris agent of Messrs. Michael Klean, Ltd., of 26, Hatton Garden, sent fifteen valuable pearls by registered post to his employers about Christmas time. On the packet being opened only cottonwool was found inside, while three of the five seals on the packet had been clearly tampered with. The value in this case was only £613, but in other respects the facts were almost identical.

With such examples before their eyes, it is not surprising that those who handled enormous sums in jewellery should see that it was well insured.

CHAPTER III

STOLEN!

MR. MAYER himself was usually to be found at his Hatton Garden office in order that the endless stream of dealers who either wanted pearls for their clients, or knew of purchasers for pearls in his possession, might have no difficulty in finding him. But in order to keep in touch with the international market, the famous merchant had organised a net-work of agents throughout the British Isles and the Continent, whose duty was to find and procure such pearls as were required to make up a necklace, and a purchaser for the completed article.

Among these agents was a Monsieur Henri Salomons, a Frenchman living in Paris, who had himself been a dealer in precious stones in a large way until he had lost the whole of his fortune in the famous, or rather infamous Madame Humbert frauds of 1902. For twenty years he had done business with Mr. Mayer and for the past eleven had been his accredited and trusted agent. It is only right to point out at once that throughout the whole proceedings no suggestion was made by any responsible person that he was not a gentleman of the very highest character.

Early in June, 1913, an enquiry reached him with regard to the necklace, which was known to be in his principal's possession, and he therefore had it sent to him in Paris, where it arrived safely on the 19th of June. As it happened, no sale was effected, and Mr. Salomons placed the necklace in his bank. A few days previous to the 15th of July he received from Mr. Mayer a further three loose pearls with instructions to return them all if no sale took place. Mr. Mayer explained this request by saying that he was going for his holiday and preferred that such valuable assets should be deposited during that time in his own London bank.

On the afternoon of the 15th of July, in accordance with the written instructions of his employer, Mr. Salomons, in the presence of his wife, proceeded to pack up the pearls for transmission to London. Whether or not this was the first time that Mrs. Salomons had seen the necklace is not recorded, but she certainly unwittingly lends a touch of humour to this melodrama by her opinion of it. It will be remembered how Mr. Mayer had described the pearls as " rosy warm " in tint, and as being " more beautiful than a woman's skin." In spite, however, of the male expert's poetic eulogy, Mrs. Salomons, the only " lady in the case," on being interviewed by the Press in the absence of her husband, remarked: " The necklace was not perhaps much to look at, but it was one of the most valuable collections of jewels of its kind that has ever passed through my husband's hands." Alas, that so much skill and artistry should be lavished on, in this case, such an unresponsive sex!

Considerable comment was made at the time on the practice of sending such valuable merchandise through the ordinary post, and interesting opinions were vouchsafed by those best qualified to speak.

E

The only alternative, it was pointed out, is a special messenger, which is certainly more expensive and universally held to be more dangerous. A single individual carrying in a tiny packet immensely valuable stones may be followed from his employer's office by members of one of the countless international gangs who so employ their time, and robbed at any one of a score of points between the office and his destination. Needless to say, the postal authorities of both countries object to the strain imposed by the obvious alternative, but they are powerless to prevent its being used. Its advantages are numerous. It is quick and cheap and it does not attract attention, while both the receipt by the Post Office from the sender and by the addressee from the Post Office are duly signed for and preserved. Add to this that the underwriters know and consent to the practice, and its advantages over the only alternative method need no further comment. So much is the Post Office in this country trusted that there is an amusing practice sometimes used by dealers who find themselves in charge of jewels of greater value than they care to leave in their offices overnight. On leaving their offices in the evening they solemnly post the jewels to themselves in a registered packet, and receive them back the following morning safe and sound.

As against this sense of security in the English Post Office, it was pointed out by the *Matin* of Paris, apparently on the authority of Mons. Calchas, a French detective of whom more will be said later, that during the previous six months nearly £30,000 had been paid over by various insurance companies in respect of jewels stolen in transit through the post

between England and France. The one weakness of
the use of the post for this purpose is, of course, that
whereas one may trust one's own emissary, the
number of officials employed by the respective Post
Offices is so large that the chance of a " black sheep "
amongst them becomes considerable, and a confederate in the Post Office would make a carefully planned
robbery from outside comparatively easy. Hence the
minute precautions taken in the Post Office to ensure
that no one man is ever alone with a packet for a
moment longer than is necessary, and hence the
elaborate system of signing receipts as the packet
moves from hand to hand.

But whatever the merits of this form of transmission, it was the one invariably used by Mr.
Salomons with the consent of his employer. Having,
therefore, fetched the necklace and the three loose
pearls from the bank, he proceeded to make up the
packet which in a few hours was to be, with its missing
contents, the chief topic of conversation throughout
England and the Continent. Mr. Salomons both lived
and worked at 71, Rue de Provence, quite close to
the Opera, and it was to this address that he took
the pearls on recovering them from the bank.
Taking the necklace from its wrappings he placed it
in a small morocco leather, plush-lined case, the case
in cotton-wool wrapped up in what he described as
" silk " paper, but which we call tissue paper, and
the " silk-paper parcel " in a wooden box, which had
been previously made for it. In addition he placed
in the wooden box a piece of paper containing the
three additional pearls. These consisted of two
" drop " pearls and a " round " pearl, the value of

the latter being about £800 and of the two drop pearls about £1,200 together. The box was then filled up with cotton wool, nailed down with three small French nails, and the whole wrapped in a sheet of the blue linen paper which Mr. Salomons always used. On this was pasted a printed label addressed to " Max Mayer, Esq., 88, Hatton Garden, London," and the parcel was then sealed up. The wax used was ordinary French red wax, and the seal was a double capital " M," standing for Max Mayer, given him by his employer for such a purpose. The parcel was sealed in seven places, three at the bottom and two at either end, and measured, when complete, 12½ inches long, 5¾ wide and 2¼ deep. Mr. Salomons took the packet thus prepared to the nearest post office, which happened to be 54, Rue de Provence, only a few minutes walk away, and arrived there about ten minutes to four. He there posted a letter to Mr. Max Mayer, advising him of the despatch of the pearls, and registered the parcel. As was afterwards proved, the number R263 was placed on it, together with Fr. 5.60 in stamps. It will be remembered throughout this story that the value of the franc in 1913 was twenty-five to the pound or, roughly speaking, tenpence a franc.

On the morning of July 16th Mr. Mayer arrived at his office in Hatton Garden at half-past nine, as was his wont, and his correspondence, which had been placed in a safe on arrival, was taken from the safe and laid before him. Among the parcels was the packet of pearls, which a clerk in Mr. Mayer's employ proceeded to open in his presence by slitting the paper with a paper-cutter round the top, thus making, as it were, a lid of the paper, without touching the seals. He removed the wooden box and handed it to a fellow clerk, who noticed that the lid of the wooden box was split, and called Mr. Mayer's attention to its condition. No suspicion was, however, roused by this peculiarity. He then prized open the lid, and noticed a smear of red wax on what was then the top, but which afterwards transpired to be the bottom of the box. Inside the box he found the leather case, a crumpled piece of newspaper, and eleven oblong lumps of sugar. Somewhat puzzled by this strange phenomenon, he called his employer's attention to it, saying: " Look! What a dirty way in which to pack the necklace up—and what does he mean by putting sugar in?" Mr. Mayer was reading his other letters and did not trouble to reply. The clerk, therefore, took out the leather case and opened it. A horrified gasp drew everyone's attention to the opened wallet as it lay in his trembling hands.

The world-famous necklace and the three loose pearls had gone!

Gone! The most famous necklace in the world! The silence in that inner office was more eloquent than words. The clerks stood motionless, their eyes on Mr. Mayer, who was vainly trying to control the varying emotions which had set his heart so uncomfortably beating. He was puzzled and alarmed, but not yet awake to the enormity of his loss. Instances of dummy packages being sent through the registered post with a view to drawing thieves' attention from the genuine article are not unknown. Hoping against hope that this was in fact the solution of the empty packet, he galvanised himself into activity and sent a telegram to Mr. Salomons in Paris saying: " Box arrived, but no necklace." No sooner was this sent than he realised that he would have to wait for many hours before he got a reply, and doubt was torturing him. He therefore ordered his clerk to telephone to Paris, and while connection was being made paced up and down his office, breathing heavily. At last he was speaking to Mr. Salomons. The line was not working well, but he gathered that the pearls had undoubtedly been sent off in the parcel, and their unfortunate owner at last realised that an astounding robbery had taken place. He could gather no more from his astonished agent save the weight of the packet when it was sent off, and that Mr. Salomons would catch the afternoon train for London.

Being a man of action in emergency, Mr. Mayer at once took steps to recover his stolen property. His first thought was for his insurers, on whom the enormous loss would ultimately fall. He therefore telephoned to his underwriters at Lloyd's, who instructed the firm of Messrs. Price and Gibbs, Assurance Assessors, of 23, St. Swithin's Lane, to send a representative without delay. Accordingly, Mr. Frank Beaumont Price, whose experience of similar robberies was considerable, and who was destined to play a considerable part in the unfolding of this story, at once set off, arriving at the office about 10.45 a.m. One glance at the situation informed this energetic gentleman that this was a case for Scotland Yard, and without delay he telephoned, with Mr. Mayer's permission, for the finest brains available.

Stolen!

What were the feelings of Chief Inspector Ward, in his office at Scotland Yard, when he placed the receiver to his ear and heard that the peaceful boredom of that summer's day had been invaded by a robbery of such world-wide interest? An interesting case is to a trained detective as an oasis to a thirsty traveller, a welcome break in the monotony of every day routine. Having sent for the nearest available subordinate, Detective-Sergeant Cornish, already one of the ablest men at the "Yard," and one who has since become a Superintendent, Ward set off for Hatton Garden, where Mr. Mayer was more impressed with his reputation than his outward form. Alfred Ward was the exact antithesis of the detective of the fiction of his day. A round and chubby face, embellished with a short moustache and the colouring of a village yokel, he was none the less a most efficient officer. Little did anyone guess in that summer of 1913 that within two years he would be blown to pieces in his own house. Yet such was his tragic end in one of the worst of the London air-raids in 1915. The bomb which killed poor Ward removed a great detective from the service of the English public.

On the morning of this 16th of July, however, he was very much alive, and proceeded to examine the only article from which a clue might be obtained, the rifled packet. Did he content himself with a single penetrating glance and announce that the thief was a Rumanian of 6ft. 4ins. with a grey moustache and a slight limp? Unfortunately, no, but sufficient material was obtained to suggest at least a few lines of enquiry. Careful examination showed that one of the two ends had been opened and re-sealed with a slightly different coloured wax, there being nine seals to replace the original two applied by Mr. Salomon the previous afternoon. These nine were all stamped with a double M, which, though a splendid imitation of the genuine seal, was even to the naked eye a forgery. Secondly, the fragment of newspaper taken from the packet was found to have been torn from a copy of the *Echo de Paris* of July 3rd, while the eleven lumps of sugar were found to be of a kind used in all French cafés and restaurants, and almost exclusively in France. Thirdly, the weight of the parcel and its substituted contents was almost identical with its weight when sent from the Paris Post Office, and finally, the box had been turned round within the blue linen paper so that what had been the top when it was originally packed appeared, on being opened, as the bottom. This was demonstrated by a smear of wax which, though found on the top, corresponded with the outside seal on the bottom.

That a carefully planned and daring robbery had been committed was therefore obvious, and as such a *coup* was probably the work of several men, and shortly would be known to many more, the immediate step towards their capture and the recovery of the pearls was clearly to make it worth the while of one of them to " split " on the others. After conference with those responsible at Lloyd's, Mr. Price accordingly proceeded to authorise the Commissioner of Police, then Sir Edward Henry, famous as the introducer of the finger-print system into the armoury of detective methods, to print and distribute a notice

of reward for the recovery of the necklace or information leading to the apprehension of the thieves. A
detailed description and life-size drawing of the
pearls was included in the document, and within a
few hours thousands of copies of which one, used as
an exhibit at the trial, is reproduced on page 56,
were displayed throughout the country. Surely no
more arresting notice had been recently presented to
the public eye! The notice read as follows:

METROPOLITAN POLICE

£10,000 REWARD

STOLEN

Between 4 p.m., 15th, and 8.30 a.m., 16th July,
1913, whilst in transit from Rue de Provence,
Paris to Hatton Garden, London:

A FINE
ORIENTAL PEARL NECKLACE

of 61 graduated pearls and weighing 1259
grains, the centre pearl weighing 47 1/16
grains, and the 30 pearls on one side of the
string weighing in rotation as follows:

grains 11 1/16, 11 1/8, 10 5/8, 12 3/8, 12, 13 3/8, 14 3/8, 14 5/8, 15 3/8, 15 5/8, 15 3/4, 15 9/16, 16 5/16, 17 3/8, 18, 17 7/8, 19 5/8, 20 5/8, 19 7/16, 21 7/16, 21 1/8, 22, 22 5/8, 23 3/8, 23 3/4, 27 3/8, 33 3/16, 34, 38 3/16, and 45 9/16, and on the other side as follows: 10 7/8, 11 1/8, 11 1/4, 12 1/4, 12 3/4, 13 7/16, 15 1/16, 15 7/8, 15 3/4, 16 7/16, 16 3/8, 16 1/2, 18, 17 7/16, 17 5/8, 17 11/16, 20 5/8, 21 5/8, 21 1/4, 23 1/4, 23 9/16, 24 13/16, 24 7/16, 27 5/8, 30 11/16, 33 3/8, 39 5/16, 40 1/16, English weight, terminating with a diamond clasp and snap; also 2 drop pearls, weighing 94½ grains, and 1 round pearl, weighing 27 grains. The property was contained in a box wrapped in blue linen paper, sealed with several large red seals, and measuring 12½ in. by 5¾ by 2¼.

(A drawing of the necklace was here reproduced)

The above reward will be paid by Messrs. Price and Gibbs, Assessors, 23, St. Swithin's Lane, E.C., who are acting on behalf of Lloyd's Underwriters, to any person giving such information as will lead to the apprehension of the thief or thieves and the recovery of the property, or in proportion to such property recovered.

Information to be given at the Metro-

METROPOLITAN POLICE.

£10,000 REWARD

STOLEN

Between 4 p.m. 15th and 8.30 a.m. 16th July, 1913, whilst in transit from Rue de Provence, Paris, to Hatton Garden, London:—

A FINE

ORIENTAL PEARL NECKLACE

of 61 graduated pearls, and weighing 1259 grains, the centre pearl weighing 47 1/16 grains, and the 30 pearls on one side of the string weighing in rotation as follows: grains 11 1/16, 11 1/8, 10 5/8, 12 3/8, 12 13 3/8, 14 5/8, 15 3/8, 15 5/8, 15 3/4, 15 9/16, 16 5/16, 17 3/8, 18, 17 7/8, 19 5/8, 20 5/8, 19 7/16, 21 1/8, 22, 22 5/8, 23 3/8, 24 3/4, 27 3/8, 33 6/16, 34, 38 3/16 and 45 9/16, and on the other side as follows : 10 7/8, 11 1/8, 11 1/4, 12 1/4, 12 3/4, 13 7/16, 15 1/16, 15 7/8, 15 3/4, 16 7/16, 16 3/8, 16 1/2, 18, 17 7/16, 17 5/8, 17 11/16, 20 5/8, 21 5/8, 21 1/4, 23 1/4, 23, 23 9/16, 24 13/16, 24 7/16, 27 5/8, 30 11/16, 33 3/8, 39 5/16, 40 1/16. English weight, terminating with a diamond clasp and snap ; also 2 drop pearls, weighing 94½ grains, and 1 round pearl, weighing 27 grains.   The property was contained in a box wrapped in blue linen paper, sealed with several large red seals, and measuring 12¼in. by 5¼in. by 2¼in.

Actual size of Pearls.

The above reward will be paid by Messrs. Price & Gibbs, Assessors, 23, St. Swithin's Lane, E.C., who are acting on behalf of Lloyd's Underwriters, to any person giving such information as will lead to the apprehension of the thief or thieves and the recovery of the property, or in proportion to such property recovered

Information to be given at the Metropolitan Police Office, New Scotland Yard, London, S.W., or at any Police Station

E. R. HENRY,
The Commissioner of Police of the Metropolis.

Metropolitan Police Office,
New Scotland Yard. S.W
19th July, 1913

Printed by the Receiver for the Metropolitan Police District, New Scotland Yard, London, SW.   (10000-7.13)

Stolen!

politan Police Office, New Scotland Yard,
London, S.W., or at any Police Station.

E. R. HENRY.
The Commissioner of Police of the Metropolis.

Metropolitan Police Office,
    New Scotland Yard, S.W.
        19th July, 1913.

Printed by the Receiver for the Metropolitan Police District, New Scotland
Yard, London. S.W.

It will be noted that no description is given of any
flaws. In fact, the " personality " of a pearl is composed partly of its colour, weight and general shape,
and partly of the tiny flaws which are never exactly
the same in any two pearls, and it is by these that an
expert remembers and identifies an individual pearl.
Enough information was nevertheless contained in
the notice to enable any honest dealer to recognise
the necklace, and any but the smallest of the individual pearls, in the event of anyone offering it to
him for sale.

Having instructed Scotland Yard to undertake
investigation this side of the Channel, Mr. Price
communicated with a firm of private detectives in
Paris, Messrs. Calchas and Debisschop, who were, in
fact, ex-police officers, and instructed them to inform
the Paris Police officially of the robbery, and instigate
their own inquiries. A notice of reward almost
identical with the English version was broadcast
throughout France, and a detailed description of the
missing pearls and the reward for their recovery was
sent all over the world.

Within a few hours of the theft the Press were fully informed, and set the wires tingling with the thrilling news. Here, at the close of the London season, was unlimited " copy " and this on a subject pregnant with " romance " and thrills of every kind. The excitement was tremendous, and it is not too much to say that the sensational robbery was the main topic of conversation wherever the news was known. Even the great " Turf Libel " and the almost forgotten Balkan War gave way before the announcement of " Ten Thousand Pounds Reward."

The inevitable result was a constant stream of useless information, and theories still more fatuous, which flowed into every police station in Europe, ranging from the suggestion that the necklace had never been posted to the dark insinuation that it would be found round the neck of the missing Mona Lisa! The only entirely unmoved person was the lady whose *mots* seem fated to provide the only " comic relief " in this story of the criminal underworld. The *Daily Express* correspondent wrote on the 17th July as follows: " The wife of Mr. Salomons . . . refuses all information. ' I really do not understand the fuss that is being made about this affair,' she said. ' If the stones are lost, the Insurance Company will pay for them, and that is all that can be said.' " Unfortunately, the underwriters, who were faced with the possibility of having to pay up £135,000, failed to achieve this philosophic calm, but, in collaboration with the police, set to work to trace and capture the criminals, as the first step towards the recovery of the necklace which they had insured.

But Press excitement alone would hardly suffice to catch the thieves and recover the famous pearls. The very audacity of the robbery informed the police that they had no mean antagonists, and the case as a whole was a definite challenge to their powers. With the assistance of Detective-Sergeants Cornish and Cooper, the latter being now a Chief Inspector and, like Cornish, one of the ablest men at the " Yard," Inspector Ward, in his own phraseology, " got down to it." Assisting them on behalf of the Underwriters was Mr. Price and ex-Superintendent Leach, whose assistance he had found invaluable before. This officer, Alfred Leach, already mentioned in these pages, is now getting on in years, and actually has a distinguished son in the Force of the rank of Divisional Inspector, but the old man's knowledge of the area of which for years he was in charge, which included Hatton Garden, is unrivalled still. These five men between them, with assistance from a score of others, were as powerful a team for the unmasking of a gang of criminals as any country could produce, and yet they failed. It was irony indeed that where the experienced professionals were all but at a loss, the efforts of a pair of enthusiastic amateurs should brilliantly succeed. And yet, even had these latter not come forward, it is more than probable that in the end the patience of the professional would have produced the same result. No one who has read Mr. Dilnot's *Triumphs of Detection* will fail to appreciate the deadly efficiency of team-work, thoroughness, and patience inexhaustible.

The detective of fiction relies upon individual brilliance; the detective of fact relies upon team-work and routine. Not that individual acumen is not required, but alone it can do little except in the rarest cases. One of the first steps taken by the police in a robbery of this sort is to close all known avenues by which the goods might be disposed of to a " smasher," that is, a receiver of stolen property. It is often said that without the " receiver " theft, as a means of livelihood, would all but cease to exist. A moment's reflection will show the uselessness of jewellery to a burglar unless he can immediately sell it for cash. Hence the host of " receivers " of every kind, from the famous few such as Grizard to the low-class " jeweller " in the slums of London's underworld, and hence the Law's regarding such men as no less criminals than those from whom they buy. But the crime of " receiving " includes "knowing it to have been stolen," and many an honest trader finds himself at times in possession of stolen property. There are all degrees of knowledge, ranging from an express agreement between the thief and receiver before ever the theft is made, to a jeweller who buys from questionable-looking customers for questionable prices without inquiring whence the property came. Above these again are honest pawnbrokers who have the greatest difficulty in preventing themselves un-wittingly buying stolen property, for many of the stories told them of hardship in the home which causes family heirlooms to be sold at pathetic prices are unquestionably true, though others are as obviously false.

One of the most important factors in the disposing of stolen property is the degree to which the article can be made unrecognisable, and carefully fitted garages exist, for instance, in which stolen cars can be altered out of recognition in a remarkably short space of time. The same applies to jewellery, though in a varying degree. Diamonds, the most valuable of all, can be easily recut, and thus divorced from all the factors by which they might be known, shape, weight, flaws and brilliance. Pearls, on the other hand, are generally considered to be untouchable. This is not strictly true, for pearls can be " skinned," a word which means what it says. An expert will sometimes remove a skin from a badly flawed pearl in hopes of finding its inner skin flawless. If this is so the " new " pearl, though smaller than the old, may still be far more valuable. On the other hand, such experts are few and far between, and still more rare are those of the criminal variety. The general proposition is, therefore, substantially correct, that in stealing a beautiful pearl one is stealing something known throughout the trade and which will be recognised the moment it is offered for sale. If this applies to any average pearl of value, how much more does it apply to a priceless string such as Mr. Mayer's, each pearl on which was perfect of its kind?

It will now be appreciated in what direction the greatest hope of the police was to be found — the difficulty of turning the necklace into cash. Verily the thief who took the necklace from its packet was encumbering himself and his companions with a dangerous " white elephant." Each one of the pearls was known and its description circulated, which meant that no one who recognised it would buy it, while any honest trader would give the police a description of the person attempting to sell it to him.

On the other hand, if once the pearls were smuggled out of the country and reached the East they would never be seen again. There is a saying in the trade: " Once East of Suez and pursuit is hopeless," and thieves of such experience could probably afford to wait, if need be for months, before making the slightest move. In these cases, the only hope is the notice of reward, and the possibility that to keep themselves in funds the thieves will try to sell a minor portion of their booty, in which case discovery of the portion may yield a clue which will lead the pursuers to the whole.

For all these reasons it is clearly the business of the police to reduce to a minimum the chances of " smashing " the stolen goods. The police and honest traders are therefore warned in the following ways. On news of the robbery being received at Scotland Yard, an " A.S." message is sent out, A.S. standing for All Stations. This is filed by each police station and shown to its officers. In addition, there is sent out four times a day a news sheet, printed at Scotland Yard, called Printed Information. This will give in greater detail a description of the stolen articles as well as the other news of interest to each member of the Force. Thirdly, there is a Pawnbrokers' List, which is sent to every registered pawnbroker to be read by him or ignored at his peril. These three methods are confined to the Metropolitan Police. Finally, there is the *Police Gazette*, the oldest and best known of the publications issued by New Scotland Yard. For over a hundred years this paper has been circulated throughout the Police Force of the country, and is regularly sent abroad in exchange for similar publications from other Forces. It is published daily and is a mine of information to those engaged in detecting and preventing crime. In this, as in the other three, a full description of the stolen necklace was set out with details of the robbery. In addition to these general precautions, individual known " receivers " were carefully observed, in the hopes that some of the pearls would be brought to them, but sharp as the look-out was in England and on the Continent, no trace of them was found.

Students of criminology may ask why the well-known method of M.O. was not available and useful here. Modus Operandi, or " M.O.," depends upon the weakness of the average criminal for doing all his " jobs " in exactly the same way. A " cat burglar " who climbs up drain-pipes in Mayfair and enters dressing-room windows while the owners are at dinner, for example, will continue to do so. You will not find him breaking open a farm-house door with a crowbar and stealing food. Now this theft had been obviously done by experienced jewel thieves, and done by pre-arranged substitution. There was here, for example, no question of " snatch and run." But, as Sir Robert Anderson, one time chief of the C.I.D., explained (I quote from Mr. Dilnot's " Scotland Yard "): " Great crimes are the work of great criminals, and great criminals are very few. And by ' great crimes ' I mean, not crimes that loom large in the public view because of their moral heinousness, but crimes that are the work of skilled and resourceful criminals. The problem in such cases is not to find the offender in a population of many millions, but to pick him out among a few definitely

F

known ' specialists ' in that particular crime." In these cases the police seek out each of the men who might have done the crime and inquire his whereabouts on the night in question, further inquiries being directed towards those unable to give a satisfactory reply. It says much for the gang who had stolen Mr. Mayer's necklace that for a month at least no action was taken against any of them. Their time, however, would have probably come if other, far more dramatic, events had not intervened.

Meanwhile the police, having thus closed all known avenues of escape for the pearls or criminals, began to follow up the remaining lines of possible inquiry, the seals on the box and the route taken by the packet from its point of departure in Paris to its arrival on Mr. Mayer's table exactly sixteen hours later. The first person to examine was, of course, Mr. Salomons, and to him the attention of all was turned.

CHAPTER IV

THE SEARCH

Mr. Salomons arrived in London on the night of the 16th, and was met at Charing Cross Station by a collection of those chiefly concerned, among them being Mr. Max Mayer, Chief Inspector Ward, ex-Superintendent Leach and Mr. Price. They travelled straight to Scotland Yard by cars waiting in attendance, and immediately launched upon an inquiry with other officials of "the Yard" which lasted until the early hours of the morning.

Meanwhile the London "dailies" were busy printing off the news with which they were to startle the world the following day. Needless to say, they had welcomed the robbery with open arms, and vied with one another in the size of their head-lines and the wealth of detail which their respective "special correspondents" were able to supply. Incidentally, the readers of this book are indebted to their industry for much of the detail herein contained. Luckily for the reporters, the principal figure in the case proved not only open to interview, but positively loquacious, and every paper had a report of "special" interviews with the famous dealer in pearls, whose views, theories, hopes and fears were at the disposal of all who cared to call. Sure enough, it was only a matter of hours before pictures appeared with pen and ink drawings of 88,

Hatton Garden, with the necklace super-imposed and the inevitable " inset " of anyone remotely connected with the case whom they were able to photograph.

The efforts of the gang concerned to draw a red herring towards Paris were entirely successful. The mere presence of the fragments of a French paper and the typically French sugar was enough to convince the searchers at the outset that the theft had occurred in Paris. " It appears certain," said the *Daily Chronicle* on the 17th, " that the pearls were abstracted on French soil, as the lumps of sugar were of the shape generally used on the Continent." Again, in the *Star* for the same evening, we are told: " The sugar was of French manufacture, and this with the presence of a scrap of French newspaper makes it clear that the robbery took place in Paris." Even *The Times* inclined towards the prevailing view, and the *Daily Telegraph* alone saw the possibilities of using the sugar and paper as a " blind." An extract from this paper on the day following the robbery may be of interest in the light of subsequent events. After stating such brief facts as were then known, the report continues: " These are the known facts regarding the robbery, and they present all the elements of a very fine mystery. . . . Somewhere between the post-office in Paris and Mr. Mayer's office the jewels disappeared. The substitution of the French sugar and the French newspaper suggests, on the face of it, that the robbery occurred on the other side of the Channel. But in official quarters sight is not lost of the fact that both this particular sugar and newspaper might have been used in this country for the purpose of throwing investigators off the track."

Needless to say, the French authorities were furious at the suggestions made against their honesty and the organisation of their postal transport, and their rage was hardly diminished by the type of letter which appeared in various quarters of the European Press, of which we have only room to quote an amusing specimen. In a letter to *The Times* of July 22nd an indignant gentleman living in the South of France gives in considerable detail a lamentable incident in which a photograph and writing case, despatched to different friends at Christmas time, were substituted in the post and sent to the wrong recipients. On the strength of this he announces that he thereby " lost faith " in the French Post Office, and was not in the least surprised to hear " that a valuable pearl necklace had been stolen in the course of transit between Paris and London!"

Some papers favoured the theory of complete substitution, suggesting that the package only contained sugar when sent off. " It is regarded," said the *Daily News*, " as a clever case of the substitution of a carefully prepared packet for the original. Recently, it will be recalled, boxes containing lead were substituted for boxes of gold in transit between the Bank of England and Alexandria," and the *Daily Mirror*, after making the same suggestion, adds: " If the theft had actually taken place in the post, as the postal authorities would probably not notice such a thing as a change of weight in transit, the substitution would have been purposeless; and it may therefore be that the substitution was worked by fraud before the package was actually posted, and that the person who posted it was really posting sugar, believing it to be pearls. This view is rather born out by the fact that the package received, with seals unbroken, bore the French postmark." One further quotation will be of interest in the light of later events. In the same article in the *Daily Telegraph* from which quotation has already been made, it is suggested, speaking of the use of the post-office for such merchandise, that " people who take this risk lose sight of the possibility —in many cases the probability—of there being a member of the gang of thieves actually in the service of the Post Office itself. With such a person in a position to gain access to the package, and with the necessity of their having it in their possession only a short time, the thieves would find it a matter of comparative ease to make the substitution, covering, as in this case, any tears which they have made in the wrapping with a few extra seals, so as to avert suspicion should the package be noticed by any other official in transit." In view of later developments, this theory of a Post Office confederate is greatly to the credit of the *Daily Telegraph*. It is true that *The Times* a few days later suggested a possible connection between the robbery and the big French Post Office strike of two years previously, when hundreds of men were taken on and subsequently retained with little or no references, but this was still subject to the prevailing conviction that the theft had taken place in France.

On the night of the 17th July Mr. Salomons and Mr. Price crossed to Paris, taking with them the rifled parcel, and the next morning, having laid formal complaint of the robbery in the proper quarter, they joined in a consultation with Mons.

Hunt for World's Most Costly Necklace.

A cutting from the *Daily Chronicle* of July 18th, 1913, two days after the robbery.

Calchas, already mentioned, Mons. Puichard, Chief of the Parisian C.I.D., and other officers. The French officials at once opened an inquiry in the French Post Office, while Inspector Ward, with the help of the English postal detectives, made the equivalent investigation in London. The report of the French inquiry, published on the 4th of August, is of such interest, as showing the extreme care with which such valuables are handled, that no excuse is made for quoting from it at length.

" The box in question was deposited at window No. 12 of the Post Office No. 22 (Rue de Provence) on Tuesday, 15th July, between 3.40 p.m., earliest, and 3.50 p.m., latest, by M. Salomons himself to M. Seince, in charge of the said window, who weighed it, franked it as a foreign registered letter, stamped it with his date stamp, registered it in the special book, No. 510, containing particulars of articles which have been registered, and then placed it in the wire case situated within reach of his right hand. These operations only took one to two minutes.

" As usual, at exactly 4 o'clock, M. Fournials, a clerk deputed to dispatch the registered packets, came and collected all the articles in the office, to the number of 158. The time taken in receiving, counting, handing over these articles and transferring them to ' la cabine,' can be estimated at five minutes. It is then about 4.5 p.m., when the box and the other 157 articles have been sorted and put in the proper compartments by M. Fournials.

" After this classification, M. Guillot, another clerk also in charge of the department for registered articles, made out a despatch memorandum for each particular parcel which he had to prepare, and on this memorandum he entered, in one number, the registered letters, and described individually each of the valuable articles which were contained therein. Concerning the parcel containing the box in question, it contained 82 other registered articles franked as letters, and 5 registered samples franked for the reduced tariff. The 83 articles composing the total of this sending had been counted and placed in a sack by M. Guillot in the presence of his colleague, M. Fournials, for the handling of the registered articles is regularly done by two persons. M. Guillot afterwards tied to the neck of the sack a label ' Etranger, Europe,' and sealed this ring with the ordinary wax ' Reddish Brown ' which is alone in use in our offices.

" This sack he placed afterwards with a second one addressed ' Outre mer ' in a covering sack, likewise sealed and having on the neck the destination ' Paris Recette Principale.'

" The whole of the operations in ' la cabine ' took hardly a quarter of an hour, as the closing of the sacks with the registered articles should commence at 4.20 p.m. at the latest, in order that the delivery of the fifth despatch for the General Post Office should take place at 4.34 p.m. From 4.20 p.m. to 4.34 p.m. the said covering sack has passed from ' la cabine ' of the registered articles to the departure room for the ordinary correspondence, and from there into the van.

" Leaving at 4.34 p.m. with five other sacks in the motor postal van No. 197, driven by the ' wattman ' Aladenise, the covering sack in question arrived at the General Post Office at 4.44 p.m. after a very short stop at No. 8 office ' Bould des Italiens.' Sergeant

Lespinasse and the porter Guereau who took the delivery on the transferring, did not see anything abnormal in its exterior state. The porter Rouvière placed the said sack and all those from the office No. 22 in ' la benne ' of the second floor, which is taken up at 4.48 p.m.

" M. Chevalier, charged with the verification of the bags of the arrival service, noticed nothing irregular.

" From the arrival service the bag in question was directed to the foreign aperture, where it was opened at 5.4 p.m. There it was assured that the despatch was in order; the registered sack containing the box was extracted; this was handed sealed to M. Fanet, clerk, who, after finding it intact, passed it at 5.8 p.m. to the ' Chargements étrangers ' service.

" At 5.10 p.m. M. Perrimond, clerk, opened the registered sack; he noticed the articles which it contained and which, he says, were all in good order; he then gave them to the distribution service. As the opening of the sacks containing registered articles is done on two tables joined together, M. M. Cherel and G. Rurand assisted in doing it. They saw nothing which drew their attention.

" At 5.12 p.m. M. Redinger, clerk, had the box in his hand in proceeding with the distribution of the foreign articles which had arrived by the 5th despatch from the Paris offices. This box remained under his safeguard until 5.20 p.m., when it was confided, with 57 other registered packages destined to England, to M. L. Durand, clerk, charged with the despatch of these articles.

" M. L. Durand sorted the said packages, and then commenced to describe individually on a special register on one side and on a memorandum form on the other, all the correspondence which was then ready to pack, and it is thus that the box figures on the fourth supplementary sheet for the London office under order No. 14. This fourth sheet and the 30 registered articles which were declared were inserted in bag No. 2 by M. M. L. Durand and Peyrondet. This bag No. 2 was itself placed in bag No. 5, which was regularly labelled and sealed about 5.40 p.m. by M. Peyrondet in the presence of M. L. Durand. Thus closed, the said bag No. 5 remained in ' la cabine ' for England until 7.10 p.m., when it was delivered with others to the route for England for insertion with other bags containing ordinary correspondence.

" At 7.35 p.m. the 7 sealed bags thus described for London were pushed into the slide; they were a minute afterwards gathered up at the bottom of the slide; then placed in the motor-van No. 314, which left for the Northern railway station at 7.45 p.m.

" Arriving at 7.55 p.m. at the ' abulant ' transhipment service of the Northern line with 72 others, of which 61 were for various foreign destinations, these seven bags for London were immediately taken out of the motor-van and placed on a truck in charge of two porters and, after each bag had been individually checked, were deposited in carriage No. 221 of the ' abulant ' office from Paris to Calais 2nd (Brigade C), which left the Northern railway station at 9.20 p.m. As soon as the van was loaded it was locked, and the key remained in the possession of the chief of the Brigade until the arrival at the Calais Maritime Station of train No. 23 at its usual time, 1.23 a.m.

" The van was then opened in the presence of the clerk of the said ' abulant ' office, who superintends the delivery, and handed to M. Roussel, caretaker of the Calais post, who verified all the bags of the despatch and took charge of them without making any criticism.

" Finally, M. Roussel delivered, in his turn, the said sacks to the English Postal Authorities, who did not make the least remark as to their exterior condition.

" It is, then, established that from the putting in of the bag in the Principal Receiving Office of Paris, neither the bag containing the necklace, nor the outer bag, both duly sealed in brown sealing wax, has been the object of any attempt at violation, for reason that all along the route and up to the boat, the first English destination, they were seen to be in good condition."

It seems, from a further report, that Mr. Price himself attended the inquiry, and though at first he " seemed to have very strong bias against us," the results " very much impressed him in favour of our staff, whose attitude, marked by entire frankness, produced upon him the best effect." Considerable stress was laid upon the fact that the line of seals found on the tampered end of the box when it arrived in London were unbroken and not even cracked, although the others were mostly cracked and in some cases broken. As one witness from the post-office said: " One thing astonished me very much, that the seals placed on the bottom are still intact, if they are those which were there when I received it. I had, to cancel the postage stamps, to strike very forcibly with my date stamp, and I should thus have certainly broken slightly the seals on the opposite side." And again: " Each of the ten officers whom Mons. Richaud asked whether it was possible that the seals would have remained in a state of integrity after the journey, replied that it appeared to them absolutely impossible that the wax should not suffer deterioration in the course of transport." Mr. Price was actually shown a quantity of débris from seals on parcels coming from Paris which had just been fetched out of the bags.

The result of this inquiry was to show conclusively that the packet handed in by Mr. Salomons on the afternoon of the 15th was handed over intact to the English authorities at Calais, so that, unless a case of substitution was accomplished in the face of Mr. Salomons' vigilance, the theft did not take place in France.

No wonder, then, that the French officials were furious at the public slur cast upon their efficiency by the English Press, and though details would be indiscreet, it is not difficult to believe that the friction which developed between the English and French officials to say the least of it frayed the edge of courtesy!

In point of fact, the arguments as to the incidence of blame became so heated that the already famous Richard Muir, then Senior Treasury Counsel, was invoked to examine and if possible improve the existing relationship. Thus it is that the great man comes upon the scene some months before, in the ordinary course of events, his assistance would be required. It is no part of Counsel's duties to act as a detective, but the famous Scot, clear-headed and far-sighted as he was, in this respect was a law unto himself. Most Counsel are content to handle the cases which are put into their hands in the form in which they find them, but Muir would frequently conduct, through those instructing him, investigations on his own. He was therefore an admirable person to advise upon the delicate situation which had arisen, for it would be his task when the criminals were caught to prosecute them at the trial.

This situation, which he discussed at length with his friend and colleague, Travers Humphreys, who was later briefed to assist him at the trial, was, as the two of them at once admitted, baffling in the last degree. The French investigation was so thorough and conclusive as to leave but two alternatives. Either the pearls were stolen after they had left French hands or before they left Mr. Salomons'. " What do you know of this man, Salomons?" said Richard Muir to the police. " It may be a ' put-up ' job from beginning to end." The police, however, headed by Chief Inspector Ward, assured him that they were satisfied that Mr. Salomons was a gentleman of unimpeachable integrity. It followed that the pearls were not stolen in France. But the English investigation was no less thorough, and apparently produced the same result. An impossible position therefore appeared. The packet was posted in Paris, arrived untouched at Dover, had reached London without anyone having the opportunity of opening it, had there been passed without comment, and later in the morning delivered at Mr. Mayer's office with his other mail. Therefore they had not been stolen!

Richard Muir seems to have accepted the French inquiry from the outset, and fastened at once on the weakness of the English chain of evidence. By thus accepting the French conclusions as correct he pacified the French, and by suggesting certain lines of inquiry in England he gave the English officials employment of more value than deploring the inefficiency of their Continental colleagues.

Meanwhile, in the course of investigation, there were incidents on both sides of the Channel which, though of little account in themselves, were sufficient to show the possibility of weak links in the chain, thereby reducing the too complacent certainty of the officials in both countries that they, at any rate, were not to blame. For example, the Paris *Matin* gave an account of a representative who, three days after the robbery, made the following experiment. " One of the most surprising things revealed by the robbery," reads the report, " is the ease with which strangers can enter the sorting-room of the General Post Office in Paris. A French journalist made a test yesterday. He went up to the second floor, where the foreign letters are sorted, and walked about without any questions being asked." This, however, may be nothing in itself. It is one thing to walk into a room filled with busy officials without being challenged, but quite another to open one of the registered packages beneath the eyes of a dozen men, re-seal it with burning wax, the smell of which would at once attract attention in a room in which no wax was ever used, and replace it where it was found.

A more alarming, and, from the legal and psychological point of view, more interesting possibility, was opened up by an incident which curiously enough occurred, though at different times, on both sides of the Channel. For the French incident we are indebted solely to *The Times* of July 25th which reports that in the course of the French inquiry two officials independently alleged that they distinctly remembered seeing the mass of seals at the damaged end of the parcel, thus showing, if they were to be believed, that the theft had taken place in France. In England, however, the equivalent incident was developed later to a far more interesting degree, for the man in question, one W. R. Loades, one of three sorters who worked together in the mail-van between Dover and Victoria Station, was deliberately omitted from the list of witnesses for the prosecution and ultimately called for the defence. In common with all other English postal officials who had handled the parcel on its way from Calais to London, Loades had made a statement to the police. This statement was thought so unsatisfactory that it was rejected by the prosecution, but, in accordance with our invariable custom handed, in the interests of fairness, to the defence. On being called for the defence, Loades repeated what had appeared in his statement that " on the morning in question I noticed a large blue-wrapped parcel, which I have since identified as this parcel (the rifled packet). After sorting it out, which would bring it into this position with me (illustrating) with the damaged end towards me, it seemed to me there was a line of wax running across this end as there is now." There was, of course, considerable cross-examination to this, but nothing would shake his stubborn certainty. On the other hand, by the time the trial took place, it was abundantly clear to the prosecution that the packet was not, in fact, opened before it reached the London office where the foreign mail is redistributed for local delivery.

Loades was therefore either lying, which, in the absence of any motive, is in a man of excellent character highly improbable, or genuinely mistaken. If the latter, where was there room for mistake? It is not as if he spoke to a vague recollection. He was quite convinced. It remained for Sir Richard Muir to suggest, and virtually prove, a third alternative. In the course of his cross-examination he elicited the fact that, prior to the statement being made, Loades had in all probability seen a photograph in the Press of the rifled packet, showing the famous "line of seals." By a process of what would nowadays be described as auto-suggestion, he had, by constantly reading a description of the packet and gazing at its photograph, imprinted its appearance on his mind until he genuinely believed that when he handled it upon the train, with hundreds of others, he not only noticed it, but remembered this particular peculiarity. Here, then, was a man prepared to swear, and who subsequently swore in the witness-box, that he had seen what in fact he never could have seen, and such a precedent has alarming possibilities. How often is the excellent character of an accused man, and his vigorous denials of his guilt, discounted and outweighed by the obvious sincerity and conviction displayed in the witness-box by a man of unblemished character who, has, it seems, no possible motive for telling anything but the truth? Yet here was such a man who swore to seeing what, in fact, he had never seen. Truly a disturbing field of possibility is opened up by this revelation of the working of the human mind.

Meanwhile, as often in these cases, an event which seemed at first sight to solve the problem almost before it was propounded startled the ears of Europe before the noise of the robbery had died away. A report from Reuter of July 21st reads as follows: " Paris.—It has just become known that a student while walking in the Bois de Boulogne last evening found a pearl necklace identical in appearance with that stolen from Mr. Max Mayer. The young man took his find to the police station at Neuilly. Mr. Salomons, the sender of the necklace, was at once sent for, and stated that the necklace was certainly identical with the one stolen, but he could not say for certain that it was it. An expert examination will be made to-day, and the question will then be settled beyond a doubt."—Reuter.

Unfortunately, by the 23rd it was definitely established that the necklace was a clever copy manufactured in Paris for a music-hall artiste then performing at Lyons. She had sent a photograph of the missing necklace to a manufacturer of imitation jewellery, who had copied it so well that it needed experts to declare its falsity. The sham necklace had, by what was presumably a curious coincidence, been dropped in the Bois de Boulogne.

Another newspaper report relates a further remarkable coincidence, for such it must have been, which occurred on the day the parcel containing the real necklace was posted from Paris. I quote from the *Daily Chronicle* of July 18th: " The fact that

79

when the packet reached London the place of the pearls had been taken by eleven lumps of sugar such as could be picked up at any café in Paris, has seized the popular imagination. In this connection a curious incident has come to light. . . .

At a café in the Boulevard Haussman, at no great distance from the post office where Mr. Salomons dispatched the packet, a waiter recalls a curious customer who called on Tuesday afternoon (the day the parcel was sent off) about 2.30 p.m. and ordered coffee. With this the waiter brought three lumps of sugar which the drinker quietly pocketed. Within a few minutes he ordered a second cup. Again the waiter saw him appropriate the sugar. (Here followed a brief description of the man.) The detectives are now engaged upon the seemingly impossible task of ferreting out the man with the black case who has such a propensity for carrying off sugar. At the moment it is impossible to say whether he will ever be found, or whether there is the remotest connection between his actions and the substitution of pieces of French sugar for the necklace." As it happens, we are on both these points no nearer the solution to-day.

So much for two of the three main lines of inquiry, the possible recipients of the stolen goods and the handling of the packet in the post. There remained a third, the nature of the wax found at the damaged end of the parcel on arrival, and the seal with which the forged impressions had been made.

A sample of the wax used by Mr. Salomons and a sample of the seal from the damaged end of the box were analysed by an expert and carefully compared. The analyst's report was quite definite that the two were not the same, and attention was therefore focussed on the seal. That it was a clever forgery was clear to the naked eye, but it was pointed out that any would-be thief, by waiting his opportunity, could make an impression of an impression of the genuine seal, and from that create an almost perfect duplicate of the original. On the other hand, a re-creation of the seal from such material would be the work of an expert, and steps were at once taken to find the maker. An invitation was published in the Press to any person having made such a die or seal to give particulars to Messrs. Price and Gibbs, and this was duly seen by the person responsible. He, however, was of a cautious nature, coming as he did from north of the Tweed, and at first only answered anonymously. On July 25th Messrs. Price and Gibbs received the following letter, marked " Strictly Private," from an unknown source. " Gentlemen," it ran, " I am an engraver, and was asked some weeks ago to engrave a seal. I have no doubt it was for the purpose of pearl robbery. Not wishing my name mentioned, kindly put adt. in personal column of *Evening News* to-morrow as to my procedure in the matter. Yours faithfully, Engraver." To this was added in pencil: " Enclosed find impression of one I did from verbal instructions, but was, I think, *not* used. Did another which I think was the one used. Have just seen reproduction in *Lloyds News*. Put ad. in such a way that no one else will understand as have reason to think I'd be in danger if known. I am giving you this information because I know the people who gave me the instructions and their where-abouts." Needless to say, a reply was published for his benefit in the next day's *Evening News* which for unintelligibility would satisfy the most fastidious. "Will engraver please give full particulars to same address or make appointment for confidential interview? P. and G." As a result of this correspondence the police eventually got in touch with him and secured a statement. His evidence was, of course, of immense importance for in conjunction with another discovery to be mentioned later it led to a man who in the absence of further information might be regarded as the actual thief.

It appeared that a Mr. Peter Robertson Gordon, of King Street, Hammersmith, was an engraver by trade, and some six weeks previously had been having a drink in the "Leather Bottle" public-house, which used to stand at the corner of Leather Lane and Charles Street, Hatton Garden. He was showing a specimen of his work to a friend when a man, whose name he did not know, asked if he were an engraver and where he lived. Nothing more was said at the time, but a week or so later the stranger called at his shop, and asked Mr. Gordon if he would cut him a die from a wax impression which he produced. The impression was made in a soft wax such as dentists use, and the stranger wanted the die as soon as possible. At Gordon's request he brought along on the following day a piece of boxwood in which to cut the die, and Gordon proceeded to make it in his dinner hour. A shilling changed hands and the transaction was closed. The die was a double M. A fortnight or so later the stranger returned, and asked Mr. Gordon to engrave a monogram, H.M., on a locket and shield which he produced, and this was duly done.

The significance of the second transaction will be noted in due course.

Meanwhile, in the course of their inquiries in the English post office, the police had made a potentially important discovery. It seemed that only a fortnight before the robbery, on June 27th, a letter had been received at the General Post Office, which ran as follows:

101-2 Hatton Garden,　　S. Silverman and Co.,
　　London, E.C.　　　Pearls and Precious Stones.
Hol. 2865, Tel. No.

Secretary, General Post Office.

I should esteem it a favour if you will instruct your postman to deliver my correspondence on the first post in the mornings to my office personally, and not to give to lift attendant under any circumstances.

Thanking you,
· Yours faithfully,
· S. SILVERMAN.

A glance at the map of this part of Hatton Garden on page 30, will make it clear that No. 101 was only a few doors from Mr. Mayer's office. Inquiries showed that Mr. Silverman's request had been granted, and that his office consisted of a single room on the third floor, that he certainly conducted a genuine business as a dealer in precious stones and bore, so far as the police were concerned, a good character.

CHAPTER V

To return to the days immediately following the theft, the barometer of hope and despair was violent in its movement, both on the part of those immediately concerned and the highly interested public. Mr. Mayer's initial optimism was based on the difficulty of disposing of the pearls when every legal outlet had been closed by the police. He argued that those clever enough to steal the necklace were probably possessed of sufficient funds to enable them to lie low for a considerable time, then to sell one or two of the smaller pearls to keep themselves in funds and finally, when the search had more or less died down, but not until then, to attempt to smuggle them through the Suez Canal to India, where no further trace of them would ever be found.

Mons. Calchas, the Parisian inquiry agent, placed his faith in the notice of reward. When interviewed and asked " Whom do you suspect?" his reply was in the best traditions of detective fiction. " Everybody," said Mons. Calchas, laughing, " that is my business." He is, however, further reported to have said to a representative of the *Petit Parisien:* " If anyone brings the necklace to us we will immediately hand him a cheque for 250,000 francs (£10,000). We shall ask him for no explanation, and he can be assured of our discretion." Unfortunately such a course, though often no doubt carried out " behind

84

the scenes," is none the less illegal in this country, for it is, in legal terminology, compounding a felony. It is virtually announcing that you will make a bargain with the thief, the terms being that he will return the property and you will forbear to prosecute. Such a course, though undoubtedly in the interests of the individual, is held to be against the interests of the community and is against the law.

However that may be, among those who saw the notice of reward in Paris, and were consumed with a desire to make that enormous sum their own, was a Mr. Samuel Brandstatter, a French Jew by birth, aged 27, and a diamond dealer by trade, carrying on business in the Rue Chateaudun in Paris. It was his practice to go to Antwerp once a fortnight to buy or sell his wares in that international centre of the diamond trade. On the 4th of August, the day when the publication of the French postal inquiry proved that the theft had not taken place in France, he was walking in the street at Antwerp when he met a distant relative, by name Leisir Gutwirth, an Austrian subject of middle age who traded as a diamond dealer between Antwerp and London. He had, in fact, conducted various business deals with Brandstatter over a period of three or four years, and naturally fell into conversation with him. In the course of what turned out to be an historic interview, Gutwirth, after talking of everything except the matter which he wished above all things to discuss, made certain mysterious statements to the effect that he had a very big deal on hand. Apparently he lacked the courage to say more at the moment, and an appointment was made the following day outside the Terminus Hotel, when further details would be disclosed. On the following day the rendezvous was faithfully kept, and without delay Gutwirth came to the point by asking Brandstatter whether he bought goods on a large scale. Brandstatter replied that he would go up to a hundred or two hundred thousand francs. Gutwirth scoffed at such an amount, and explained that his deal was a matter of a million or a million and a half. The whole interview only lasted about twenty minutes, but in that time Gutwirth had with obvious pride confessed that the deal related to no less an article than the widely sought, and still more widely discussed, Max Mayer necklace stolen a fortnight before. Brandstatter, with visions of ten thousand pounds reward, at once proceeded to extract from his presumably dishonest relative all the information that he could. This, however, did not amount to much, for Gutwirth refused to commit himself beyond saying they were " in the hands of his friends in London " and that, save for the diamond clasp, which had been sold, the necklace was intact. At this moment other persons joined them, and after eliciting a promise from Gutwirth to send him further particulars in Paris, Brandstatter walked away. On the next day he returned to Paris to await the longed-for " further particulars." On the 12th of August, hearing nothing more, he wrote to Gutwirth, saying, what was, in fact, untrue, that he had a potential buyer for the " article." In reply he received from Gutwirth, who was now in London, a telegram in German, saying that a letter followed at once. At this point, Brandstatter, seeing that negotiations were definitely about to be opened, wisely decided to

increase his chances of success by enlisting the aid of
a cleverer mind than his own, even if it meant the
halving of the reward. As subsequent events made
clear, it needed skill, nerve and judgment, as well as
unlimited " cheek," to bluff an international gang of
criminals, and it was a sound move on the part of
Brandstatter to double the chances of success in the
way he did. He at once got into touch with his
cousin, Myer Cohen Quadratstein, who proved himself to be the brains of the partnership, and from that
moment took control.

Quadratstein was a young man of twenty-nine,
born in London, though he had lived most of his life
in Paris. He, too, was a diamond merchant, and in
that capacity occasionally travelled between Paris and
London. He knew of Gutwirth by reputation, and
had once done business with him by acting as " intermediary " in the sale of some sapphires to the famous
" Cammi " Grizard. No one suggested, at least in so
far as the young Parisian was concerned, that this was
other than a perfectly honest deal.

When Brandstatter showed his cousin the telegram
from Gutwirth they discussed their plans, and decided
to wait until the letter came before taking further
action. The letter arrived next day, and was the first
occasion on which one of the gang committed himself
in writing. This letter, which arrived registered and
expressed, was written in Yiddish, and the following
is a translation of the relative parts.

It was sent from 2, Charles St., Hatton Garden,
and was dated August 13th. " My dear Samuel," it
read, " I am now writing to you explicitly that you
shall leave to-morrow for London and send me a

telegram when you are leaving. I will then meet
you at the station and we can arrange matters.

"Bring with you 1½—you know what I mean—
what we have spoken about. . . .

"Now, dear Samuel, about what you have told me
that you can get the 1½. If you can come yourself
I shall be very pleased, but if the man does not want
to give it to you he can come with you, but be sure
that the man is all right. Bring with you what I am
asking you. . . ." The letter ended: "Your always
loving, Leisir." The "1½" referred, of course, to
the Antwerp conversation and proved valuable corroboration of Brandstatter's story. On receipt of this
letter Quadratstein dictated to his cousin a reply,
"asking for a photograph of the necklace or a few
pearls on approval so that we should be able to convince our would-be buyer that it was really the string
belonging to Mr. Max Mayer." He also said that
his buyer had told him that the price was very
exaggerated, as he would have to put the pearls away
for at least five years. At least this self-appointed
amateur detective was not wanting in the necessary
imagination and "nerve"! In reply he received a
wire from Gutwirth in London, saying in German,
"Come at once. Telegraph if left." The invitation
was definite and tempting. All Europe was searching for the necklace, the fortunate discoverer of which
would earn ten thousand pounds, and here were a
couple of young men who, alone of honest members
of the public, were invited by those who knew its
whereabouts to negotiate for its sale. Should they
invite the co-operation of the police, or at least the
underwriters, or play out the game alone? The

whole affair might be another hoax or, far more probable, an attempt to get two foolish young men to London with £60,000 upon them in cash and then, by robbery with violence or by fraud, deprive them of it, giving nothing in return.

It may be that a wiser pair would have at least told the police what they were about to do, but they were young, and the rôle of amateur detective was as exciting as it was new. The notice of reward was dazzling to their eyes, and Quadratstein at least, as he later confessed in the witness-box, had no illusions as to his brilliant gifts of lying when occasion arose. They hesitated no longer. Whatever the outcome the die was cast, and in a few hours, having wired to Gutwirth, they were on their way to London to earn their vast reward.

They arrived at Charing Cross on the night of August 15th at 10.45 p.m., just one month after Mr. Salomons had arrived at the same platform to give his account of the sending off of the pearls. But whereas the latter was met by representatives of the Law, our young conspirators were met by Mr. Gutwirth as a representative of those who fight the Law. To explain the presence of Quadratstein, whom Gutwirth did not remember, Brandstatter, according to a plan concocted on the way from France, introduced him as a cousin who knew of a likely buyer for the pearls. From the station they went to the bar of the Golden Cross Hotel opposite, where they were at once joined by the same Mr. Silverman whose office was so close to Mr. Mayer's, and whose taste in seals was curiously enough, like his, a double " M." Silverman was presented to the two young men, though, in fact, no names was mentioned, and Quadratstein slipped out with Gutwirth to explain to him that he was authorised by his (imaginary) principal to offer half a million francs for the necklace, on being satisfied that they were really Mr. Mayer's. Gutwirth's reply was emphatic. "You had better take the next train home." He added that the lowest price would be a million francs, and he wanted in addition a hundred thousand as commission for himself. Silverman and Brandstatter joined them at this moment, and the former confirmed that a million was their lowest price, adding that it would have to be in French notes rather than the far more dangerous, because more easily traceable, English equivalents. At Gutwirth's suggestion they then adjourned to his private house in Petherton Road, Canonbury, but the taxi was ordered to stop a few yards short of the address given, and the four of them got out. Quadratstein, in his new capacity of amateur detective, had his senses fully alert for any clue which might conceivably lead the faster to the pearls, and at once noticed a man wearing a tweed cap and white silk scarf, who seemed to have been waiting out of sight, slip across in the darkness and speak to Silverman. He could not see his features, however, and followed Brandstatter and Gutwirth into the house.

Ten minutes later the door of the room in which they were seated opened, and Silverman announced the master criminal himself, the "Cammi" of the criminal underworld. This was the first time Brandstatter had seen the "King of 'Fences,'" though Quadratstein had met him once before, as already mentioned, in a business deal. Gutwirth formally introduced his " Chief " to the two young men, stating, what was news to them, that Silverman and Grizard were the owners of the pearls, though whether Mr. Mayer, who, of course, knew nothing of this meeting, would have agreed with this proposition is a question he was never asked. At Gutwirth's request Quadratstein repeated the offer of 500,000 francs for the necklace as a whole, but Grizard curtly replied that he had an American customer who was ready to take it for a million francs. As Gutwirth had called them in, however, he would give them the " first refusal " until the following Friday, but if the money was not by then in his hands he would sell to the American. Whether or not this gentleman existed outside Grizard's brain, we do not know. If not, it was an element of bluff which the two Parisians had no intention of calling while they still had better cards to play. Quadratstein's concern was to see the pearls, and if possible find their temporary whereabouts, partly to satisfy himself that these scoundrels really had some pearls to sell, and partly to prove that they were part of the necklace for which the underwriters offered the reward. He therefore asked for an appointment to be made for the following day when he might see the necklace for himself, saying that this was his purchaser's desire. An appointment was accordingly made for the following morning in a way peculiar to the underworld, for while Gutwirth and Grizard were to meet in a place not fully disclosed, the two young men were to wait in a nearby café until fetched to the common rendezvous. As it was by this time very late, Gutwirth offered to put his visitors up for the night, and they agreed to accept his hospitality. Grizard left with Silverman, and the remaining three, after chatting until the early hours of the morning, retired to bed, the two visitors sleeping together in a second bed in Gutwirth's room. The next morning, the 16th, all three went off by tram to Islington, where they had breakfast. After breakfast the two Parisians were taken by Gutwirth to the tea-shop previously arranged, having left their luggage in a cloak-room on the way. The meeting-place was a Lyons tea-shop close to Hatton Garden, where Gutwirth was to pick up Grizard at half-past ten. Shortly after this, Gutwirth rejoined the two excited amateurs, and the three of them waited in silence.

A few minutes later Grizard passed by the door, whereupon Gutwirth joined him and called the others out. All four of them took a 'bus along Holborn, going West, until they came to a Lipton's tea-room near the Holborn Restaurant. Grizard went in first and asked if the smoking-room was open. He was told that it was not, but that they could smoke where they were. All four went in and sat at the corner table furthest from the door. They ordered refreshments and prepared to wait. There were then about a dozen other people in the room. A few minutes later a stranger entered, but a stranger wearing a tweed cap and white silk scarf which to Quadratstein seemed familiar. He later described the man as of " medium height, fair hair, fair drooping moustache, grey watery eyes and wearing a black band on his arm." The stranger sat down near them, and the silence which ensued was a sore trial to the self-control of the two young men, for they realised that at last they were about to see, and maybe handle, the necklace for which all Europe was seeking, and for which there was ten thousand pounds reward. It was Grizard, apparently satisfied that they were neither watched nor overheard, who gave the signal by pulling out a cigarette and asking for a match. Without a sound the stranger, whom the two young men were later able to identify as Lockett, took from his pocket a box of matches and tossed it carelessly on to the table between them. All five of them leant over the table as Grizard, imperturbable as ever, slowly opened the box and showed it to contain, on a layer of wadding, three enormous, round rose-tinted pearls. Little did the customers at the other tables on that August morning realise that close beside them sat the master criminal with, in his hands, the finest of the missing pearls! As afterwards transpired, the largest of the three was worth alone £10,000, for it weighed over forty-seven grains and was the crowning glory of the necklace as a whole. Quadratstein removed the largest and examined it, while Brandstatter examined the other two. The three conspirators, whose conduct, if the two young experts were believed, had already earned them penal servitude, sat watching anxiously. When the examination was finished, Gutwirth asked: " Well, are you satisfied that they are real pearls?" Quadratstein replied that though he was satisfied they were genuine pearls, he still awaited proof that they were part of the necklace, and that he could only be sure by weighing them and comparing them with the weights as published in the notice of reward. Grizard hesitated a moment, and then agreed that the request was reasonable. He instructed Gutwirth to take the two of them to some place where they could weigh the pearls in secrecy, and Gutwirth, pocketing the precious box, told them to follow him outside.

Once in the street, the older, more experienced man betrayed the constant fear of the police in which such criminals pass their lives. Whether or not they had other evidence against him of complicity in the theft and subsequent disposal of the pearls, he had no intention of being arrested with them actually in his possession, and handed them to Quadratstein, preferring to trust his new confederate rather than risk arrest with the goods upon him. Quadratstein was tempted to act at once. Here he was, within twenty-four hours of leaving Paris on his great adventure, with three of the finest pearls in his pocket, one of the gang within his power and police within easy hail. But he was out for bigger game than his dishonest relative. He wanted all the pearls and all the gang and all of the reward. He therefore quietly followed Gutwirth to the " George," which, typical of such rendezvous, was down a narrow turning such as men like Gutwirth loved. It was then about noon, and the three of them, entering by a side door, walked upstairs under Gutwirth's guidance to a first-floor dining-room, then unoccupied. Here they locked themselves in, and Brandstatter, producing a pair of jeweller's scales, weighed the pearls and compared them with the weights upon the notice of reward. Quadratstein, being satisfied that they were three of the finest pearls on the string, made a careful note of the weights for future reference, and with Gutwirth's permission proceeded to thread them on a piece of silk, the ends of which he doubly sealed, one with Brandstatter's seal and one with his own. This is a common way of identifying pearls sent on approval, so that both parties may be satisfied that they are dealing with the self-same pearls. Quadratstein replaced the three pearls on the wadding in the box and the box in his pocket, after which the three of them returned to Holborn. On their way back to the tea-shop they met the redoubtable Grizard, whose first care was to ask for the return of the pearls. Quadratstein informed him he was satisfied that the pearls were part of the stolen necklace, and would return to Paris at once to collect the money from his principal. Grizard gave them until the following Friday, the 22nd, to collect the million francs, and an appointment was made on that day at the First Avenue Hotel. The four then separated, but the two young amateurs, elated with the rapidity of their success, had no intention of returning to Paris. On the other hand, they realised that they had done as much as was possible alone, and that for any further step they must produce either a " buyer " or a large sum of money, or both. They therefore collected their luggage from the cloak-room and drove to Charing Cross, arriving at the station a few minutes before the Continental boat train was due to leave. Having sent off certain telegrams, however, they considered their efforts at throwing possible followers off the scent had been carried far enough, and drove back to the City, this time to the Great Eastern Hotel, where they booked a double room. Leaving their luggage there, they went without delay to Messrs. Price and Gibbs, whose address was printed on the document which never left their consciousness, the notice of reward. Being a Saturday afternoon there was no one there, but they subsequently found Mr. Price at his business address and made an appointment with him for the Tuesday morning at their hotel. This gentleman had been untiring in his efforts during the last four weeks to trace the criminals, and had interviewed innumerable persons in London, in the Provinces and on the Continent, who purported to be in possession of information which would earn for them at least a portion of the reward, but the value of such " information " can be left to the imagination. This was, in fact, the first occasion when the information offered promised to be really valuable.

On Tuesday morning, August 19th, he therefore met the two young men at their hotel, and listened to their story, taking careful notes of all they had to tell. Brandstatter spoke very little English, but his cousin translated to him what was said, even as he had done at previous conversations with the members of the gang. Mr. Price was naturally non-committal in his opinion of the story which they told. For all he knew they might be emissaries of the persons who held the necklace, or simply telling a circumstantial story with a view to obtaining money for " expenses," as so many others had done. On the other hand, their request that he should produce someone whom they could put forward as a prospective buyer, willing to pay a million francs, was, if their story were true, a reasonable one, and provided that a suitable man could be found, at least no harm could ensue. He, therefore, took full notes of their story, with the weights and details of the pearls, asked for and was

given references, and finally left them, well pleased
with their morning's work. Meanwhile Quadratstein had realised that he and Brandstatter were supposed to be in Paris, and that any communication with
Gutwirth must purport to come from that address.
He therefore invented a simple artifice for the next
move in the game. Having with such little difficulty
discovered three of the finest pearls, he set to work to
trace the necklace as a whole. He instructed Brandstatter to write to his wife in Paris, asking her to
stamp and post the letter to Gutwirth which he
enclosed. This letter has been since destroyed, but
its contents can be gleaned from Quadratstein's
account of it in evidence. " He (Brandstatter) wrote
to say that we had seen our buyer, and that by the
description we gave of the three pearls he (the buyer)
was satisfied they were three of Mr. Mayer's string,
but that he still doubted whether they had the whole
string, and that it would be necessary for us to come
to London to see the string to convince him." This
letter had its due effect. Gutwirth replied at once, in
Yiddish, addressing his letter to Paris. On receiving
it Mrs. Brandstatter, thrilled with the adventure in
which her husband was concerned, showed it to Mrs.
Quadratstein who, at her husband's request, brought
it to London without delay, arriving on the 20th at
the platform at which successive characters in this
drama of real life seemed fated to appear. A translation of the letter reads as follows: " London.
19/8/13. I have received your letter and am
antonished that your man should believe that I have
only what you have seen. Therefore, my dear
Samuel . . . you must come, and send me a wire.

Bring one, and we shall only ask the money of you after you have seen the whole thing. I wish to remark that if you play about with me you will be sorry, as I can dispose of it at once to a foreigner to-day . . . your friend, L. Gutwirth." The language speaks for itself. In answer to this a telegram was sent to Gutwirth from Paris, saying that the two men were returning to London at once and would meet him, Gutwirth, the following morning at the First Avenue Hotel at 11 a.m.

As they were then in fact staying at the Great Eastern Hotel, they hurriedly packed their luggage and moved to the First Avenue, where they booked a double room on the first floor, No. 197, which was destined to be the scene of the next dramatic interview. The position of the two Parisians had now been made secure. From the moment they had officially invoked Mr. Price's aid they had agreed to work together under his guidance and control, and though they were still to handle the actual negotiations, they no longer did so on their own responsibility, but under the watchful, anxious and all-seeing eye of Mr. Price, who had himself, of course, to work behind the scenes.

The two conspirators were only just in time in moving to their new hotel. Gutwirth had already called that morning and then gone away, but a note to his address in Charles Street, Hatton Garden, fetched him back, and at noon they were all together in the lounge. Gutwirth's first request was characteristic of the man, and has had many parallels before and since. He asked if Quadratstein had made it clear to the Paris buyer that he wanted paid to him a special commission of 5 per cent without the others, Grizard, Silverman and Lockett, knowing that any such commission had been paid. Fortunately for the interests of justice, " honour among thieves " is the exception rather than the rule, and these rings within rings very often give the police their only method of breaking up a gang. Presumably one of the four was the actual thief, probably Silverman with Lockett's help, while Grizard was the master mind that planned the robbery and subsequent disposition of the goods. Gutwirth's only part was to get in touch with someone who would buy the pearls or see that they were sold. Yet not only did he ask for an equal share with those who had borne the heat and burden of the criminal day, but also for a first or special commission to be given him behind his partners' backs. Quadratstein's disgust at the man's mentality was fortunately kept in check, and he replied that he had spoken to " the buyer " about the commission, but that he had better speak to him himself when he arrived. Gutwirth then asked if Quadratstein had got the money with him, and the latter replied that the buyer was still arranging with various Parisian banks for the provision of the required amount in London when he arrived. This was a brilliant effort on the young man's part, for even Gutwirth would appreciate the undesirability of crossing the Channel with £40,000 upon one in cold cash. A few minutes later Silverman arrived and was told the same story. An appointment was therefore made for the following day.

Meanwhile Mr. Price had been in anxious consultation with Max Mayer as to the best man to play

the rôle of buyer. It was realised that certain of
the pearls would have to be bought from the thieves
for cash, partly to incriminate them when arrested
in possession of the numbered notes, and partly as
the next step towards finding and recovering the
remaining pearls. For this task a person would have
to be found of discretion, tact and skill. The choice
was narrowed by the fact that he would have to be
a pearl expert who was, or could pretend to be,
Parisian. The final choice was a Mr. Spanier, a
Frenchman by birth but a naturalised Englishman,
who was a pearl merchant living in the Rue Lafay-
ette, Paris. On the night of the 19th, after his first
long talk with Brandstatter and Quadratstein, Mr.
Price wrote to Mr. Spanier, explaining the difficulty
in which he found himself. The letter continued:
" Above all things you must not come to my office,
because I am being shadowed, and it would spoil
everything if it were known that you and I were in
collaboration." He concluded with specific directions
as to writing or telephoning, to put the above admoni-
tion into effect. Mr. Price's caution was probably a
genuine need. He was known to be responsible for
the investigations, and knew that the gang concerned,
having a vast amount at stake, would probably
shadow him, to learn, if possible, how much the
authorities knew.

Mr. Spanier accepted the offer at once, and
travelled to Hardelot, near Boulogne, as requested in
Mr. Price's letter, to confer with Mr. Mayer, who
was there on holiday. From there he crossed to
London on the Friday afternoon, arriving in London,
as most of the characters in this story, at Charing

Cross at 10.45 p.m. He was met by Mr. Price, who bore him away for a lengthy conference, at which it was arranged in detail just what part Mr. Spanier was to play. Though in fact a naturalised Englishman since 1894, he was a Latin in temperament, with the inborn capacity of such for playing a dramatic part. He made it quite clear at once, however, that he was intervening as a personal friend of Mr. Mayer's, for whom he had great personal regard, and not as a detective, amateur or professional, and he expressly stipulated that he should have no connection with the police aspect of the coming drama. As he said at the time, and more than once subsequently, " I am not a policeman—I am an expert!"

This being understood, it was agreed that he should act the part of a foreign " receiver," who knew no English and only spoke German. Having a healthy regard for his own personal safety, shared by Mr. Price, who would be responsible for it to the underwriters, it was further agreed that under no circumstances should he permit himself to be inveigled into a private house, where, in the hands of such international criminals, in an expressive phrase, " almost anything was rather more than likely to happen " to him. From the moment he undertook his new duties he was, in fact, watched by Mr. Price's own police wherever he went.

Meanwhile, on the Friday morning, Gutwirth, Silverman and the two Parisians met in the lounge of the First Avenue Hotel, as previously arranged, and Quadratstein had to explain why the buyer was not there. He gave the same explanation as on the previous day, and added that he, the buyer, could not afford to buy the necklace all at once, but would begin with the three pearls which had been seen and weighed. The point of this remark is obvious. It was bad enough to have to produce £4,000 and risk it being lost, but if the underwriters were to have to buy back the necklace for the price demanded for it there would be little value remaining in it when ultimately found. The two young men, having seen their guests depart, went off to Mr. Price, as was their daily wont, and received instructions for the following morning. They were given a green identity card, numbered 123437, and told that they would know Mr. Spanier the next morning because he would produce a similar one numbered 123438. It is these little touches, so beloved of detective fiction, which make it so hard to believe that this was a drama of real life, a battle of wits with £150,000 at stake, and not a " thriller " written for the screen.

Early the following morning, August 23rd, Mr. Spanier arrived at the First Avenue Hotel, where he asked for Mr. Quadratstein, and on his appearance solemnly presented his green card. Quadratstein presented his and the two Parisians shook hands. Brandstatter was then fetched and a conference ensued. Mr. Spanier then departed, having learnt the part he was to play, and fetched from Mr. Price's office the hundred thousand francs which Quadratstein had told Mr. Price was the price at which he hoped to buy the three examined pearls. Needless to say, a careful note had been taken of the numbers of the hundred one-thousand franc notes which were given him, in hopes that they would change hands and then be found again.

Meanwhile Gutwirth arrived and once more demanded his doubly dishonest commission of 5 per cent. While they were talking Mr. Spanier returned, with instructions from Mr. Price as to what pearls he was to attempt to buy and a warning to take no risks.

In the notes which Mr. Price wrote down each day of the progress of events, the following entry appears for Friday, the 22nd. " Met Spanier. Long talk with him. Agreed to act part. Agreed to hold him indemnified. Warned him how not to act and what not to do. Good chap. Seems a game one; Southern temperament, however." This agreement to hold him indemnified showed that Mr. Price was quite alive to the dangers of his emissary's task. The gang concerned were hardened criminals, and though no one of them had a record of violence, the size of the amount at stake might well cause men of finer sensibility than they to resort to it if once they realised that they were being betrayed. Mr. Spanier, however, knew of the risk he ran, and Quadratstein and Brandstatter were prepared to risk a little shooting to secure the promised reward.

To return from these considerations to the First Avenue Hotel, on Mr. Spanier's return Quadratstein took him aside with Brandstatter, and arranged that Gutwirth should be told that Spanier had 100,000 francs upon him to exchange with the three examined pearls. Gutwirth was then introduced to Spanier, but before any suggestion could be made reiterated his demand for a private commission of 5 per cent and Spanier, to put in time, proceeded to haggle over the amount. At the same time he was forming his own impression of his two confederates, and told Mr. Price that night that he was satisfied they had no secret understanding with the other side. The conversation was carried on in German, as it was agreed that Spanier should pretend to know no English in the hopes of overhearing comments which it was not intended he should understand. From this moment events began to move rapidly, and it is not very easy to follow, from the contradictory evidence, their exact sequence. Quadratstein, in his evidence, said that Spanier got impatient when Silverman did not arrive, and left, but as Mr. Spanier not only said that he was there, but described what happened and what was said, it would seem that on this occasion it is Quadratstein whose memory was at fault. Mr. Spanier says that the next arrival in the lounge of the hotel was Silverman, who suddenly appeared at their table, sat down and joined in the conversation without introduction of any kind, apparently another habit of the criminal fraternity. Gutwirth, however, introduced him as one of the men who held the necklace, and retired with Brandstatter and Quadratstein to another corner of the lounge. Silverman, alone with Spanier, said that everything was all right and he would see the necklace shortly, but not on that day, as his " friend who had the necklace," whom Spanier in his mind put down as Lockett, was motoring near Southampton with some girls. He added, by way of explanation of this behaviour, that the man in question had lost his wife some six months' previously and in order to forget his sorrows was leading rather a fast life. Lockett had in fact arrived by car at Southampton on the Monday previously, with his niece and daughter and another man, and Silverman had spent the night at the same hotel on the 21st.

Mr. Spanier pretended to be furious at the delay, and threatened to call off all negotiations and return to Paris at once. He agreed, however, to meet Silverman again at 2 p.m. to see whether he could by telegraphing then produce his man. He then left the hotel, and went straight to the Holborn Viaduct Hotel, where Mr. Price was anxiously awaiting news. Meanwhile Gutwirth had departed, leaving Silverman and the two cousins in the lounge. At Silverman's suggestion these three set off for the Lipton's teashop near the Holborn Restaurant, to find and report to Grizard the progress of the sale. Close to the teashop Quadratstein made a vague excuse and slipped away to the Holborn Viaduct Hotel to report to Mr. Price, and receive instructions for his future moves in the game.

For the moment the allies' plans had certainly miscarried, and every day's delay was serious. It was only a matter of time before a mind like Grizard's grew suspicious of the " purchasers," or stumbled on some connection between them and the underwriters, in which case not only would their very lives be in jeopardy, but all hope of recovering the pearls would be at an end. Quadratstein was therefore instructed to return to the rendezvous and make a definite appointment, which would be kept by all concerned. This he did, only to find the outwardly respectable and always imperturbable Grizard quietly sitting in the teashop, sipping his cup of coffee, with the hunched-up figure of Silverman and the nervous Brandstatter on either side trying to appear completely unconcerned. It would be interesting to know what Quadratstein would have replied had the great man asked him where he had so quietly disappeared on leaving the hotel! However, no such awkward riddle was propounded to him and Quadratstein, in pursuance of his instructions, told them that the next day, being Sunday, would be inconvenient for the purchaser, but that on Monday morning, the 25th, he would be at the First Avenue Hotel at 11.30 sharp, to give the holders of the necklace a final chance. If it were not then forthcoming negotiations would be considered at an end. All agreed to this appointment and the meeting then broke up.

At 2 p.m. Mr. Spanier returned to the First Avenue Hotel, only to be told by Silverman of the new appointment. He therefore went back to the Holborn Viaduct Hotel, returned to Mr. Price the unused bundle of notes and joined in a conference with all concerned.

So ended an eventful week which was, however, but a prelude to the following. Pending the resumed negotiations which were arranged to take place on the following Monday, Mr. Spanier felt himself at liberty to return to Hardelot for a resumption of his holiday. August in London is a matter of little interest to a Londoner, but of even less to a tired Parisian. Mr. Price, however, who had by now thoroughly worked himself up into the true " detective story " frame of mind, was convinced that Spanier was being shadowed night and day by representatives of the criminals, and feared that for him to be seen in consultation with Mr. Mayer would be fatal to their plans. As Mr. Spanier, however, insisted on returning, a plan was conceived, and duly carried out, in complete accordance with the canons of detective fiction. He had to leave his luggage at the Carlton Hotel, where he was then ostensibly staying, and go by taxi with a small valise to a rendezvous, of all romantic places, in the Old Kent Road. He was there met by the traditional "fast car," which drove him, we trust at not excessive speed, to Folkestone, where he caught the afternoon mail boat, thereby eluding the watchers who were probably on the lookout at the London terminus to see if he left town. By the same unusual methods he returned to London on the Sunday night, prepared for the interview on the Monday following.

CHAPTER VI

THE morning of August 25th was filled with joyous expectation for all concerned. The members of the gang expected to sell at least a couple of the pearls for £4,000 in cash, and possibly arrange for the subsequent sale of the necklace as a whole. Mr. Price, as representing the underwriters at Lloyds, with whom the necklace was insured, Mr. Mayer, who confidently hoped to get it back, and Messrs. Brandstatter and Quadratstein, who hoped before the day was out to earn at least a portion of the vast reward, were equally elated, though the latter were naturally somewhat nervous at the outcome of the interview. However, they had been accepted by the authorities as collaborators, and Mr. Spanier was to accompany them, not only in the rôle of buyer but to lend his moral, and if need be physical, support.

The first arrival at the rendezvous was Silverman, who met the two young amateur detectives in the lounge of the hotel, and told them that during the last two days he had succeeded in getting in touch with " the gentleman who was motoring with several ladies in the country " in an attempt to drown the memory of his lately departed wife, and that it was this gentleman who had the pearls in his possession. Before the two could ask him the vital question, whether the said possessor was to appear that morning at the rendezvous, the elusive Silverman made some excuse and left them, saying he would be back in a few minutes.

The next arrival was Mr. Spanier, who was a few minutes late, as he had had to call at Mr. Price's office to collect the 100,000 francs. Ten minutes later Silverman returned from his mysterious pilgrimage and took control of the proceedings. He courteously invited the " buyer " and his " agents " to a rendezvous where he assured them they would be quiet and undisturbed. Mr. Spanier, somewhat suspicious and perturbed, was inclined to remonstrate, but the cheerful acquiescence of the younger men decided him to see where Silverman intended them to go. At Silverman's suggestion, therefore, they watched him leave the hotel and turn up Holborn to the West. A few seconds later all three followed him, highly intrigued if somewhat nervous at this mysterious procession to an unknown end. Matters were not simplified when a few hundred yards up the road their leader stopped, returned to where they awaited him and, explaining that he had started off in the wrong direction, led them back again past the hotel and onward to the East. At the Chancery Lane Tube Station Silverman went in, and the others followed him. Silverman, without informing them where they were to go, went to the booking office to buy tickets, but the others failed to hear the destination which he named. Spanier, whose suspicions suddenly returned with this uncertainty, asked Quadratstein in German to enquire of Silverman to what address they were being taken. Silverman, seeing they were suspicious, hesitated, and then admitted that the rendezvous was the private house of a friend in Golders Green.

As Quadratstein turned back to pass this information on to Spanier his eye fell on a figure which, with its usual placid imperturbability, was standing in the entrance, framed against the light outside. To Spanier's over-excited nerves, this vision of " Cammi " silently appearing at their backs was the final touch to his suspicions of a trap. He therefore firmly announced that under no circumstances would he be taken to a private house of any kind. Grizard intervened and argued with him, saying that he knew of a " quiet and stylish " house where they could inspect and weigh the pearls without the slightest chance of being disturbed or overheard.

Mr. Spanier, however, had by now thoroughly worked out the rôle which he intended to play, and, deciding that the boldest course was the best, as being the most likely to allay the criminals' suspicions, began to " put over " an elaborate bluff which he maintained successfully to the end. His part was that of a French receiver of stolen property, a criminal like themselves, and therefore equally in fear of the police. When tenderly invited to a private house he cleverly evaded that unpleasant suggestion by refusing on the grounds that *he*, the French receiver, was afraid of *them!* " I do not know you," he said, " I have never seen you before. How do I know that you will not lure me into a trap and then betray me to the police?" Warming to his work, and thoroughly enjoying himself, he went much further. " How do I know," he said suspiciously, that you yourselves

A photograph, reduced in size, of the £150,000 necklace and the match-box in which it was subsequently found.

are not policemen in disguise?" Grizard, who had
been called many names in his time but never anything quite so flattering as this, was somewhat taken
aback, while the others roared with laughter. The
Frenchman, following up an obvious advantage, went
on: " You pretend to be suspicious of me. It is I
who am far more afraid of you!" As later events
proved, he kept up this pose of being frightened of
the men he was in fact assisting to betray, throughout the whole of the subsequent negotiations, and
with great success.

Whether Grizard really intended any harm to Mr.
Spanier at such a private interview must remain a
matter of surmise. He knew that he had on him a
considerable sum of money, and that if this were
stolen he, the presumed " receiver," would not dare
to prosecute, but such a crime was alien to his ordinary
practice for, as already said, the swindling type of
criminal is, generally speaking, faithful to his speciality, and avoids all forms of violence as carefully as
any peaceful citizen. On the other hand, the
" buyer," at an address unknown to his accomplices,
if any, would be absolutely at their mercy, but with
every hope of becoming peacefully possessed of at
least £4,000 in a few hours' time, and this by parting
with a very small percentage of a necklace which in
its entirety had only cost him at the most £500, there
was little point in shattering all chance of further
lucrative " arrangements " by the use of force. However that may be, Mr. Spanier was adamant, and
Silverman and Grizard drew apart to change their
plans. Spanier's remarks had of course been made in
German, and Silverman had had to act as interpreter.

They now, for Grizard's benefit, talked in English to each other, and Spanier, gazing round him with exaggerated lack of interest strove to overhear their words. Telephone numbers were mentioned, which he memorised and later wrote down, but he heard nothing more. In a few minutes they apparently came to some decision, and Silverman returned to the booking office to sell back the tickets he had taken to Golders Green. A fresh appointment was discussed, and Grizard, always the tactful strategist, suggested as a rendezvous the Frenchman's own hotel, thus tending to allay, as he supposed, the other's nervous apprehensions. The time was arranged as 1.45 that afternoon, and the place of meeting the billiard room of the First Avenue Hotel. It was then about noon, and the four men parted. Silverman and Grizard had presumably expected their three " clients " to agree to the suggested rendezvous, and the other members of the gang were probably waiting with what patience they could muster for the five men to arrive. However that may be, the two " decoys " allowed themselves sufficient time to acquaint the Golders Green contingent of their change of plans.

Meanwhile Spanier and his two collaborators, though disappointed at the morning's waste of time, were anxious to inform Mr. Price of the postponement. They accordingly went to lunch at the Holborn Viaduct Hotel, which the latter had adopted as his advance base of operations, in preference to his office, where none of the conspirators might dare be seen. Even at the hotel he refused to lunch with the other three for fear of being seen with them, but gleaned from Mr. Spanier in his room upstairs the change of plans.

Punctually at 1.45 p.m. the three men reached their own hotel for the fateful interview, and crossed the lounge to the billiard room, where they encountered Grizard placidly watching a game of pool. Gutwirth was also present, and Mr. Spanier, faithful to his rôle, renewed his protestations of suspicion. " I know your friends Mr. Quadratstein and Mr. Brandstatter," he said, " but who is this?" Grizard assured him he was " safe " (not knowing how little he deserved that term!), and Mr. Spanier grudgingly accepted him. At this moment Silverman arrived, and the five men, with a common instinct, turned to Grizard as the master mind to suggest a stage for the next scene in the drama. The Englishman, for he was the only native of this country present, quietly took command, and suggested, as a meeting place acceptable to all, the bedroom on the first floor occupied by Quadratstein and Brandstatter.

Gutwirth, with his " far too long a tongue," was to wait downstairs, while Spanier and his " agents " were to lead the way, he and Silverman joining them in five minutes' time. Spanier was relieved at the suggestion and gladly acquiesced. In a private house, even of the " quiet and stylish " variety, anything might happen in one's dealings with a gang of criminals. In a bedroom in a large hotel, however, it was difficult to see how anything untoward could occur. The three men accordingly went upstairs, and were followed a few minutes later by Silverman. The room was a double bedroom of a type to be found in every such hotel before the War, with nothing to suggest the meeting place of famous thieves and the market for their stolen property. A few minutes later Grizard quietly entered and the circle was complete. The door was locked, and at Spanier's suggestion the table which stood between the two beds was moved to the window so that they might have better light for inspecting and weighing the pearls. All but Brandstatter sat down round the table, but the wily Grizard, with the ring-craft of the master criminal, was careful to place his chair and Silverman's upon that side of the table which put the two of them between the three men and the door. Brandstatter remained standing behind his cousin's chair.

The stage was set for the all-important interview, and it is none too easy to appreciate the thoughts which passed through Mr. Spanier's mind. Blasé as we are in 1929 with the endless stream of " thrillers " which flows from a hundred publishers, it is difficult to tune one's consciousness from the world of fiction into the world of fact. The artificial excitement of the detective novel, and its still more blatant brother the " thriller " sold as such, almost warps the mind from the ability to understand such excitement in reality, and to one of Mr. Spanier's temperament the excitement which anticipation had engendered lacks description save in cheap superlatives. Here was the whole of Europe searching for the most famous necklace in the world. The centre of the search was London, the deserted London of a sultry and uninteresting August in which even the Press could find but little to report. Yet here in London, unknown to the public who pursued their avocations undisturbed, the finest brains in the Metropolis, from

Scotland Yard, from Hatton Garden and from Lloyd's, were hot on the scent of the greatest criminal organiser of his day and £150,000 worth of incomparable pearls.

The pearls! Everyone was talking about them, in trams and trains, in clubs and business premises, at lunch and in the home, yet here, in a first-floor bedroom in the heart of London, he, Mr. Spanier, was to handle, actually handle, what the world was looking for! Fact was fact, however, and a part had to be played. It was therefore Mr. Spanier who insisted on locking the door. The others were surprised. "We don't want interruptions," said Mr. Spanier, in his best criminal-conspiracy manner, "and I don't trust you not to have told the police!"

It would seem that the others were armed with revolvers, ready for all emergencies, but Mr. Spanier wisely appreciated the danger and futility of such a course, and preferred to bluff this detail as he had bluffed the rest. He therefore kept his right hand in his trousers pocket throughout the interview whenever possible, to maintain the impression that he trusted no-one save himself.

When the table had been moved into the window, that the precious daylight might more easily fall upon the famous pearls, Grizard, the chief conspirator in silence opened the interview by taking from his right-hand trouser pocket a parcel wrapped up in brown paper. This he handed to Silverman, the "little Jew" as Spanier, who had not heard his name, described him to Mr. Price that evening, and Silverman undid the parcel which the great man would not trouble to undo. He proceeded to empty onto the

table all that it contained, which proved to be a small
tin box and two Bryant and May's match boxes. These
were carefully opened in turn. In one of the two
match boxes were the pearls which Quadratstein and
Brandstatter had examined, weighed and sealed in the
" George " public-house the preceding Saturday
week; in the second were the three pearls, two of
the " round " variety and a " drop " pearl, which Mr.
Salomons had packed up with the necklace on the 15th
of July; while, in the small tin box, with scarcely
any wrapping, lay the rest of the missing necklace,
which was valued by its owner at £150,000! The
effect on the three Parisians can be better imagined
than described. All three were violently excited, and
allowed themselves to toy with the thought of keeping there and then, if need be at the point of the
revolver, the prize for which all three of them, the
young men in particular, had worked so hard. But
orders were orders, and the game must be played to
the finish as their absent " chief " had ordered.
Spanier's instructions were explicit and allowed no
compromise, to choose and buy the finest of the pearls
and to run no risks. Mr. Price was no mean judge
of human nature and saw the necessity of making
such a " tempermental " subject, as he had described
him, promise to obey his more experienced friend. A
revolver is a dangerous toy, and to force the hand of
a man of Grizard's reputation and experience would
more than likely end in losing the necklace, the
criminals, and maybe even the soundness of their life
and limb.

Spanier therefore controlled his excitement and
carefully examined the pearls. Once so occupied, the

connoisseur predominated, as with loving care he handled and then weighed each individual pearl. Meanwhile Quadratstein was satisfying himself that the seals upon the three examined pearls were still unbroken, and that the pearls were the same three. At a single glance Mr. Spanier was satisfied that the necklace was in fact Max Mayer's, having compared the weights as he had found them with the weights as published on the notice of reward. He went further. In an earlier chapter of this book was given an extract from the account of an interview with Mr. Mayer in which he said that he had recognised a pearl which someone brought to him for sale as one which he himself had owned some twenty years before. Mr. Spanier here displayed the same remarkable faculty, for he said in evidence at a later stage that he recognised one of the pearls in the necklace, when he handled it, as one which he had sold to a gentleman about two years before, and knew as a fact that this dealer had later sold it to Max Mayer for his famous string.

At this moment, however, while Spanier was examining the pearls and the other men were watching him in interested silence, there came, to the horror of all, a totally unexpected knock at the bedroom door. The atmosphere became electrical, and all eyed one another with angry suspicion to know at whose instigation the interruption had occurred. Silverman and Grizard glared at the other three, Spanier was distrustful of all four of them, while Brandstatter and Quadratstein were uncertain what to think. Who was it? The police, as the three Parisians hoped and the criminals feared, or one or more of the gang, as

Silverman and Grizard hoped and the other three most definitely feared? Apparently when the knock came all the men got up, nor would their agitation allow them to stand still for, as Mr. Spanier said, " we walked about in the room." Finally, Quadratstein, the man of action, advanced past the others to the door, none hindering him in their anxiety to know the nature of the man or men outside. Swiftly he opened it. Alas, that there should follow here another of those anti-climaxes with which this story is so full. The object which had terrified and agitated five armed men into pacing round the room for minutes on end was a diminutive page, who could almost have been placed in Grizard's pocket with the pearls! To Quadratstein, who was standing staring at him, he handed a note from Gutwirth, who was waiting in the hall below, to know if he might come up. Quadratstein asked Grizard over his shoulder what he should reply. " Tell him," was the answer, " that we're busy. He can come back in an hour or two." Leisur Gutwirth was a useful man to Grizard in this pearl transaction, but his presence at such an interview might be more embarrassing than useful. The five men, somewhat ashamed at their display of excitement, slowly returned to their seats, breathing heavily.

Finally the examination was concluded, and the expert eyes and fingers of Mr. Spanier were satisfied that before him lay at least the greater part of the necklace stolen on the 16th of July. He was thinking hard, for the watchful eyes of Silverman and Grizard were boring into him. It was one thing to secure the whereabouts of the necklace, quite another to leave the room in possession of part of it. The crucial question was the price, and with the lightest possible touch the wily actor casually remarked: " You're right. These are the pearls. I know them well by repute. You have kept your promise." Silverman assumed such dignity as he could muster. " Of course," he replied, " we always keep our promises!" " How much?" demanded Mr. Spanier in the most casual voice he could command. " A million francs for the lot," was Grizard's quiet reply. This was an enormous sum, £40,000, and yet it was only a little more than quarter what the necklace was really worth. Truly the receiver's part is the safer and more lucrative game to play! Provided care were taken he ran little risk of the police, and with an outlay to confederates of, possibly, £10,000, could pocket for himself, without suspicion, fear or blame, the remaining £30,000. Mr. Spanier, of course, had no intention of purchasing the necklace as a whole but, to play his part, proceeded to haggle with Grizard for a few of the finest pearls, Grizard trying to get as much cash as he could before the time came for "lying low," Spanier to get as many of the pearls as possible for the money he was authorised to spend on their recovery. Quadratstein and Brandstatter, fidgeting about with excitement, left the talking to their leader, as did Silverman. Gutwirth, with his reputation of having " too long a tongue," had been left downstairs. In the end the " buyer " played his final card and offered the hundred thousand francs, whose numbers were so carefully taken, for the three pearls which had been weighed and sealed by Quadratstein.

As their true value was between twelve and fourteen thousand pounds the bargain would have been a good one for Spanier had he been what he pretended to be, a Parisian purchaser of stolen goods, and " the little Jew " demurred. He took from his inside pocket a little book and solemnly referred to it. After an anxious pause he announced: " I can't do it. Those three pearls cost me more than that! " Mr. Spanier's nervous excitement was for the moment all but overcome by his inborn sense of humour, but to laugh in the faces of his adversaries would have been fatal to his plans. He therefore began to argue with equal solemnity about the value to be placed on the pearls, and Silverman became the spokesman for the rest. While general negotiations for the necklace were in progress he had left the bargaining to Grizard, but on questions of the proper value to be placed on a specific pearl the Austrian's expert knowledge gave him an advantage over the older man, who never dealt in pearls when he could find a less embarrassing commodity. So fierce was Silverman's bargaining that Mr. Spanier feared a premature end to the interview, and as his orders were at all costs to exchange his hundred thousand francs for at least two of the pearls he finally offered that sum for the largest two of the three. This offer was to his great relief accepted, and the sale was made. With an inward smile of satisfaction Mr. Spanier took the roll of notes from his pocket, slowly counted out to Grizard one hundred notes on the Bank of France for a thousand francs each, and took his pearls. Grizard handed the money without a word to Silverman, who counted it again and gave it back. Four thousand pounds! Not a bad morning's work when one is selling other people's property!

Grizard put the money in his inside pocket and then turned to the remaining pearls. As it was part of Mr. Spanier's orders to keep up the pretence of further negotiations, even though the underwriters had no intention of spending further money in the recovery of the pearls by purchase, he spoke at length of buying the remainder at a later date. It was finally agreed that he should return the following Wednesday with a further four hundred thousand francs (£16,000), if he could collect that sum in notes in time, and with it buy at least a large portion of the necklace as a whole. Grizard asked him to re-seal the remaining pearls in a way which he would recognise, and this he did, placing them in two plain envelopes which Silverman produced. He was also asked to seal up the two drop pearls and the round pearl, which were not part of the necklace, and as Silverman had no more envelopes, he used a tinted one which Brandstatter produced, which had his name and address printed on the back. The three envelopes were then sealed up, though Spanier, having heard the story of the robbery, was none too trustful of the value of his seal. Finally, Grizard took the envelopes and placed them in his trousers pocket.

While all concerned were clearing from the table the burnt matches and other debris which resulted from the sealing of the envelopes, Quadratstein took up a piece of paper on which he had written the weights and descriptions of the three pearls which he had weighed in the George public-house the previous Saturday week. Grizard, seeing this, became suspicious, and with the criminal's instinct to leave no trace of his nefarious operations, pointing to it, said to him: " You don't want that any more. It's no use to you now and you had better destroy it." Quadratstein, having no reasonable excuse for argument, obeyed and tore it up. Luckily Mr. Price had taken a copy at the interview at which the two young men had described their adventures up to date, so nothing valuable had been destroyed.

The interview was over, and the temptation in the minds of the three Parisians came back with doubled force. Here they were, in a first-floor bedroom in a large hotel, surrounded by persons who, if called to their aid, could be relied upon to support them against the captured criminals, outnumbering the latter by three to two and at least as efficiently armed, with no escape for their quarry save through the door twelve feet away and through the whole hotel. And what a capture if it could be made! There, in Grizard's pocket lay the £150,000 worth of pearls, and there, in another pocket, lay the money he had taken for the pearls which were not his. Grizard caught red-handed, " Cammi," the greatest receiver of his time! It would be too good to be true.

Counsel defending Grizard at the trial appreciated their temptation and cross-examined Quadratstein at length, suggesting that their self-control was so unlikely and so unreasonable as to vitiate the likelihood of the jury accepting the rest of their evidence as true.

Q. You actually at one time had the necklace produced in your own bedroom in the First Avenue Hotel? Quite so.

Q. Three of you? Yes.

Q. All armed with loaded revolvers? Yes.

Q. How many of the accused were with you when you handled the necklace? Two.

Q. Three against two? Quite so.

Q. Could you give me any reason, Mr. Quadratstein, if that was so, why you did not seize that opportunity of putting the necklace in your pocket and keeping it there? I was working on the instructions of Mr. Price and he did not tell me to do so.

Q. You were out after the reward? Quite so.

Q. And you had the cherished object actually in your hand? Yes.

Q. And you had two men with you as against two? Quite so.

Q. And you could have walked out of the hotel? I don't know if they would have let me.

Q. How could they prevent you? Grizard is a man about twice as big as any of us.

Q. Is he a sort of Goliath who could overwhelm the three of you? I thought it very possible!

Q. Then you handed back the necklace which was worth, if your ambitions were to be fulfilled, £10,000, when you could have put it in your pocket and kept it there, and, protected by two men, you calmly allowed it to be given back under circumstances when you might never see it again?

It was not for me to do it. If anybody had to put the necklace in his pocket it was Mr. Spanier who was the representative of Lloyd's."

And so it was left, for Mr. Spanier was never asked his version of his prudent conduct, but his reply would have been that he was acting under orders, and followed the dictates of his commonsense. The interview was over, and Mr. Spanier, his nerves at the end of his self-control, was anxious to be gone. He moved towards the door. " One moment, Mr. Spanier, please "! The voice was Grizard's and his eyes brooked no refusal. In ominous silence the famous criminal walked over to the door and turned to face his audience. " No one leaves this room for ten minutes after we have left. Do you understand?" Had his hand held the revolver which all knew to be lying in his pocket, his words would not have been more menacing, and none of the " buyers " had the least intention of disobeying the orders so imperatively given. Satisfied that his commands would be obeyed, the great man beckoned to his underling and left the room. For ten full minutes the remaining three sat waiting and then Mr. Spanier, valiant in action, but fretting his nerves to pieces with delay, led the way downstairs. In the hall he saw no one that he knew, and without troubling to speak to the men who followed him downstairs he hastened to the outside door.

Standing at the curb in front of him was an empty taxi, the one thing he required. Without a second's thought he sprang inside and gave the first address which came into his head, which happened to be Hyde Park Corner. On the way, however, a dreadful thought assailed him. Was it coincidence that the taxi was so opportunely waiting for him? Or had it been drawn up there on purpose to decoy him to some unknown destination at which he would be robbed of his precious pearls? In his calmer movements Mr. Spanier would have appreciated the enormous difficulties in the way of such a form of abduction, but his nerve was shattered by the strain of the momentous interview, and he acted without delay.

In Southampton Row the taxi was held up in a traffic block. Seizing the opportunity, the astonished driver's "fare" leapt out, paid for his drive and disappeared. In Kingsway he took a second taxi and drove due west to Hammersmith, the bogey of pursuit still thundering at his heels. At intervals he peered out through the window at the back, and seeing no signs of followers, dismissed the cab at Hammersmith and took a third to the Midland Hotel, St. Pancras, in North London. There he got out and walked into the hotel dining room, leaving by a separate door which gave onto the platform, and so, by devious routes, returned to the street. He there took a fourth taxi and drove, in comparative sense of security, to his original destination, which was due East of his point of departure, the Holborn Viaduct Hotel! One is inclined to say: "There's imagination for you!" Looking back on the event at an interval of sixteen years Mr. Spanier laughs at his exaggerated fears, but he feels again to-day the terror which inspired him then.

"When I arrived at Mr. Price's room," he said, when reminiscing at request, "Mr. Price gave one look at me and sent for a glass of brandy," and this is corroborated by the notes which the unemotional "O.C. operations" made at the time. When he had calmed down sufficiently to tell his story he did so, and handed over the pearls. Mr. Price at once went off with them to his superiors, and it was agreed that as soon as possible they should be shown to Mr. Mayer for his identification. The success of the scheme produced another necessity. So long as the story of the two young amateurs was uncorroborated, the Underwriters did not feel justified in invoking the assistance of the police. Now, however, that the best possible corroboration was at hand, it was only fair to inform them of the momentous interview. Mr. Price therefore sent for his trusted ally, Ex-Superintendent Leach, and explained the position. At the latter's suggestion Inspector Ward was summoned to a joint conference of all concerned, in order that the evidence obtained might be used to the best advantage. When the police officers arrived Mr. Price asked Ward to procure a warrant immediately, but Ward refused to move until Mr. Mayer had formally identified the pearls. The result was a deadlock, and the meeting came to an end.

Meanwhile Mr. Spanier, still obsessed with the fear of being followed, which was rather fostered than allayed by Mr. Price, had used the same circuitous taxi peregrinations to visit his niece in Bayswater, and was still in a highly imaginative mood when he returned to the Carlton Hotel after the police conference.

Convinced that he was being followed at the orders of those he was attempting to betray, he asked at the bureau who was occupying the next room to his, and was told " a lady." Somewhat mollified to hear that it was not a doubtful-looking gentleman with a ferocious expression and bulging hip-pocket, he retired to bed. No sooner in bed than he heard a scratching at the door which divided the next room from his own. He turned on the light, got out of bed, listened at the communicating door, and satisfied himself that the noise must have had some innocent cause. He retired to bed again. The scratching recommenced. Thoroughly alarmed, he abandoned thoughts of sleep and sat up all night in an armchair within easy reach of the bell. As he said when recalling the incident to memory; " How did I know the ' lady ' was still there? A man might have taken her place, or she might have been a man in disguise!"

In the morning he inquired about the lady, and heard that she had left early. His suspicions turned to certainty, he got permission to enter the room. Alas for melodrama! The bed was placed with its head to the communicating door, to which it was pressed too close. The result was that every movement of the person in bed caused the bed rail to rub against the door, and so produce the " scratching " which had deprived the excited expert of his sleep!

CHAPTER VII

THE TRAP

WHILE Mr. Spanier was preparing to defend himself against imaginary assailants, Mr. Price, Inspector Ward and ex-Superintendent Leach were planning future events as soon as Mr. Mayer's identification of the pearls was formally obtained. It was agreed that the safest plan would be to proceed on the basis of negotiating for the entire necklace, and that a conference should be arranged at which all parties would be present, as in the bedroom scene of that afternoon, but with this difference. Inspector Ward and his men would be all round the building awaiting a signal from Mr. Spanier, upon which they would " rush " the room and arrest the criminals with the necklace actually before them. There was only one scheme better than this, to arrest not only the criminals but the two decoys and Mr. Spanier while negotiations were proceeding, the last three to be later released, but Mr. Spanier flatly refused to be party to such a scheme. As he repeated with dignity, " I am not a policeman. I am an expert." He agreed, however, to lure the criminals into the trap and then abandon them to those who were, metaphorically, thirsting for their blood, and so it was arranged. Mr. Price was to instruct Mr. Spanier in his part before leaving for Folkestone in the morning, and on Wednesday, if possible, the trap would be sprung.

As events turned out, however, the climax was not so easily attained, and there were thrilling scenes to be enacted before the robbers were under lock and key.

On Tuesday morning, the 26th, Mr. Spanier called on Mr. Price at the Holborn Viaduct Hotel, received his instructions and set off for the First Avenue Hotel, where he had agreed to meet Quadratstein to tell him to what extent he was empowered to buy a further consignment of the pearls. Mr. Price, on his part, set off for Folkestone to get Mr. Mayer's identification of the two already obtained.

On arriving in the lounge, Mr. Spanier found Silverman with his two collaborators, and announced for the former's benefit that he was empowered by his " principal " to take up the whole of the necklace the following day for 400,000 francs. Silverman, to Mr. Spanier's relief, seemed satisfied with this arrangement, little knowing he was thereby giving Mr. Price sufficient time to get the pearls identified, and wire to Scotland Yard, where an Assistant Commissioner was awaiting the word to obtain a warrant for the arrest of all four men.

This concluded the interview, and Mr. Spanier left. He turned East, crossed the road, and was walking along the pavement when suddenly he saw Grizard himself, who did not, however, see him. He was thus witness to an incident which is a commonplace to criminals and well known to the police. Mr. Spanier, however, had never seen it before and was duly impressed and interested. As he walked along behind the " King of the Underworld," he saw what appeared to be a sailor step out from a corner and fall into step with Grizard, who neither acknowledged his presence nor turned his head. The sailor, however, spoke a few words, apparently into the air, and then as silently and swiftly disappeared. Intrigued by this method of conveying messages Mr. Spanier continued to follow his quarry, and was soon rewarded for his pertinacity. A few yards further on, an old woman, or so the figure seemed to be, did exactly the same thing, Grizard slightly reducing his pace to allow the " decrepit " individual at his side to keep up with him. Another message seemed to pass between them, and the second messenger likewise disappeared.

As it turned out, both these messengers were members of the gang, and used this immemorial method to convey their news without attracting attention to themselves or the person they were there to warn. The same principal is adopted in conveying stolen property from the place of stealing to the receiver waiting to dispose of it, and by this " human chain " the property is swiftly passed from one end of the town to the other, changing hands, it may be, a dozen times en route.

Meanwhile Mr. Price was lunching with Mr. Mayer at the Imperial Hotel at Folkestone in a private sitting room, Mr. Mayer having crossed from France to meet him at this rendezvous. He there showed him the two pearls, which the delighted owner at once identified as the finest two of the sixty-one which formed his famous necklace, and signed the statement which Mr. Price wrote out for him to that effect. Mr. Price refused to tell the famous collector anything which had transpired, and bound

him over to secrecy that he had even seen the two
pearls shown to him. He then saw him off by the
4.30 boat back to Boulogne, wired to Scotland Yard
that the identification had been made, and returned
to London, where he went at once to the rendezvous
arranged in room No. 6 at the Berkeley. He there
met the police and made plans for the following day.
The trap was prepared, but would the quarry enter
it?

Wednesday, the 27th, dawned as other days, but
in the drama being unfolded a new factor had arrived
upon the scene. The forces of the underworld, as
represented by the four conspirators and Grizard's
countless allies and subordinates, were of the same
strength as on the preceding day. The opposing
army, on the other hand, had now the united strength
of Scotland Yard to reinforce them. Hitherto they
had relied on amateurs, with such assistance as was
possible from ex-Superintendent Leach and his subordinates. Now, however, they had Chief-Inspector
Ward, Detective-Sergeants Cornish and Cooper, and
a dozen other men, not only to shadow all the protagonists but, when feasible, to arrest the criminals
and so bring the long-drawn battle to an end.

Immediately after breakfast Mr. Price went to his
office, took from his safe one hundred notes of
1,000 francs each, and proceeded to the rendezvous
arranged with Quadratstein, which this time was the
refreshment room by the booking office in Vauxhall
Station. He then arranged communication with him,
handed over the notes, and returned home.

Quadratstein and his cousin set off for the First
Avenue Hotel and arrived there about 11.30. Mean-

while Mr. Spanier set off from the Charing Cross Hotel (which, it would seem, was one of the few London Hotels at which he had not previously stayed in the course of this story!) and, duly shadowed by Detective-Sergeant Cooper, arrived at the rendezvous shortly afterwards. Silverman seems to have already arrived.

The hotel was now surrounded by Inspector Ward's men, while Ward himself, with Sergeant Cornish, ex-Superintendent Leach and others were concealed in a van at the corner of a turning almost opposite the entrance to the hotel. Mr. Spanier, whose respect for our police methods was not excessive, states that as he approached the building it was obvious to him what the silent van contained, and thinks its presence helps to explain the subsequent developments.

On entering the hotel he found Silverman with Quadratstein and Brandstatter, but no signs of Gutwirth or the far more important master criminal himself. Until the latter arrived the trap would not be sprung.

The nervous tension was considerable, and to put in time Mr. Spanier got into conversation with Silverman. He told him that he had managed to raise a further 400,000 francs for the whole of the pearls, and actually showed him the notes which had been done up in two packets of 200,000 francs each. Silverman seemed immensely pleased, and once more made the suspicious suggestion that they should adjourn to a room which he had taken in a nearby hotel, in which they could conclude the transaction without fear of interruption. This did not suit Mr.

Spanier at all. The present meeting place, innocent in the sunshine of an August morning, was alive with hidden police, but the wily Austrian's suggested rendezvous would be not only unprotected as far as his £16,000 of cash was concerned, but useless as a trap. He therefore once more demurred at accompanying the criminals to any private room, and stated finally that all negotiations were to take place in public restaurants or in his own hotel. Silverman pleaded vehemently, but only confirmed Mr. Spanier's suspicions of foul play. Finally, he stated that if Silverman refused to announce the address of the suggested rendezvous, thereby showing that he did not trust the Parisian " buyer " he, Mr. Spanier, failed to see why he should trust Mr. Silverman. Having no answer ready to this conclusive argument, the hunch-back said that he would have to consult the others and forthwith left the hotel.

What had alarmed the cautious Grizard? Why was he so suspicious of a trap that he refused to enter the hotel in which, on preceding days, negotiations had so peacefully taken place? On this occasion he had obviously sent in Silverman to lure the " buyer," with his bank notes, from the potential danger-spot to a meeting place known only to the gang. Why? Was it because of the suspicious van drawn up in front of the hotel door? Grizard had certainly come to the rendezvous, for he was seen by the police approaching the hotel but carefully remaining at a certain distance from it. Ex-Superintendent Leach maintains that he could see him from the van not only cross to the South side of the road, where it was standing, but actually, while waiting for a signal from his ally, lean on the mudguard of the van within which Ward sat waiting with a warrant for his arrest! Was this marvellous bravado or surprising ignorance? Detectives, like a certain type of furniture, are delivered, free of cost, in plain and unobtrusive vans, but it is surely odd that Grizard should have chosen this spot of all others from which to observe the battle field, and yet, if he knew the nature of its contents, what consummate nerve! The orders of the police, however, were to await a signal from Mr. Spanier, and before such signal could be given the infuriated officers saw Silverman walk out of the hotel. Before they could decide whether to follow him or to await developments, the self-contained and placid figure of the " O.C. Criminal Negotiations " rose from his recumbent position on the radiator and moved off in the same direction as his subordinate!

The time was now about 11.50 and Mr. Spanier was impatiently waiting in the lounge for the expiration of the five minutes which Silverman had said was all that he required. The five minutes came and went, as also ten, twenty and then half an hour. At 12.20 Mr. Spanier's patience came to an end. He suddenly announced that he was returning to Paris, at once and finally. Quadratstein argued with him, but in vain, and at half-past twelve he left.

Scarcely had he vanished from sight than the watching police saw Silverman return. Quadratstein, his nerves on edge at the imminent failure of their plans, fiercely attacked the little Jew in answer to his complaints that Mr. Spanier had not waited, and told him it was his fault for taking forty minutes when he had said that he needed five. He sent off Brandstatter, nevertheless, to fetch back Spanier as quickly as possible. Brandstatter left, and Silverman announced that he would wait for Spanier in the hotel smoking room. Quadratstein remained impatiently pacing up and down the lounge while Brandstatter telephoned to Mr. Spanier, who had gone at once to Mr. Price and handed back the money which had not been used. He told Mr. Spanier to return at once and left the telephone box. Outside it he met Gutwirth, who began to tell him an incoherent and excited story of Grizard having recognised no less than four detectives in the vicinity and of having, therefore, broken off negotiations. Not feeling competent to deal with this deplorable development, the amateur detective returned to his more experienced partner, who proceeded to cross-examine Gutwith as to the true state of affairs. The message resolved itself into a demand by Grizard to see Quadratstein or Brandstatter at once outside the hotel, as he had seen and recognised, with his marvellous knowledge of the " Yard " officials, four of their men, and was returning home.

But Gutwirth, true to type, had another message— this time of his own. He said that he had five thousand francs on him in cash and " in case anything happened," that is, in connnection with the detectives waiting outside, Brandstatter was to say that he had lent them to him, as " everyone knew that Brandstatter could afford to lend him that amount."

In pursuance of the first request, Quadratstein followed Gutwirth to a bar nearby in Holborn, where the latter expected to find his "chief," but the search was fruitless and he returned to the hotel. A few minutes later Mr. Spanier returned. The two men sent for Silverman and Mr. Spanier told him that as far as he was concerned the deal was off. That he had waited forty minutes in vain and was tired of waiting. That he was also suspicious that he was being followed for the large sum in his pocket and that, in short, he "had had enough of it." He explained, however, that he would authorise Quadratstein to act as his agent, and would send him money from time to time with which to buy consignments of the pearls until he had bought them all. He then left the hotel, reported his decision to Mr. Price, metaphorically washed his hands of the whole matter, and returned to Paris the same afternoon. He thus walks out of the story in which he took so prominent a rôle, having, as it turned out, performed with no little skill a difficult and somewhat dangerous part in the ultimate capture of the famous criminals. His elaborate bluff all through was marvellously done, and he says that in the famous bedroom scene, when all five men were agitated by the visit to the door, he pretended, when they had sat down again, to be so agitated that the kindly Grizard had actually patted him on the shoulder and announced, "There, there, I will protect you. Have no fear!" To obtain such a result needs no mean dramatic ability, and his conduct certainly justified Mr. Price's choice.

On Mr. Spanier's departure, Quadratstein made another appointment with Silverman for that afternoon at 4 o'clock, and the three men separated. At four o'clock the wily Silverman made another attempt to lure the Frenchman to an unknown rendezvous, but in vain. He even produced the key of a room in some hotel, and said that there " they would not be disturbed." Quadratstein was adamant, but he agreed to buy a further three pearls of the necklace for 100,000 francs which Mr. Spanier had given him, and specified the three. Silverman demurred at such a sum, and said that he could not have any two of them for that amount, thus repeating the bedroom scene transaction. Quadratstein, who had no intention of buying any of them, and was only playing for time, eventually agreed, and an appointment was made for Thursday, the 28th, at the " J.P. Restaurant " nearby.

And that was all. The police dispersed and the great trap was unsprung. Whether the police blundered in allowing the watchful eyes of Grizard to observe and recognise them is not known. It may have been that members of his own gang were detailed to watch for such eventualities, in which case it would be all but impossible to prevent the officers being seen. Certainly, no sooner did he realise that he was being watched, than " Cammi " placed his own men on the track of the police, who, realising in turn that they were being spied upon, set other men to keep an eye on them. And so the amazing " follow-my-leader " queue set forth to trail round London, in the search, on the one hand for a gang of criminals and the most famous necklace in the world, on the other, for all the money they could raise with safety, and a clear escape.

On the following morning, Thursday, August 28th, the procession re-formed. Quadratstein and

Brandstatter, shadowed by detectives, entered the J.P. Restaurant at the Holborn end of Chancery Lane and there met Silverman. The time was then about 11 o'clock and the meeting only lasted a few minutes. Grizard, very suspicious and rather anxious about the future course of events, was clearly using Silverman as a go-between until he was satisfied that he could meet the two Parisians with safety. Silverman therefore announced that he wished to make an appointment later in the morning, at which Grizard would be present, for a brief, decisive interview. An appointment was made for 12.30 in the Lyons tea-shop next door, and the three men left, Quadratstein and his cousin going back to the First Avenue Hotel, Silverman leaving a few minutes later and turning towards the city. The solemn procession of watchers and counter-spies no doubt proceeded to shadow them and each other until 12.30, when the three men met again. One is tempted to enquire how much unwanted coffee and soft drinks were consumed at these innumerable café meetings in the Holborn neighbourhood, and whether the various proprietors were duly grateful to their unknown benefactors! At 12.30 the blow fell. Silverman was waiting in the café alone and at once explained the absence of his principal. Grizard, he said, was frankly frightened. He had seen the detectives outside the hotel on the previous day, and was sure that the police were watching him. He thought that their suspicions had been aroused by Mr. Spanier's drawing such large quantities of French bank notes from the London banks, and that no more business would be possible for a month.

The remark as to the cause of the police suspicion is interesting, for it shows that Mr. Spanier had played his part so well that Grizard had no doubts of his authenticity.

Quadratstein tried to convince the Jew that his " chief's " suspicions were absurd, but the latter was not there to argue, merely to give the message he had come to give. " It is no business of mine," he said. " You had better come and see Grizard in person." As this was just what Quadratstein desired, he accepted the suggestion, and the three men left the café for the Lipton's tea shop further up the road which had been used before. At this rendezvous, the third within three hours, the attacking forces once more met the brains of the enemy in person, for Grizard was already sitting there. Not, however, the swaggering and self-complacent " Cammi " of the previous interview, but an anxious and extremely nervous man.

His first words showed that he still had no suspicions of the men who were betraying him. " You have had a very narrow escape," he said. " The police are on our tracks on account of Spanier drawing so much French money, and we must be very careful." He said that all negotiations would have to be suspended for a month, but that in the meantime he would not sell the necklace to anyone else. " You two had better return to Paris," he said to the two cousins. " Tell Spanier to return the notes to his bankers in London and draw fresh ones in Paris, and return in a month's time, when you can buy the remainder of the necklace in one lot." He added that he would be at the station to meet them when they returned, and would see that they were not watched.

Quadratstein, playing for time in which to adjust his plans to this unfortunate development, asked how the pearls were to be taken from London when the sale was made.

" That's easy," was the reply. " Bring your wife over with you and she can wear the pearls going back."

Quadratstein agreed to this suggestion for the moment, but added that he must see Mr. Spanier before the arrangement could finally stand. He then very cleverly asked his opponent where he could find him in the interim, and the latter gave the address of Mr. Levi, c/o Mr. Goldberg, 45, Hatton Garden, " but the letter must be registered."

Whether Grizard had had reason to doubt the bona fides of his colleague, Gutwirth, is not known, but he suddenly volunteered the statement that the cousins would not have to deal with him in future as he had " too long a tongue." " From now on," he said, " you will only have to deal with gentlemen!"

Silverman, too, was to be eliminated from further negotiations, as the detectives would get to know him if he appeared so much. This was the first time Silverman had been mentioned by name, and the information was duly handed over to the police at a later interview. According to instructions, cleverly devised by Mr. Price, the astute young amateur then mentioned that he had an unpaid bill from his hotel and asked for a little money on account. Silverman, entirely unsuspicious of the trap, produced two £5 notes and handed them over together with some

change, and the interview closed with a parting remark from Grizard that the lives of the two young
men would be quite safe in his hands!

One of the £5 notes was later cashed by Quadratstein at Victoria Station, but the other was duly
handed over to the police and later used as evidence.

So the interview ended, and the plans of another
day had failed. Quadratstein had done his best to
find where the necklace was being kept, but Grizard
would not commit himself beyond saying that it was
in a place as safe as the Bank of England. Whether
this is a fair description of the pocket of a notorious
criminal is a matter of opinion, for such the truth
turned out to be, but for the moment Quadratstein
could do no more.

He and his cousin, who had understood but little
of the interview, which had been carried on in
English, therefore returned to Mr. Price to revise
their future plans.

Realising that it would be difficult to get at
Grizard for the future save through his associates,
Inspector Ward instructed Brandstatter to write to
Gutwirth in Yiddish, asking him to meet him at the
Inns of Court Hotel the following morning at 11
a.m., where he was to ask for Monsieur Dubois,
under which name he would then be staying there.
Mr. Price's name was changed to the less euphonious
one of Bloch, under which he would be waiting at
the telephone, in touch with the police, in case of
interesting developments. The fertile brain of the
Inspector concentrated on some tale which would induce the frightened Grizard to forego his plan of
a month's delay, and finally a most attractive story

was evolved. The letter was duly written and despatched by special messenger, and the battle ended for the day.

The position was becoming critical. The forces of law and order had lost touch with the necklace, and frightened the man they wanted to arrest red-handed, while each day's delay increased the chances of the necklace leaving the country and of the criminals " running to ground." The long drawn-out anxiety of all concerned was not improved by the hot and sultry weather, and the nerves of the leaders of both " armies " were becoming sorely frayed. It was in these circumstances that the fifth day of the drama opened on a fresh hotel but by no means fresh antagonists.

Punctually at 11 a.m. on the 29th, Gutwirth entered the Inns of Court Hotel and was shown up to " Mr. Dubois." Quadratstein then told him, as instructed the night before, that he had found an Indian Rajah who was anxious to buy the pearls, but that he was returning to India shortly and was therefore anxious to make the purchase at once. He added that if this potential buyer was allowed to leave the country without buying the pearls they would have great difficulty in finding another purchaser, and that it was therefore imperative to put the sale through with all possible speed. Finally, if he, Gutwirth, would assist to get the deal through quickly they would give him a special commission of £1,000 in addition to the 5 per cent for which he had been bargaining all through.

This story was extremely clever. Grizard's chief desire was speed and immediate payment in cash, while the fact that the pearls would immediately leave the country was an additional advantage. Gutwirth, again, could be safely "bought" with the promise of a special bribe, and would henceforth do all he could to bring the deal off quickly, that is, bring his unsuspecting leader back into the trap. Gutwirth swallowed the bait with alacrity, and promised to see Grizard without delay. It was still necessary, however, to bring in Silverman, so Quadratstein explained that he wanted to see him first, to secure his agreement to the need for speed. In this attempt he was quite successful, for Gutwirth went off to see Silverman, who telephoned within the hour and made an appointment at once, in the gardens opposite the hotel. Quadratstein there repeated to him the story of the Rajah, and Silverman agreed to make an appointment with Grizard at the earliest opportunity. This was excellent, for the principals were being slowly re-collected into the net. On some excuse he persuaded Silverman to give him his business card, and this was duly filed for evidence.

Silverman then asked the delighted Quadratstein whether he wanted any more money, and it is not difficult to guess the answer given. He promptly departed and returned with four more £5 Bank of England notes, which the other accepted gratefully and later handed to Mr. Price. A provisional appointment was then made with Grizard and the meeting closed.

The available supply of local rendezvous must by now have been running short, but the meeting with the once more joyful "Cammi" was arranged for the " Bun Shop " opposite Lipton's café in High Holborn. Once more the procession of watchers and the watched adjourned to the latest meeting-place, and there was " Cammi " waiting for the news. Once more the story of the Rajah was unfolded, and, like the others, Grizard accepted it with alacrity. He said that he would go to Brighton to " see his friend " about the pearls, and would bring them with him to a general conference on the following Monday at 2 p.m. in the Lyons' tea-shop opposite the Holborn Restaurant. This was definite and sounded promising. If something was not accomplished on this occasion, it would not be for want of a desperate attempt. Grizard departed, and the two young men reported to Mr. Price.

On Saturday, the 30th, Gutwirth called upon them at their hotel, and in the course of conversation made some interesting statements which more than earned for him the opinion held by Grizard that he " had too long a tongue." He began by announcing vaguely that they were quite safe, as Grizard and Jim Lockett were " looking over them." This meant, apparently, that they were looking after them, protecting them. The interesting point about the remark, however, was the mention of Jim Lockett, the notorious burglar, for his name had never before been mentioned as being a member of the gang. His next remark, however, was of far more importance. With his incurable habit of chattering about affairs which he had been told to keep secret, he suddenly began to talk about two post-men. He explained that they had been promised £200 each for their work, and had already been given

£100 of it. Quadratstein forbore to inquire for what the postmen were being paid, it being obvious, but tactfully inquired the nature of the accounts or figures from which the garrulous Austrian was then reading. The various items, he was told, represented the expenses of the thieves " in getting the pearls." He thought the total figure mentioned was about £1,200.

" He added up several sums," said Quadratstein in evidence at the trial, " starting with £200, £200, £400, £800; I cannot remember the exact figures. He did not say what the other items represented, only £200 each for the two postmen."

So ended the interview, and Quadratstein hastened to write down this all-important evidence. The conversation had been in Yiddish, so that Brandstatter could understand what was said, and the latter remembered a remark which his cousin did not hear. This, too, was important, for it gave the belief existing in the Austrian's mind as to the hiding-place of the pearls. According to him it was held by a brother-in-law of Lockett, " a man with a pointed black beard." The importance of this will appear at a later stage.

The cousins then went off to Brighton for the rest of the week-end, but saw nothing of the conspirators, and returned on the Sunday night.

On the Monday morning Gutwirth returned to the hotel, and Quadratstein informed him that at the interview that afternoon he would be in a position to buy the remainder of the pearls for 900,000 francs. Gutwirth, thinking only of his personal, dishonest commission, if it be dishonest to steal from your fellow-thieves, asked when this would be paid.

"This evening," was the reply, "if I safely buy the pearls." Gutwirth, delighted at this news, went off, as was intended, to draw the principals into the baited trap.

The next to arrive was Silverman, excited and suspicious of the very walls. He led his supposed accomplice into Lincoln's Inn Fields, and there discussed the best place to hand over and count the money when the deal had been arranged. Quadratstein says he even took him to his office in Hatton Garden to show him the easiest approach in case that meeting-place was chosen.

At 2 p.m. the Lyons' restaurant chosen for the final rendezvous was surrounded by the police, and a score of practised eyes were trained on the doorway whence alone the wanted men, once entered, could escape. The cousins were the first to arrive, closely followed by Grizard and Gutwirth. The former entered and joined the others, but Gutwirth remained outside, pacing up and down as if on guard to see that the others were not observed. Considering that there were at least twelve people watching *him* as well as the other three inside, it would appear that watching was not his strongest card! Inside the great man came to the point. "Have you got the money?" Quadratstein, of course, had nothing of the sort, and hurriedly explained that his buyer had changed his mind, would not trust him with so much money in the crowd, and would still prefer to buy 200,000 francs' worth at a time. The "agent" showed him the 200,000 francs which he had on him and, in spite of the absence of Silverman, asked to be allowed to choose at once a few more of the pearls. His agony of mind while he waited for the answer can be imagined better than described. Should the pearls be produced and laid upon the table, a single gesture of the hand, and the famous " Cammi " would be instantly surrounded with the pearls in front of him. Once more, however, the caution of the older man destroyed his plans. " I would rather wait until Silverman is present," he said. " He is the only one who can properly value the pearls, and I might give you too much." Quadratstein, however, could not stand another day's delay, and pressed for an appointment the same afternoon. In the end it was agreed that the final rendezvous should be for 3.15 at the British Museum Tube Station. The meeting then adjourned.

Mr. Price and the police were puzzled. Was " Cammi " merely vaguely suspicious, or was he playing a deep game of his own? Day after day, in countless cafés, tea-shops, restaurants and similar rendezvous, the criminals were meeting, singly or at the most in couples, but never altogether, and never with the pearls. At one time it seemed as if the sale of the pearls was indefinitely suspended; later, the clever handling of the young Parisian had brought the suspicious principals back into the wide-flung net. Ward was getting desperate and, it may be, a trifle careless. Certainly the afternoon's anti-climax proved to the hilt, either that Grizard had once more recognised his enemies, or else that such were his suspicions that he preferred a " try-out " meeting before he produced the pearls.

The police preparations were perfect in point of organisation. In the words of Inspector Ward's report: " I arranged with Sergeant Cooper to be disguised as a uniform sergeant of the Public Carriage Branch; Sergeants Cornish, Hayman and Goodwillie were concealed in a van, and other C.I.D. officers in various disguises were posted by me in the vicinity of the Tube station." The report continues, heartbreaking in its brevity: " At about 3.15 Grizard came up and went into the Tube station with Quadratstein and Brandstatter. Soon after I saw Lockett and Gutwirth outside the Tube station. They did not enter, but went up a passage by the station, and did not return. Grizard and the others remained in the station about an hour, then separated, Grizard going away by train."

By way of comment, I cannot do better than continue in the words of the report.

" This meeting seems to have been a test one to see if they were being followed, and it speaks for itself that the observation was well kept, as they made the same meeting-place the following day at 10.30 a.m. I again saw Quadratstein, who told me that they were to meet at the time mentioned, and proceed from there by Tube to some station, and from thence to a public-house, the name or locality of which he (Grizard) would not divulge. The following of these men on the Tube without being seen is, in ordinary circumstances, most difficult, and I decided that if I could get them together I would cause them to be arrested, rather than run the risk of being seen or of losing them in attempting to follow them. I therefore arranged for the observation to be kept as on the day previous, with the further instructions that if they all met at the station they were to be arrested."

The Trap

So ended the long preliminaries, for on the following day the trap was sprung. What happened among the subordinates of Grizard who were told off to keep watch on those who were watching him, and those of the police who were ordered to keep an eye on *them*, has never appeared. Grizard seems to have been suspicious of some form of treachery from the day he saw the detectives following him, but the greed of gold was stronger than the voice of caution, and so the great man fell. The lion was captured, but . . . we anticipate.

CHAPTER VIII

ARRESTED!

At 10.30 a.m. on the following day, September 2nd, the stage was set for the climax of the drama. The first to arrive was Silverman, though no one seems to have seen him come. Quadratstein and Brandstatter had informed the police the way they would approach the rendezvous, and on their way were shadowed by Sergeant Prosser in appropriate disguise. On arriving at the British Museum Tube Station the two men spoke to Silverman, who seemed relieved at seeing them, as if the waiting was getting on his nerves. It may be that he " sensed " that something untoward was afoot, but apparently he had not up to then identified in the usual loafers of the neighbourhood his hidden enemies, the police. Yet the approach to the station was " alive " with hidden watchers, none of whom dare to approach the rendezvous sufficiently closely to get a good look at the wanted man. What a brilliant mind that thought of the one infallible disguise for a C.I.D. detective—a uniformed constable! How should the criminals suspect the usual constable in blue as he paced the front of the station at his regulation two miles an hour? Did he not, on the contrary, tend to prove to the suspicious Silverman that on that sultry morning all was as he would have it be?

The trap was set and could not this time fail, but

though the capture of the men seemed certain, would they be found to have the pearls? Time alone would show, and time was passing rapidly. On meeting Silverman the two young men walked up and down the pavement with him for about ten minutes, while the ring of disguised and waiting men crept gradually closer to the trap. As Quadratstein was speaking, Silverman was keeping a constant watch upon his surroundings on the look-out for the slightest sign of anything abnormal, and it argues well for the police that nothing suspicious was seen. Each time that he and his two (supposed) confederates reached the end of the beat which they were pacing, he would wheel round suddenly to see whether anyone was watching him, but nothing outwardly disturbed the hum-drum monotony of a public thoroughfare. Such passing Londoners, as circumstance had kept away from the sea, were all oblivious of the drama being openly performed within their midst.

Suddenly Grizard appeared at the entrance of the station, dramatic as ever in his appearances, and a thrill ran through the waiting, watching men. It was now ten minutes to eleven, and Ward was getting anxious. Where were the other two? Not that Gutwirth mattered. He was known to be but a pawn, but Lockett, the famous thief and burglar, was the man on whom most likely the pearls would be found concealed. Why had he kept away, unless because he was suspicious of the rendezvous and all that it implied? A moment later, however, he appeared, having apparently arrived below ground by the next train after Grizard's, and come up in the lift which followed his. Meanwhile the waiting three had noticed Grizard and hastened to meet him at the entrance to the Tube. Lockett, apparently not seeing them at first, began to cross the road, but a secret signal from his " chief " recalled him to the pavement, where he joined the waiting four. The lions were in the trap, and held there by the trained decoys. The moment for action had come, and Cornish, by a pre-arranged signal, drew his men in closer still. At the same time Grizard led the way back into the station and proceeded to take tickets to Oxford Circus, which were destined never to be used. The five men passed into the lift, the doors were closed and the lift disappeared from view.

Cornish gave the pre-arranged signal, and the waiting officers, slipped from the leash at last, rushed from their various hiding-places to the station entrance, thence through the booking hall to the emergency stairs and down them in a cataract of eager speed. Poor " Cammi "! He was, as the lift descended, murmuring to Quadratstein that he was " taking them to a nice quiet bar where everything would be all right." Lockett nodded and smiled in confirmation of his leader's words. The lift arrived, and in common with its other occupants, the five men passed through its doors and so to the station platform to wait for a West-bound train. Scarcely had they arrived when the avalanche was on them, each man with his " bracelets " ready, and schooled by Ward beforehand as to the part he was to play. Cornish and Cooper made for Silverman, Hayman made for Grizard, Goodwillie and Soden arrested Lockett, and Prosser, Gimblett and Moorman cut off all escape. A moment of wild confusion, the briefest struggle, a string of oaths from someone and the " bracelets " clicked. The arrest was made and " Cammi," the genius of the underworld, was caught at last. The procession slowly formed and began to ascend the stairs back to the street, the prisoners dazed by the swiftness of the unexpected end to all their dreams of luxury, the eight police exultant at their swift success, the two confederates, following behind, perhaps a little sorry at the unpleasant part that they had lately had to play. In the early days of their adventure they had been filled with the splendour of the reward they hoped to earn and the sheer excitement of the game, but when the game was over they were, as all other sportsmen, a little sorry for the prey.

On arresting the criminals Sergeant Cornish, who was in charge of the arrest, announced to all three men: " We are police officers, and will arrest you for being concerned together and with others in stealing and receiving between the 15th and 16th of July last a pearl necklace, value about £150,000, between Paris and 88, Hatton Garden, the property of Max Mayer." No mean speech on such an occasion, to which he added in his statement: " Neither of them made any reply." The three men were so dazed at the swift dénouement to their carefully worked-out schemes that they could think of nothing for the moment, certainly not of an appropriate reply. Silverman, however, very quickly recovered his presence of mind. " He became very violent and flung himself on the stairs." Whether this was out of sheer annoyance at the arrest, in a vain attempt to free himself from what to him seemed his innumerable adversaries, or in a wild attempt to jettison the embarrassing possessions found upon him later when he was carefully searched, will never be known, but in none of these was he successful, and he was quickly jerked to his feet. His statement, shouted to those who held him, perhaps provides a clue: " I have not got them on me," he protested, to which the officer replied: " Haven't got what on you?" Silverman, thinking perhaps he had given himself away, was heard to mutter: " You've just told us it's for the pearls." Later, in the street, the full importance of the morning's anti-climax seemed to dawn on him, for he said to Sergeant Cornish, who was holding him: " I don't like this. Life is short, and I expect it will be a long time before I come round here again."

Meanwhile Lockett, in the course of the spiral journey up the staircase, said to his captor: " What's your name?" Sergeant Goodwillie gave his name. " Well, you needn't hold me so tight," said Lockett, " I have nothing to get rid of. I have plenty of money, but nothing that will get me into trouble," a statement which, though bravely said, was unfortunately for him not founded upon fact. Grizard, as became the greatness of the man, was the calmest of the three. On being arrested, he said to his captor: " I know what it is all about. I shan't give any trouble." And for the rest of the mournful journey to the police station at Bow Street he neither by word nor gesture betrayed what was passing through his mind.

On arrival at the " station " all three men were searched by their respective captors and locked up in the cells. The search being very thorough took some time, and Ward's anxiety was growing fast. The whole point of the capture at that moment was lest the thieves should be alarmed at their discovery of the watching and dispose of the necklace where it would never again be found. The greatest care had been taken to see that none of the arrested men had had the opportunity to dispose of anything upon his person, from the moment of arrest to the time when they were searched. One by one his officers reported to him the result of their examinations. Lockett, he was told, had enormous sums of money on him for a man in his position, but no pearls. Silverman had money and jewellers' implements of various kinds, but not a single pearl. The only hope was Grizard. A little money . . . a jeweller's gauge . . . " pieces of pearls in a leather card case " . . . sealing-wax and keys on a ring . . . no more. The pearls were not there! So far as the necklace was concerned, the mighty coup had failed! Ward's only hope was Gutwirth, and he knew where he would be found. He gave instructions to his subordinates, and turned to examine the property found upon the men and to hear what they had said while it was being found.

Sergeants Cornish and Cooper searched the prisoner Silverman, and on him found four £5 Bank of England notes, of which they took the numbers, eight one-thousand franc notes on the Bank of France, the numbers of which they seemed to recognise, some gold, silver and bronze, various jewellers' instruments and a piece of sealing-wax which figured later in the case, and the usual stamps, keys, pen and handkerchief, etcetera, which are found in the pocket of most men on their innocent daily round. A contract note with a pawnbroker proved that the paths of crime are not always paths of luxury. The French notes were, of course, the damning articles, and as they were found he was asked by the officer what they were. His reply spoke volumes in the minimum of words. " I wish I had not had them on me."

Sergeant Hayman searched the "prisoner Grizard," as the King of the Underworld had now become. On him was found a little money and a number of jeweller's instruments, but nothing else, except the tickets he had taken for the party an hour before. No clever criminal of Grizard's standing would allow himself to be arrested with the damning evidence of noted money and the like in his possession. Not by such a simple means was Cammi Grizard to be " downed."

Lockett, on the other hand, was a perfect mine of wealth. In addition to the usual possessions he was found to have no less than £355 in cash upon his person, of which £25 10s. was in that vanished every-day commodity, gold. The rest consisted of two £50 Bank of England notes, seven £10 notes, and thirty-two £5 notes, all of which the sergeant took the numbers. On reaching the " station " Lockett had been self-contained to the point of facetiousness. " This is a bit of all right," he said. " I have been to France for a bit of a holiday only yesterday, and this is a nice way to treat me when I get back." But amongst the papers found upon him was a slip which had been torn in two, but which was obviously a note of the exchange of foreign money in the offices of Thomas Cook and Sons at Southampton, and the details showed that he, too, had been handling the marked French notes. Seeing that it was discovered he tried to bluff it out. " I changed the money," he said, referring to it, " into English money. That is the paper that refers to it."

Meanwhile Detective Percy Worth had travelled post-haste under the anxious orders of his " chief " to Hatton Garden, in search of the unsuspecting Gutwirth. He found him in Charles Street, which runs parallel to Hatton Garden, at about 12.10 p.m. Having stopped him, he repeated the neat little speech which was delivered to the other men on the platform of the Central London Tube. Gutwirth's reply was typical: " All right. Don't make a scene. Take a taxi. I am well known about here." On the way to Bow Street in the taxi he said: " Have you got a warrant for me?" The answer was in the negative, but his sole reply as they arrived was: " Treat me fairly. That is all I ask." Nor was it a request which, in spite of popular belief at times, is ever made to our police in vain.

On being searched he was found to possess, beside the usual articles, nothing of importance save a card with a name and address upon it, that of Quadrat-stein. The four men were arrested, but the pearls had not been found!

One final hope remained. It will be remembered that while going down in the lift at the British Museum Station Grizard had mentioned to Quadrat-stein that he was taking them all to a " nice quiet bar " where they could transact their business in peace. Now the only type of bar at which one can buy and sell large quantities of jewellery without attracting attention is that which abounded in those days in the neighbourhood of Hatton Garden, and this fact, with other reasons of his own, made Chief Inspector Cornish fairly confident that it was to some such spot that Grizard meant to lead his followers.

Another point must here be mentioned, to which but passing reference has up to now been made. The ramifications of a man like Grizard through the criminal underworld are as numerous as they are intricate, and his confederates range from the " bosom ally " to the " down and out " who is an ignorant but useful pawn, in that he asks no questions, and accepts the payment for his services without inquiring of what larger scheme they form a part. The chief conspirators in this most brilliantly worked-out robbery were now in custody, but lesser members of the same confederacy might well be in possession of the pearls which those who knew that they were shadowed would not dare to carry upon them in the light of day. Of such a type was a poor old man called Daniel McCarthy, then aged eighty-two, who was known to be friendly with several of the prisoners, and was strongly suspected of having assisted in the disposal of stolen property in the past. In his younger days he had acquired the reputation of being a thoroughly up-to-date Continental thief, though he seems to have omitted England from his hunting-ground. At a later stage the English police attempted to trace particulars of a conviction against him somewhere on the Continent for receiving stolen property, but in this they failed.

If Ward's deductions were correct, it was this type of man who would in all probability be waiting at what he assumed to be the final rendezvous to which the five men had been about to go when they were arrested. He therefore went to Hatton Garden at top speed and from there to the public-house, already mentioned previously, where he knew that Gutwirth was a frequent visitor, the " George." Sure enough, in the first bar which he entered he found McCarthy, obviously waiting for someone to arrive. He questioned him, and asked him for whom he was waiting, and the reply, as expected, was Leisir Gutwirth. Ward told him he would arrest him for being concerned with other men in custody in stealing and receiving the stolen pearls. McCarthy was an old man, but his brain still worked at high speed in emergency. The reply was most ingenuous. " I know nothing about it. All I did was to bring some flowers here for Gutwirth, whom I have only known for five weeks or so. He told me the other day that his little girl was ill, so I brought him some flowers along to give to her." It seems unnecessary to say that Ward was not exactly satisfied with this reply, and asked him what he had about him. McCarthy said that he had four £5 Bank of England notes. " What else? " demanded the suspicious officer, and proceeded to produce, like a drawing-room conjuror, a bag of gold, containing £29 10s., and other smaller sums. He naturally asked McCarthy to account for such enormous wealth, and the second reply was as glib as the first. " It is all mine " (though no one had suggested to that moment it was not!) I have just sold a house for £500 and also received compensation for an injury." Ward was insistent. " Where did you get the money and the notes?" McCarthy's reply was illuminating. " I received the

Bank of England notes from Cook's at Ludgate Hill in exchange for two 500 franc French notes on Saturday last. The French notes I got from a Continental gentleman whose name I decline to give. I heard them talking at Hatton Garden about some diamonds, and volunteered to change the notes."
" In consequence of this statement," Ward's report continues, " he was formally arrested, taken to Bow Street Police Station in a cab and there detained while further inquiries were being made." The French notes turned out to be 1,000 franc notes, and had been, of course, given him by one of the arrested men, presumably for services rendered. When formally charged with complicity in the crime, McCarthy's statement was a model of brevity. " All that I can say it that I am innocent." It is well for the administration of justice that other men when arrested and charged are not so reticent. When thoroughly searched a list of property found upon him was made and added to the other four. In its brevity it is illuminating, when it is realised that this is *all* that was found upon him except the clothes in which he stood. Truly a curious list, as much for what is not there as for that which is. The note in the police report reads as follows:

Daniel McCarthy.
Found on person.
£29 10s. gold, 14/- silver, 2/4½ bronze.
1 Foreign coin.
4 £5 Bank of England notes.
1 Letter.
1 Latch-key.

At a later stage a statement was taken from MCcarthy's brother, a man of seventy-one, who stated that his brother lived with him and his wife at their address in Clerkenwell, where his wife had died about twelve months ago. " He has never done any work," the statement continued, " but lived independently, having had some house property left him some years ago. This he has lately sold. I think he has about £450 in the bank. He pays me 5/- a week for a bedroom and allows my wife 5/- a week for food." The remainder of the statement, dealing with his excellent character, was hardly borne out by information in possession of the police, and though the brother's statement corroborated his legitimate possession of plenty of money, it hardly assisted his remarkable account of the way in which he became possessed of the French notes.

Meanwhile Inspector Ward hurried off to Silverman's office in Hatton Garden to see what incriminating evidence, if any, he could find upon his business premises. His search was well rewarded, for he found not only sealing-wax, of which more will be heard at the trial, but also a spirit lamp and a ladle used for melting wax. A quantity of modelling wax was of equal interest in the light of the evidence of experts, who were later called to speak to the condition of the seals which had been added to the parcel on its way to Mr. Mayer's office. He also found a seal with J.T. on it, which, though produced at the trial, was apparently not thought of much importance, for it was never mentioned again. Finally, he found a locket and shield which Mr. Gordon later identified as the one which had been brought to him by Silver-

man a few days after the handing over of the copied
M.M. seal. The importance of this, as corroborating
the curious and damning story of the Hammersmith
engraver, need not be emphasised.

From Hatton Garden the anxious officer, bent upon
the recovery of the pearls, repaired to Dalston to
search the house of the greatest of his captives,
Grizard. Here, however, if there had been anything
to find, he was too late. Beyond a quantity of correspondence of no value as evidence against the famous
receiver, he found nothing which would incriminate
him. If Grizard had, in fact, left anything incriminating at his home address some kind friend had
forestalled the police in removing it before they came.
News travels fast in the criminal underworld, and
Grizard, thanks to the reputation which he had
acquired for " playing straight " with those who dealt
with him, had many friends. On the other hand, it
may be that as soon as he noticed that he was being
watched by men who were obviously detectives, he
hastened to prepare his home for the search which
could not be long delayed. It is true that in addition
the inspector took away a quantity of jewellery, but
most of it was subsequently proved to be the property
of Mrs. Grizard and the rest of it his own. Certainly
none of it could be traced as being stolen property.

Nothing daunted, the indefatigable detective
turned his attention to Gutwirth, whom he knew to
have a safe in the Safe Depository in Chancery Lane.
This form of hiding-place is a well known one among
such criminals, for it has the merits of reducing the
amount of property to be concealed from prying eyes
to the key which one is given on renting the safe.

Provided that this can be successfully concealed until one's " time " has been served, the proceeds of one's larceny can be safely hidden until the time comes for their enjoyment in the years to come. If, on the other hand, the key is found, the marvellous organisation of the police will sooner or later find the safe which it will open, and the criminal will lose his hard-earned winnings in addition to his liberty. In this case, however, Ward was unfortunate, for when, having armed himself with a search warrant from the magistrate, he opened the safe which was rented in Gutwirth's name he found, as appears in his own laconic wording in the report, " nothing."

He was no more fortunate in his search of Gutwirth's private house at Canonbury, where the two young amateurs had spent the first night of their great adventures, for he found there nothing but a quantity of memoranda of no importance in proving his complicity. As it happened, Gutwirth had another house at Southend, to which Ward at once despatched two officers with orders to make a careful search, while he returned to Bow Street to extend his inquiries further afield.

Officers were sent to Silverman's private house with no more fortunate result, and another to the Viennese Café in Charles Street, Hatton Garden, where Gutwirth used a drawer of the propietor's desk for the purpose of his business in that locality. The list of property found there contained nothing of note, unless it was " 1 receipt book in Belgian "!

A few hours later he heard from Southend that the search there had produced the same result. By this time it was close on midnight, and Ward had the four men brought up from the cells to be formally charged. He read them the formal charge while they faced him in a row, gauging the man who week by week had been organising all the resources of the police machinery to bring about this moment. On being charged they made, however, no reply.

Having made arrangements for the representative of the Director of Public Prosecutions to be present at the police court on the following day, the inspector summoned all the officers who had been working under him, and in a lengthy consultation discussed their future activities and the case against the four men as it stood. At 1 a.m. they parted, Ward reminding himself no doubt that if the pearls had not yet been recovered, at least the greatest criminal of his day was at last, and, as he hoped, for a long time to come, behind the bars.

The men were caught, but it remained to prove that they were guilty of the offences charged. All who have read accounts of French proceedings on the arrest of a suspected man will not need to be told that it is for the prisoner when arrested to prove that he is innocent, and every means is used to " persuade " him to confess. Not physical bullying, it is true, but there is pressure of a far more subtle kind which can be brought to bear on a suspected man to make him confess his guilt, or at least give information which will lead to the recovery of the property stolen or incriminate his fellow-prisoners.

In England such a course is quite unknown. Not only is it strictly forbidden by police regulations, but it is quite alien in spirit and in practice to the methods of the Force. In the police station as at the trial, an arrested man in this country is deemed to be innocent of all offence until the case against him has been proved " beyond reasonable doubt " in a court of law. It is not enough that the police are satisfied of his guilt; they must produce such evidence as will satisfy a magistrate that there is a *prima facie* case of guilt to lay before a jury. On being arrested, a prisoner is perfectly entitled to say nothing at all, and to wait in silence while the case for the prosecution is laid before the magistrate. If, when the case for the Crown is closed, the prisoner considers that the police have failed to prove their case, he can so plead to the magistrate who may, and often does, accede to the plea and let him go. There are certain exceptions to this rule, but the principle remains, and long may it continue to govern the administration of our law.

By way of illustrating the chasm which may exist between arrest and conviction, the following example may be of interest, and as the writer was present it has the merits of being first hand. During the General Strike of 1926 a procession of strikers was moving slowly up the Ealing High Street, past the police station, on its way to the Uxbridge Road and so to Ealing Common, where a meeting was to be held. Knowing of the approach of the procession, a large body of special constables were told to " stand by " in the station yard, as well as an adequate force of professional police. As the head of the procession reached this very yard, behind whose doors two score of " Specials " were thirsting for a fray, an omnibus, driven by volunteers, was seen approaching from the opposite direction. The sight of such an expanse of still unbroken glass was too much for the strikers, and the atmosphere became electric with suspense. Suddenly, from the midst of the crowd, a hand was raised, a hand which held a stone. The stone flew and the sound of broken glass shattered the silence. There was a crash as the police station doors flew open, a streak of blue as a uniformed thunderbolt clove the crowd asunder, and a roar from fifty voices of " Got 'im " as the hand of the Law descended on the shoulder of the miscreant! With what seemed a single movement the bewildered individual was plucked from the crowd and all but flung into the open doors of the abode of Law. The constable followed, the door slammed to, and the crowd, recovering slowly from its astonishment, proceeded, less one member, on its way. Yet when, on the following morning, that wretched man was brought before the local magistrates, it was with the greatest difficulty that a conviction was secured! The magistrates seemed to think there was some doubt as to the identity of the accused, and this when every officer in the station, not to mention a score of " Specials," had watched the offence from the commencement to its sudden end! No wonder the men in blue occasionally blaspheme against the administrators of our lenient Law.

To return to the case in hand, however, the evidence, if carefully marshalled and properly handled, was, though circumstantial, almost conclusive both in quantity and kind. So notable, however, were the criminals in custody that the officer in charge, mindful that the pearls were not yet found, decided to invoke the best brains at his disposal to prove his prisoner's guilt.

CHAPTER IX

BOW STREET

At half-past ten the following morning, September 3rd, the five men appeared at Bow Street Police Court before the Magistrate then sitting, who happened to be Mr. Graham Campbell. Needless to say, the case against them was scarcely begun, and only formal notice of arrest could be given to the magistrate. It is a rule, however, of English law that no man may be kept in custody a moment longer than is necessary before being taken before a magistrate, and as the courts are sitting every day of the year except on Sundays and certain holidays, this means that no man can be kept waiting more than forty-eight hours, and only rarely more than twenty-four. Even when brought before the magistrate, he cannot be remanded in custody for longer than eight days at a time, though if allowed on bail he may, with his consent, be remanded for much longer periods. There is thus in England no equivalent of the Continental system of throwing a man into prison to wait, it may be, months before he is so much as brought before a magistrate, much less properly tried. In England, if the above rule is infringed in any way, the prisoner, through his solicitor or friends, will apply to the High Court of Justice for a Writ of Habeas Corpus to make the magistrate show cause why the man so held against his will should not be at once set free, all of which it is useful to remember

when, as periodically happens, some public outcry is
aroused against the behaviour of officialdom to
" British citizens."

From the report of the proceedings on September 3rd, which appears in *The Times* for September 4th, it will be seen that Mr. Margetts
appeared for Lockett and Grizard, and Mr. Albert
Osborn for Silverman and Gutwirth. No one
appeared for the venerable McCarthy but Mr. Poole,
now Sir Reginald Poole, of Lewis and Lewis, the
famous solicitors, appeared to " watch " for the
underwriters at Lloyds. Among the distinguished
persons present on the bench with Mr. Graham
Campbell were, it seems, Mr. Stephenson, now Sir
Guy Stephenson, Assistant Director of Public Prosecutions, and Mr. Basil Thompson, later Sir Basil
Thompson, the Assistant-Commissioner of the Metropolitan Police.

The proceedings were soon over. The various
officers gave evidence of arresting the five men in
the dock, and a formal remand was asked for and
obtained. Some slight attempt at obtaining bail was
made, but curtly refused by the Magistrate, who
probably considered such a request as bordering on
the impudent. The five men were then taken from
the dock to the cells below and from there in separate
vehicles, closely guarded, back to the prison whence
they came. The proceedings were for the moment
over and the prosecution, who at this hearing were
represented by Mr. Williamson, began to prepare the
evidence on which they would rely in obtaining a conviction against the criminals.

The importance of the case warranted the some-

Mr. Samuel Brandstatter and ex-Superintendent Leach leaving Bow
Street Police Court.

[*Photo : Topical Press Agency*]

what unusual course of briefing Senior Treasury
Counsel at the police court, and for this reason. In
the vast majority of cases which are tried upon Assize,
whether in the country or at the Central Criminal
Court, which is the Assize Court for the County of
London, the conduct of the case at the preliminary
hearing is left to a salaried representative of the
Director of Public Prosecutions, who may be a
solicitor or barrister, and the depositions and exhibits,
with comment thereon, and other papers are made up
into the Brief which is laid before Counsel as soon
as may be before the trial. There are some cases,
however, which by their length, intricacy or public
importance, warrant the additional expense to the
community of briefing Treasury Counsel in the first
instance. The basis of a trial at Assize is the Depositions, sworn statements signed by the witnesses, and if
the case is badly handled at the police court it may be
very hard for Counsel at the trial to present his
evidence in the way which he would like. As Counsel
have the responsibility of conducting the case at the
trial, it is only fair that in issues of importance they
should handle the situation from the first. The position is analogous to a general practitioner handing
over a case to the specialist before any treatment has
been given which might embarrass the latter's own.

It is therefore quite common for Junior Treasury
Counsel to appear at a police court for the prosecution, but far more rare for Senior Treasury Counsel
to be briefed. There are three Junior and three Senior
Treasury Counsel, their name being derived from the
days when they were specially retained by the
Treasury, in whose hands the work of the present

Director's office then lay, to assist or represent the Attorney-General at the Central Criminal Court. When, however, in 1908, Sir Charles Matthews was appointed to the Directorship of Public Prosecutions as a separate office, having no connection with the Treasury, the name became a misnomer, but has still remained. These Counsel are still entitled to practise in all other capacities, but the Director has a " first call " upon their services at each Sessions of the Central Criminal Court. As between themselves the position of the Senior to the Junior three is virtually that of King's Counsel to a junior, but in the eyes of the Bar as a whole they are equally Juniors, and cannot, in fact, " take silk."

In 1913 one of the Senior Treasury Counsel was that master of criminal law, Mr. Richard Muir, afterwards Sir Richard Muir. Like many other famous lawyers, he had started life in the gallery of the House of Commons, where for many years he was on the Parliamentary reporting staff of *The Times*. By 1893, however, his work at the Bar had, by its painstaking thoroughness and sound common sense, brought him so much recognition that he had to resign from his reporting and devote his time to the practice of the law. He was that rare combination—a great advocate and a great lawyer, while in his methods of advocacy he became the greatest exponent in his time of the cold, impartial, deadly fair presentation of pure fact. He was a serious-minded, almost ponderous-minded man, but possessed, as so many of those who come from North of the Tweed, of a large and kindly heart. If genius be defined as the infinite capacity for taking pains " Dicky " Muir was a genius, for the preparation of the smallest of his cases was a work of art. His variety of coloured pencils was known wherever he practised, and the papers from which so much of this story has been taken, the very papers which he used at the trial, are scored and underlined all through with colours of every hue, one for each of the prisoners and others to distinguish points for cross-examination or other matters which needed to be kept clear. If I may quote from the life of Sir Richard Muir, compiled by S. T. Felstead and Lady Muir, he " had a unique method of preparing his cases. By means of small cards, about the size of playing cards, and various coloured pencils, he marshalled his facts and analysed the salient points of his cases. He always took about with him a bundle of pencils held by a rubber band. One colour was for examination-in-chief, one for cross-examination, and another for re-examination. All the judges knew Muir's ' playing cards,' as they called them. By their aid he noted the points of attack to be made in cross-examination, and further analysed them under A.B.C. headings, further sub-dividing them by numbers." In this way the whole of the evidence, however long and complicated, was elaborately analysed.

We have already said that Treasury Counsel are in no sense Public Prosecutors as the French, for example, understand the term. They have no interest in the outcome of the cases in which they appear. Their sole duty is to conduct the case for the prosecution in a dignified, impersonal way, leaving to the jury the question of deciding whether the evidence which they have laid before them is sufficient to make it their duty to convict. Hence at the Central Criminal Court one frequently sees one of the Treasury Counsel prosecuting in some case and then, when the next case is called on, making way for some brother barrister, with whom, maybe, he had just been collaborating, and retire to the other end of the bench to defend the next prisoner.

Such is the nature of our Law, however, and such the nature of our national psychology, that it is this very impersonal attitude which often wins the case. The prisoner is never allowed a grievance and is helped in every way, and when the verdict goes against him he can only admit that, like so many before him, he has nothing more to say. If not the founder of this method of " killing by fairness," as it is sometimes called, Muir was its most able exponent, though all who practise at the Criminal Bar will agree that one of his closest friends, who later stepped into his shoes as Senior of the Treasury Counsel, the writer of the Foreword to this book, was an able pupil, if not the equal, of the master of whom he was so fond.

Such was Richard Muir, and Grizard knew to the full, when he heard the name of the man who was to face him at the trial, that he had an opponent worthy of his steel. Fresh from the laurels of the Crippen case, Muir was known through the criminal under-world as a man to be feared, and his Junior, Travers Humphreys as he then was, proved himself a valuable ally. Muir was briefed alone at the Police Court, but he was told by the Director that he would be assisted at the trial by the already well-known criminal lawyer who, being in his own chambers, had unique opportunities for helping him. The two of them, from the day when briefs were delivered shortly after the arrest, began to work on the case in earnest, and within the seven days of the adjournment had prepared such a perfect exposition of the facts as all the wiles of the mighty " Cammi " would be unable to escape.

On September 10th Bow Street Police Court was crowded to the utmost of its capacity.

When the usual " night charges " were concluded, the five men were once more placed in the dock and Mr. Muir, his famous " playing cards " in hand, rose to present to the Magistrate the case against the prisoners which he hoped to prove. The only report of this " opening " is to be found in the newspaper files for that evening and the following day, but none of these do more than give in outline the story as already told, and nothing will be served by reproducing any of them here.

Mr. Muir remarked of Gutwirth that it was probably his " far too long a tongue," as Grizard called it, that had given the honest dealer, Brandstatter, at Antwerp, the chance of tracking the criminals to earth, and maybe Gutwirth from his position in the dock regarded those who were watching him as possible protectors from the vengeance of his " colleagues " for his indiscretion, rather than as the jailors of his liberty which in fact they were. The fault, however, lay in those who had entrusted such a babbler with so delicate a mission on their behalf.

At the close of the opening speech, the Prosecution began to call their witnesses, and so the first day of the hearing ended. Application was made by those representing the prisoners for their friends to be

allowed to see them in prison, and the police very
naturally intervened to submit that such an interview, if granted, should be subject to the closest
scrutiny. It would be remembered, their representative, Inspector Ward, reminded the magistrate, that
the pearls had yet to be found, and it might well be
that the prisoners alone knew where they were, and
would desire to confide in some confederate the position of the hiding-place so that others might complete the work which they, the prisoners, had left un-
done. Mr. Graham Campbell wisely gave the
required permission subject to the prison regulations
governing such interviews, and left the Inspector free
to arrange with the prison governor in what way the
meetings might with safety take place.

The hearing was then adjourned to the 14th, when
Quadratstein was called, and from then to the 15th,
at the close of which hearing Mr. Muir announced to
the Magistrate that all the evidence available against
McCarthy of his complicity in the robbery had then
been given. He summarised it by saying that he was
an associate of Gutwirth's, that he had upon him when
arrested bank-notes which he admittedly had received
from members of the gang for *some* consideration,
and that he had given to the police a most unsatisfactory, and obviously untrue, account of how they
came into his possession. He, Mr. Muir, however,
did not suggest that this alone would be evidence
upon which a jury could, with fairness, be asked to
convict, and McCarthy was accordingly discharged.
His friends received the old man with effusive con-
gratulations on his return to liberty, while the remaining four, knowing that their shrewd opponent would

never make the same remark on their behalf, were removed once more by separate vans to the prison where they could but wait for the next move in the game.

Little did they think as they were trundled back to prison that within twenty-four hours their final hope of ultimate gain from their nefarious deeds would be taken from them, for on the next day, August 16th, the pearls were found.

It will by now have been made clear that Mr. Price, as representing the underwriters, with his own inquiry agents, and the official police, as represented by Inspector Ward, were primarily concerned in recovering two different things. Mr. Price was interested in the pearls, and only incidentally in the men who had so brilliantly stolen them; Inspector Ward was out for the capture of the men, and only interested in the pearls to the extent that their discovery might provide additional evidence of his prisoners' guilt. The latter had been working, from the moment when, on the 25th, he was informed of the bedroom interview, towards luring the criminals into a trap where he could arrest them with the pearls in front of them, and when, through someone's carelessness, the wily " Cammi " noticed he was being followed and refused to negotiate further, it became imperative to make an arrest as soon as possible to make certain at least of capturing the men. The result we have already seen. " Cammi " was far too clever to be arrested with the pearls upon him, or in the hands of those who accompanied him to the rendezvous, and only when he was convinced that they were not being watched or followed would he have given the signal to a confederate to fetch the pearls from where they were in relatively safe keeping to the meeting-place where they could be quickly sold.

The method of working of such criminals is usually as follows. The principals concerned assemble at a selected rendezvous, and having, either by careful tests, or else by swift and intricate movements thrown all possible pursuers off the scent, adjourn to a second rendezvous, where a member of the gang is deputed to fetch the stolen property from its hiding-place. The deal would then be hurriedly concluded and the gang would scatter with their welcome but ill-gotten gains.

Such, it is thought, was the programme for the second of September. Grizard was convinced that he was being followed, but though an experienced detective can do marvels in following a man who does not know that anyone is following him, it is a matter of comparative ease in a city the size of London to throw pursuers off the track when once they are realised for what in fact they are. Clearly one of the easiest methods of escaping from such unwelcome companionship is to make use of the Tubes. Trains come and go at frequent intervals. Provided that the followed man can slip into a train a second or two ahead of his followers he has to all intents and purposes got clean away. His followers in the next train cannot know what station he has left the train in front of them, or whither he went on leaving it. No better method of escaping pursuit exists for the harassed criminal.

It was probably with some such thought in his mind that Grizard had suggested the British Museum Tube

Station as a rendezvous. Once he was satisfied that he and his fellow-criminals were not observed in going down in the lift, he reckoned that he would be safely away from the platform before any possible watchers realised the plan he had in mind. He would then have taken the other four to a public-house or restaurant where the presence of the five would not provoke any comment, and thence despatch an emissary to the actual holder of the pearls who was waiting, maybe, in a distant part of London for the emissary to appear. And who would be this unknown and unmentioned personality, whose sole part in the drama was to hold in careful keeping the treasure round which all the plot and counter-plot revolved? McCarthy, for example, was such a person, but in approaching and arresting him Inspector Ward was frankly " drawing a bow at a venture." It may be that he looked upon the venerable associate of thieves as so unlikely to be carrying a fragrant bunch of flowers in a public-house in Hatton Garden on a summer's afternoon for any but a nefarious purpose that his rough examination of the posy, to see whether it did not contain at its heart a form of fruit more valuable to men than was apparent to the eye, may be excused. As it turned out, however, he was wrong, for McCarthy, though possessed of money the acquisition of which he could not satisfactorily explain, was innocent of pearls.

It has been suggested, nevertheless, that he need not have left to chance the finding of the actual holder. He must have known that none of the four men at the Holborn rendezvous would be in possession of the pearls, especially when the leader of the gang suspected he was being watched, but he equally must have known that just before the meeting some-one must have handed over the necklace to a fifth confederate to hold in safety until informed that the men were waiting where they knew they would not be pursued. Then why did he not watch, not only the houses of all four men, but the members of their families and those whom he knew to be associates of each of them? At a matter of historic fact, no one has ever discovered with any certainty where the pearls were hidden during those fateful days between the arrest of the thieves and the dramatic finding of their spoils. The police have their theories, but as the persons whom they suspect have never been arrested for this or any other crime it would be neither wise nor fair to publish their identity. The underwriters did not even trouble to inquire. It was enough that after days of fierce anxiety and sleepless nights they finally recovered the necklace which they had insured, and thereby saved themselves consider-ably more than a hundred thousand pounds.

The story of the actual finding of the pearls is not the least dramatic incident in this tale of London's underworld, and certainly lends itself to being " written up." As an example of its possibilities, the following quotation is taken from the *Premier Magazine* of December, 1927, in which a story entitled " Peerless Pearls " contains a highly coloured, though tolerably accurate, version of the subject-matter of this book.

" Furtively the woman, walking slowly down the London street, glanced around her. It was early morning, only just past eight o'clock, and the street was not yet wholly awakened to life. In many of the top-floor windows blinds were still down; the windows of the shops were blank with the drop curtains not yet drawn to reveal the stage on which the wares played out their little parts; at the doors women, with pails and brushes, bustled to give the shops their morning toilets. But crowded omnibuses were plying along the road and, on the pavements, men and girls were scurrying on their way to work, their faces tense with the fear that prevails at such morning times of arriving late." (All of which is one way of saying that the time was eight a.m.)

"No such fear apparently oppressed this woman. She seemed in no hurry to get anywhere. She walked slowly, pausing now and again to look around her; now turning and retracing her steps while the furtive, sleepless-looking eyes scanned the hurrying passers-by. With the hand concealed beneath the cloak she wore she clutched something close to her.

"A pause seemed to come at last in the stream of passing folk, and with a last quick glance around, the woman threw what she had been clutching into the gutter of the roadway and walked swiftly away. For some minutes the thing lay there—a small brown-paper parcel tied with string. At last it attracted the notice of a man, evidently a workman, who, picking it up, took it aside and breaking the string, opened the paper to discover what the packet contained. Only a large match-box! He slid it open and looked; then with a grunt of disgust, thrust the thing into his pocket . . ."

In point of dull and unromantic fact, nothing is precisely known as to the laying of the packet in the gutter, though the police have "theories" which may, for all the public know, be true. However that may be, there is no doubt that a Mr. Augustus George Horn, a " pianoforte back maker," living at Islington, was walking to his work in the early morning of September 16th, thinking of nothing in particular, when he saw a small brown parcel lying in the gutter. The sight recalled him from his vacant reverie and he prodded it with his walking-stick in idle curiosity. He naturally glanced about him to see if anyone was still in sight who might have dropped it in the course of stepping off the kerb. All he saw was a man and woman getting on to a passing 44 omnibus which was going towards Highbury. He shouted to them, but they did not seem to hear. He afterwards described the couple with that remarkable precision which many of us could not attempt to imitate, but the description covered far too many people to be of any use to the police in tracing them. Being somewhat undecided as to what to do with his treasure trove, he proceeded on his way with the parcel in his pocket, but later called, as was his wont, at the Swan public-house at Highbury, which in 1913 was open at that hour. In the course of his journey he took the parcel from his pocket, and, his curiosity being aroused once more, proceeded to open it. Within the paper he found a match-box of the Bryant and May variety, rather larger than the present penny one, and his disgust at such an apparent anti-climax was profound. He opened it, however, and found it to be filled with what he took to be some coloured marbles, so tightly packed that many of them fell out into the gutter and had to be retrieved. On entering the public-

The Hon. Mr. Justice Humphreys, Junior Counsel for the Prosecution at the Trial.

[*Photo : Barratt's*]

The late Sir Richard Muir arriving at Bow Street Police Court with his clerk.

[*Photo : Topical Press Agency*]

house he showed his find to a Mr. Lewis, a fellow-employee, and a Mr. Yates, who worked nearby. Both men handled the " marbles " thoughtfully, and said they were " no good." Horn, however, was not so sure, basing his opinion on the fact that they were curiously packed for marbles, but for the moment he said nothing more, and after finishing his drink went out. From there he went to his shop, and having shown the " marbles " to his mates announced that he was going to take them to the police station nearby. Lewis, and another man called Jacobs, accompanied him to the " station," where he gave them to the officer in charge. The latter examined them, and gave the finder a receipt for " imitation pearls "!

The lucky finder, all unconscious that he had exchanged a necklace valued at £135,000 for a brief acknowledgment of imitation pearls, proceeded to the nearest public-house (the morning being very hot) and ordered himself a drink. On the way, however, he felt in his pocket and found another pearl which had been overlooked in emptying its contents on the table in the sergeant's presence. He showed it to Lewis, and asked him, " What about this?" " Throw it down the gutter," was that worthy's brief reply. At the Railway public-house, a little further on (the morning, as we have said, was *very* hot), he met a friend called Owen, to whom he offered the pearl for the price of drinks for three. The offer was refused! " Throw it down the drain," said Mr. Owen, and that was the last seen of the pearl. The temptation to moralise is irresistible. On the one hand, we have a widespread industry employing thousands of men throughout the world in procuring and collecting pearls, with experts such as Mr. Mayer and others of his kind spending their lives in matching, grading and selling them, all for the greater adornment of the basis of their livelihood, " the eternal feminine." On the other hand, we have Mr. Horn and his associates, to whom these priceless products of long years of careful work were merely " marbles " of so little value that a perfect specimen was not considered worth a pint of beer, and, when all is said and done, *pace* the inhabitants of Hatton Garden, who shall say that the judgment of these working men upon the coloured marbles from the ocean bed was not, in the eye of eternal values, of the two more accurate?

Meanwhile the Station Sergeant, as in duty bound, sent on the pearls to Scotland Yard to be identified, but not before he had reversed his judgment of their worth by taking them across to a local jeweller, who pronounced them without hesitation not only real, but the most perfect specimens which he had ever handled in his long career. At Scotland Yard they were at once identified, and Mr. Mayer was sent for with all speed. On his arrival he had but to glance at the contents of the match-box to know that there, before his eyes, after two months of anxiety, his famous necklace lay in all its glory, and his joy was indescribable. It is true that he was insured, and that in the event of the pearls being held as finally lost, he would recover their value to the full, but no true connoisseur will regard mere money as a perfect substitute for his choicest works of art. Mr. Mayer loved his necklace, and described the pearls as he handled them as the " prettiest things in the world."

The news was telephoned to Lloyd's without

delay, and apparently for the first time in its history the famous Lutine Bell, which is rung when a ship long overdue with valuable cargo safely reaches port, was rung for the recovery in London of the stolen pearls. When the hall was filled in answer to the summons, and the announcer shouted from the rostrum that the necklace had been found, the walls re-echoed with a rousing cheer. Lloyd's had had its lesson, and in future £50,000 became the maximum for which a single item would be insured upon the previous terms, while premiums for such insurance were in future raised by 10 per cent.

The news spread to the Press, and on the following morning the doors of the police court were besieged by a crowd of the inevitable kind, ambitious to gaze for themselves upon the famous piece of jewellery. The original necklace had consisted of sixty-one pearls. Fifty-seven had been found by Horn and handed over, and one he had for ever lost. Two more had been bought by Mr. Spanier from the criminals, and the last was never found. The diamond clasp, as we have seen, was the first thing to be sold by the criminals. Of the sixty-one pearls and the clasp, however, fifty-nine pearls had been recovered, and with such a result Mr. Mayer was well satisfied.

When the court assembled on the morning of the 18th Mr. Mayer was the first witness to be called. The pearls had been brought from the strong room at Scotland Yard by Chief Inspector Ward, who handed them to Mr. Mayer in the witness-box. Mr. Muir, in his usual unemotional tones, inquired of the witness: " Would you look at those pearls, Mr.

Mayer. Are they yours, and part of the stolen necklace, fifty-nine in all?" "They are," replied Mr. Mayer, and held them up for all to see. What were the thoughts of the four men in the dock as they gazed on the "coloured marbles" which had brought them where they were? If only Silverman, on seeing that the packet contained pearls and not the longed-for diamonds, had put them back and sealed the broken end, to let the packet be delivered with its contents as they were, would Mr. Mayer or his clerks have noticed the unusual number of seals, and if he had, would he have had the least suspicion of the cause of the abnormality? Probably not, and the thieves would have waited in all safety for a parcel of diamonds which they could "smash" with comparative ease. Again, if Gutwirth had only curbed his "far too long a tongue" at Antwerp, and arranged to sell the pearls through channels which he knew to be too implicated in dishonest dealing to attempt to "double cross" him in the endeavour to earn the underwriters' reward! But the time had passed for speculation on the might-have-been, and the future held sufficient trouble for the day.

When Mr. Mayer had identified the pearls he handed them back to the officer who, buttoning them up in his inside coat pocket, left the court with two men to escort him and returned his precious "exhibit" to the strong room at "the Yard."

Other witnesses were then examined on that and subsequent days, but any comment upon the evidence will be reserved for the description of the trial. Mr. Spanier made it quite clear that he regarded himself all through the negotiations as an expert in identifying Mr. Mayer's pearls and as that alone. When cross-examined to know why, at the bedroom scene in the First Avenue Hotel, he did not take the opportunity of keeping the necklace and claiming the reward, he explained that his orders were to weigh, examine and buy as many pearls as possible for the £4,000 which he had been given for that purpose. When asked, " But you are an able-bodied man?" he tartly replied, " I am not a policeman—I am an expert." Save for this incident there was little to enliven the monotony of the preliminary proceedings, and in the course of time the case for the Prosecution came to a close, the Defence reserved what explanation or excuse they had to give, and the four men were committed for trial to the Central Criminal Court. The charges on the committal were couched in general terms, and amounted to the stealing of the necklace and the three loose pearls in the course of their transmission by post, and the felonious receiving of them, knowing them to have been stolen. Without delay both Prosecution and Defence began to prepare for the forthcoming struggle at the trial.

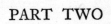

PART TWO

CHAPTER X

THE TRIAL

On Monday morning, November 17th, 1913, the curtain rose on the last scene in this drama of real life, and the stage was Court No. 1 in the Central Criminal Court. This building, better known to the public as the " Old Bailey," so called from the street in which it stands, it built on the site of Newgate Gaol, outside whose walls so many felons, sentenced maybe for what now would be called a trivial offence, have paid for their misbehaviour with their lives. There are three courts sitting at the commencement of each Session, presided over by the Recorder, Common Serjeant, and Commissioner repectively, while on the third day, usually a Thursday, a " red Judge," that is to say a judge of the King's Bench Division of the High Court, comes under special Commission to try the most serious cases at the Assize. All Englishmen are familiar with the principal of Assizes, in which a duly appointed Judge of the King's Bench Division travels round his " Circuit " from town to town with instructions from His Majesty, for " Oyer and Terminer " and " General Gaol Delivery." London, having itself as large a population as all the counties in the average Circuit put together, has a permanent Assize Court of its own, to which all prisoners are committed from the Metropolitan and other Police Courts in the artificial County of London and adjacent areas. This building is the Central Criminal Court, opened by King Edward in 1907, and here it was that the outwitted gang were destined to be tried. Needless to say, their case was of sufficient importance to be placed in the Judge's List.

The Court was crowded to its utmost capacity long before the trial was due to commence, for having searched all over Europe for the pearls which were to give them such a vast reward, the public were agog to see the master-criminal who had so brilliantly but unavailingly stolen them.

At half-past ten precisely Mr. Justice A. T. Lawrence entered the Court, bowed to Counsel and the waiting Jurymen, and took his seat. All four of the prisoners were represented at the trial by Counsel, many of whom are names well known to-day. In the words of the shorthand note: " Mr. R. D. Muir, Mr. Travers Humphreys and Mr. B. Leycester Muir appeared for the Prosecution. Mr. Curtis Bennett and Mr. Ivan Snell appeared for the prisoner Lockett. Mr. George Elliott, K.C., and Mr. G. W. H. Jones appeared for Grizard. Mr. J. P. Valetta and Mr. E. K. Corrie appeared for Silverman. Mr. Walter Frampton apeared for Gutwirth."

Of these, Mr. Curtis Bennett, son of the late Chief Magistrate at Bow Street, is now Sir Henry Curtis Bennett, K.C., with a son, Mr. Derek Curtis Bennett, also at the Bar. Sir Henry has become famous in recent years as one of the leading defending Counsel of his day, but it is seldom that he argues Law as strenuously as circumstances proved to be necessary in this case. His Junior, Mr. Ivan

Snell, is now a Police Court Magistrate. Grizard's name happened to be third on the Indictment, although in fact he was the most dangerous of all, and for his Counsel chose the great George Elliott, K.C., who also had a son to follow after him. George Elliott was a notable character in his time, and practised mainly at the Criminal Bar with prolonged excursions into Licensing. He was a great exponent of the suave, apologetic manner, and was known to his intimate friends as " genial George." He was never known to be rude to anyone, and always gave the witness whom he happened to be cross-examining the impression that he apologised for troubling him to answer the questions put, but *would* he mind just clearing up a point which he, the stupid Counsel, did not *quite* understand. The unsuspicious witness would naturally comply, and only when it was too late to retrace his footsteps find the embarrassing nature of the admission he had innocently made.

His Junior, Mr. G. W. H. Jones, is now Sir George Jones, M.P., with a large and varied practice in the High Court punctuated with occasional visits to the arena of crime. Mr. Valetta's practice is equally varied, but he is a great deal younger than his veteran junior, Mr. E. K. Corrie, who was called to the Bar over fifty years ago.

For Gutwirth Mr. Walter Frampton, also with a son at the Bar, appeared alone. Mr. Frampton now has a larger " all-round " practice than almost anyone else at the Bar. He will visit in the course of day, with the help of innumerable juniors or " Leaders " as the case may be, the Admiralty, Divorce and Appeal Courts, look in at a police court on his way to an inquest, settle some little matter in a County Court, and return by way of the Bankruptcy Court to a High Court action in the Strand. If this is not actual fact it is at least the impression made upon his admiring juniors!

But able as these Counsel were they had two difficulties to overcome, the facts as provable in evidence and the experience and skill of the men who would handle it at the trial. Of Sir Richard Muir, as he afterwards became, and Sir Travers Humphreys, afterwards himself a High Court Judge, we have already spoken, and they were assisted, though unofficially, by Mr. Burleigh Muir, Sir Richard's son, who later died while serving in the War. It is a noticeable example of the hereditary nature of the Bar that of the nine men briefed at the Trial no less than five had sons who followed after them, and the same applied to the Learned Judge.

This eminent lawyer was born in 1843 and was therefore seventy years old at the date of trial. He was educated at Trinity Hall, Cambridge, which college, though small in numbers, has produced for its size a larger proportion of distinguished lawyers than any other in the British Isles. Mr. Justice Humphreys is another " old Hall man " who apppeared in the case, though he followed the Judge to Cambridge at an interval of twenty years, and the writer of this story followed his father thirty years after that. Yet even the total interval of fifty years does not prevent all three appearing together at an old " Hall " gathering, for the College prides itself on · the comradeship between its members present and past. Mr. Justice Lawrence was raised to

the Bench in 1904, and in 1921, on the retirement
of Lord Reading to become Viceroy of the Indian
Empire, was appointed Lord Chief Justice of
England in his place with the title of Lord Trevethin
of Blaengawney. His tenure of this great office was,
however, short, for in 1922 he retired in favour of
the then Attorney General, Sir Gordon Hewart, now
Lord Hewart of Bury. In 1913, with half a
century's experience of criminal law and practice to
his credit, Mr. Justice Lawrence was an admirable
" referee " between the famous " Cammi " Grizard
and his redoubtable antagonist, Sir Richard Muir.

The procedure at a criminal trial is well known
to all readers of such famous cases, though alas but
little known it seems to those who write of them in
fiction, where the wildest errors, libellous to British
justice, are too frequently displayed.

In the ordinary way the Indictment is read to the
prisoner by the Clerk of the Court and the prisoner,
in consultation with those defending him, pleads
Guilty or Not Guilty as the case may be. Issue is then
joined between the parties, who in criminal cases are
the Crown and the " Prisoner at the Bar," and a Jury
is sworn to deliver " a true verdict according to the
evidence." The prisoner is then placed into their
charge, and the trial begins. On this occasion, however, Mr. Curtis Bennett, as he then was, on behalf
of Lockett, took objection to the form in which the
Indictment was laid and moved, as was his right,
to have it quashed on the ground of its invalidity.
The rules for drawing up indictments are naturally
very strict, as it is only fair to the prisoner that he
should know exactly for what offence he is being

tried. But in the course of centuries the spirit of accuracy which was the basis of a good indictment had degenerated into a pointless clinging to the letter of the form, and even in the first decade of the present century the slightest technical inaccuracy in the drafting, or even copying out, of an indictment might render it bad on objection being taken, and the prisoner, who maybe was not only guilty but, failing his legal objection, was prepared to admit his guilt, would leave the dock forthwith. Nevertheless, in spite of what is sometimes quoted as being popular opinion on the subject, the Law is not " an ass," and when matters reached a point at which a dangerous murderer would again be let loose upon society as the reward for a slip of the pen, a movement arose to return the law on the subject to the basis of commonsense. The passing of the Indictments Act in 1915 was in part the result of this very case, in which once more the attention of the public was drawn to the uncertain and unsatisfactory state of the law. At the time of the trial, however, the old procedure still obtained.

The Indictment contained six Counts, or separate charges, each of them against all four of the defendants, who were regarded as a gang of men united by a common purpose, working jointly to a common end. In view of the technical nautre of the Indictment and the objections which they realised would at once be raised, Sir Richard and his Junior, Travers Humphreys, spent many weary hours in drafting it, and the net result was a legal masterpiece. As it was in a form which is now obsolete, it may be of interest to reproduce the Abstract of it.

CENTRAL CRIMINAL COURT

THE JURORS FOR OUR LORD THE KING upon their oath present that JAMES LOCKETT, JOSEPH GRIZARD, SIMON SILVERMAN AND LEISER GUTWIRTH on the 16th of July in the County of London and within the jurisdiction of the Central Criminal Court certain chattels to wit one pearl necklace consisting of 61 pearls and one diamond clasp, one loose round pearl and two loose pear shaped pearls the chattels and property of His Majesty's Post Master General feloniously did steal take and carry away out of a certain postal packet addressed to one Max Mayer posted and registered in Paris in the French Republic and then in course of transmission by post in England to No. 88 Hatton Garden in the said County of London.

2. That the said James Lockett Joseph Grizard Simon Silverman and Leiser Gutwirth on the day and in the year aforesaid at the parish and within the jurisdiction aforesaid feloniously did receive the chattels and property aforesaid before then feloniously stolen taken and carried away out of a certain postal packet addressed to the said Max Mayer and registered in Paris in the French Republic and then in course of transmission by post in England to No. 88 Hatton Garden in the said County and that they the said James Lockett Joseph Grizard

Simon Silverman and Leiser Gutwirth when they so received the said chattels well knew that the same had been sent by post and had been feloniously stolen while in course of transmission by post in England.

3. That the said James Lockett Joseph Grizard Simon Silverman and Leiser Gutwirth on the day and in the year aforesaid at the parish and within the jurisdiction aforesaid certain chattels to wit one pearl necklace consisting of 61 pearls and one diamond clasp one loose round pearl and two loose pear shaped pearls the chattels and property of the said Max Mayer feloniously did steal take and carry away.

4. That the said James Lockett Joseph Grizard Simon Silverman and Leiser Gutwirth on the day and in the year aforesaid at the parish and within the jurisdiction aforesaid the chattels and property last aforesaid feloniously did receive and have they the said James Lockett Joseph Grizard Simon Silverman and Leiser Gutwirth then knowing the said chattels and property to have been feloniously stolen taken and carried away.

PRELIMINARY AVERMENT TO 5TH AND 6TH COUNTS

That heretofore and before the committing of the offences and felonies hereinafter in the 5th and 6th Counts charged and stated to wit on

the 15th day of July A.D. 1913 certain property
to wit one pearl necklace consisting of 61 pearls
and one diamond clasp one loose round pearl and
two loose pear shaped pearls the chattels and
property of one Max Mayer had been stolen
and taken outside the United Kingdom to wit
at some place the name of which is to the jurors
aforesaid unknown within the French Republic
under such circumstances that if the said stealing and taking had been committed within that
part of the United Kingdom called England
the person so stealing and taking the said
property would have been guilty of felony and
the indictable offence of larceny to wit the said
property had been stolen and taken unlawfully
and without claim of right and against the will
of the said Max Mayer and with the intention
of permanently converting the said property to
the use of persons other than the said Max
Mayer.

5. That the said James Lockett Joseph
Grizard Simon Silverman and Leiser Gutwirth
on the 16th day of July A.D. 1913 at the parish
and within the jurisdiction aforesaid the chattels
and property last aforesaid before then stolen
and taken outside the United Kingdom to wit
at some place the name of which is to the jurors
unknown in the French Republic feloniously
and without lawful excuse did receive and have
they the said J. Lockett J. Grizard S. Silverman
and L. Gutwirth when they so received the said
property knowing the same to have been stolen.

6. That the said J. Lockett J. Grizard S. Silverman and L. Gutwirth afterwards to wit on the day and in the year last aforesaid at the parish and within the jurisdiction aforesaid the chattels and property last aforesaid before then stolen and taken outside the United Kingdom to wit at some place the name of which is to the jurors aforesaid unknown in the French Republic feloniously and without lawful excuse did have in their possession they the said J. Lockett J. Grizard S. Silverman and L. Gutwirth when they so had in their possession the said last mentioned chattels and property knowing the same to have been stolen.

PREVIOUS CONVICTION

That before the commission of the offences herein before charged to wit at the Court of Oyer and Terminer sitting at the Assize Courts Liverpool in and for the County of Lancaster on the 14th day of February A.D. 1906 the said James Lockett was by the name of William Preston convicted of felony to wit burglary and sentenced to five years penal servitude.

That before the commission of the offences hereinbefore charged to wit at the General Session of the delivery of the lawfully appointed prisons holden for the jurisdiction of the Central Criminal Court at Justice Hall in the Old Bailey in the suburbs of the City of London before certain Justices of our Lord the King appointed to deliver the said prisons of the

prisoners then being therein on the 14th day of
March A.D. 1910 the said Joseph Grizard was
by the name of Joseph Grizard convicted of
felony to wit feloniously receiving harbouring
comforting and maintaining one Samuel Barnett
well knowing that he had feloniously stolen a
leather bag.

To summarise this flow of words, the first Count
charges the prisoners with stealing the necklace and
the other pearls " in the course of transmission by
post to England," and while in the possession of the
post office. The second Count charges them with
receiving the property well knowing it to have been
stolen. This is, as we have seen at an earlier page,
an offence, and a serious offence, in itself. It is usual
when a number of men are charged with stealing
under circumstances such as these to include a count
for " receiving " the stolen property, so that should
any one of them satisfy the jury that he was not
present or conniving at the larceny, he can still be
convicted, maybe, for the subsequent offence. To continue in the words of Mr. Curtis Bennett, as shown
on the shorthand note: " The third Count varies only
in this particular, that the property is put in Max
Mayer instead of the Postmaster General, and this
again is a stealing Count, and the fourth Count is for
receiving the same property, putting it in Max
Mayer's name." In other words, the third and
fourth are a second pair, the same as the first pair but
with a technical difference, that the possession of the
property is given as Max Mayer's to cover the possibility of the pearls having been stolen after they left

the postman's hands and before reaching Mr. Mayer's. These four Counts were framed, as is shown, under the Larceny Act of 1861, and as Counsel said, "if they stood alone I should have no objection to them. But, my Lord, after those four your Lordship will see there is an averment (which readers will find in the Indictment, beginning 'The Jurors upon their oath to further present . . .') which of course is made under the Larceny Act of 1896, which made it an offence for any person to receive property in this country which had in fact been stolen outside the United Kingdom," in other words, whether the necklace had been stolen in this country or abroad it was an offence to receive it in this country knowing it to have been stolen—somewhere.

"Now, my Lord," Mr. Bennett continued, "the 5th Count charges the prisoners with receiving the necklace which is alleged to have been stolen outside the United Kingdom, and the 6th Count charges them with having the necklace in their possession, it having been stolen outside the United Kingdom. Now, my Lord, my reason for moving to quash this Indictment is that it is embarrassing to the prisoners, in that it charges two distinct offences here, of stealing a necklace and receiving a necklace stolen in this country; it further charges the offence of receiving, not stealing but receiving, a necklace which was stolen outside this country. For instance, supposing the first four counts here stood alone, for stealing in this country, the defence might be that the necklace was not stolen in this country at all; there might be evidence in the possession of the defence to prove conclusively that the necklace was stolen in France. But by putting forward that defence here they would be proving the last two counts upon the indictment."

All this was most ingenious, and at least an arguable point of view. The point of it, stripped of all technicality, is this. Either the pearls were stolen in France or in England. The Prosecution, said Counsel, could not have it both ways. Did they allege the pearls were stolen in France or England? If the latter they must remove the French Counts from the Indictment; if the former, they must eliminate the English Counts and rely on the French. But here they were in a difficulty. As already stated earlier in the book, the very conclusiveness of the admirable Report of the French Police made the question of the necklace being stolen in France a matter almost of impossibility, and in the face of such evidence Sir Richard had no right to indict the prisoners for doing something he was going to prove they never could have done. He must therefore, said Sir Henry, cut out the French counts and thus, he added to himself, at least leave a loophole through which his clients might escape, though analysis of the evidence did not show that loophole to be very big.

The point was put so cleverly that His Lordship was for the moment lured from his judicial calm. He was beginning to grow restless when Sir Henry's next words brought his objection to a head. "Speaking of embarrassment," the learned Counsel continued, "Is the case to be put to the jury: 'We do not know where the larceny took place: you can guess whether it was in England or France?' Surely, my Lord, that is an embarrassment to the prisoners. There must be evidence of first, the offence in England, and secondly the offence in France—two, as I submit to your Lordship, absolutely distinct offences . . . My Lord, I know this is purely a legal point which I am putting to your Lordship, but the question of indictment in this country has been greatly discussed over a number of years, and great care is taken in Criminal Courts that a prisoner shall not be embarrassed by being charged in one indictment with two distinct offences which may embarrass him in his defence."

At this point the Judge intervened, and in cutting tones remarked: " I do not know of ' embarrassment ' ever being implied unless it would embarrass an innocent person. The question of embarrassment, as I understand it, is that if a person is innocent he might be embarrassed by being tried in this way. You cannot come forward and say, ' Though I am guilty I shall be embarrassed by having these two things tried together; I shall be more certain of being convicted.' As I understand, you are saying that the argument is: ' Though guilty I am entitled to be tried in the way least embarrassing to myself.' That is what it comes to."

Mr. George Elliott for Grizard, and the other Counsel for the two remaining prisoners, rose to concur with the argument put forward by Sir Henry, to show that the submission was addressed to the Bench on behalf of all four men. Mr. Elliott in fact put a further point to the Judge, but as there was little substance in it, and as it was of a nature which, with the abolition of much technicality, would have no meaning now, it is not proposed to take up space discussing it. His Lordship then gave judgment on the first, substantial point. His first words dashed the hopes which showed themselves in the strained attention of the men who sat in the dock: " I do not think that I can accede to this argument. I think the two sets of Counts merely deal with the same transaction in two different aspects, and the embarrassment is that which anybody feels when he has a possible loophole, and it is the duty of the Prosecution when they frame the Indictment to close all possible loopholes . . . It is not in order to allow a guilty man to escape and so snap his fingers in the face of the Court, that the doctrine of embarrassment is to apply." The learned Judge then dismissed with equal promptitude the argument of Mr. Elliott, and the Clerk of the Court rose slowly to his feet to read the Indictment, as it stood, to the waiting prisoners. The point of law had failed, and they were now faced with the task of combating the facts, those facts which all the genius and experience of Sir Richard Muir and those assisting him had with such care arranged and prepared in their most deadly form. The four men rose to their feet while the Indictment was read to them and stood, each guarded by a warder, at the rail of the Dock from which, before and since, so many famous criminals have looked their last upon the world of men. The prisoners were then asked to plead, and one by one pronounced the words in no uncertain tones—Not Guilty. A Jury of " twelve good men and true " was then empanelled, and its members severally sworn that they would " well and truly try, and true deliverance make between their Sovereign Lord the

King and the prisoner at the Bar whom they should have in charge, and a true verdict give according to the evidence." The Jury at this time was composed of men alone, for it was not until five years later that women began to share the labours and responsibilities of this work with men. Having heard the Jury duly sworn, Sir Henry Curtis Bennett rose to his feet to make one final effort to divert the course of justice into the technical and far more hopeful paths of law. " I submit," he said, " that the Prosecution ought to be put to their election as to whether they proceed upon the first four Counts, the necklace having been stolen in England, or on the last two Counts, the necklace having been stolen in France." The submission failed and Counsel resumed his seat. Without delay Sir Richard Muir rose slowly to his feet and paused before the first words of his opening speech.

Sir Richard Muir had the ideal mind for such a task. Slow, remorseless, deadly fair, he would build up word by word the case against the prisoner until, when he resumed his seat, it seemed that there was nothing more to say. He would take the most elaborate precautions to ensure that all he said was accurate, in its proper order, and useful to his case. He not only made notes but wrote them out at considerable length, underlining various parts of them with the many-coloured pencils which he always used. His " note " was not so much a series of headings as an elaborate analysis and index of the evidence, and reads, to the laymen unacquainted with the law or facts of the case in hand, as a logical, coherent narrative of the facts about to be proved. It is a great

misfortune that the note from which Sir Richard
spoke on this occasion has been destroyed, but an
admirable example of his methods may be seen in
a far more famous trial, the Crippen Case, which
takes up no less than twenty pages of Mr. Felstead's
Life of Sir Richard Muir. The material contained
in this opening speech was enormous. No less than
sixty-seven witnesses were called by the Prosecution and ninety-six Exhibits " put in," that is, made
evidence. These latter included letters and their
envelopes, translations and replies, extracts from
bank accounts, pass books, plans and photographs,
bank notes, pieces of sealing wax and seals, receipts
and counterfoils, and the famous articles which
figured in the case, which varied in value from a
lump of sugar to the necklace which, with its royal
history, was worth £150,000. Surely the latter was
the most valuable exhibit ever produced by a witness
in a Court of Law. Sir Richard spoke for several
hours and when he finally resumed his seat the case,
to use an expressive term which is common among
lawyers, was completely " dead."

We have shown how strenuously the defending
Counsel fought to reduce the inclusive nature of the
Indictment, for by doing so they would have left a
loophole for escape. Having failed in their endeavour there was little more which they could do.
In spite of the public's pathetic faith in those defending them, they cannot make bricks without straw any
more than the Israelites, and the ablest Counsel cannot effectively cross-examine without material. The
only hope of the Defence was to prove that Quadratstein and Brandstatter were such liars on their own

confession that they could not be believed on oath. But there still remained Mr. Spanier and a number of minor witnesses and then, more deadly still, the " silent " evidence of the letters, and the numbers of the bank notes handed to the prisoners which they in turn had cashed all over London on succeeding days. In the absence of elaborate cross-examination the evidence at the Trial is largely a repetition of the story we have already told, and there is no advantage in repeating it in detail. At the same time there were incidents which made the trial of interest quite apart from the famous criminal whose freedom was at stake, and these will be given as a running commentary upon the evidence produced.

This evidence falls naturally into four divisions.

1. The witnesses from the French and English Post Offices who handled the packet in the post.
2. The evidence of the pseudo-purchasers, Messrs. Spanier, Quadratstein and Brandstatter, and those instructing them, Mr. Price and Mr. Mayer himself.
3. The tracing of the bank notes, English and French.
4. The evidence of the Police as to arrest, searching, and the like.

There were, of course, a few more witnesses who do not fall into any of these categories, but this division covers the great majority. Sir Richard tried to arrange the order in which they were called in a manner which would make their story a coherent one, and seems to have succeeded admirably.

CHAPTER XI

THE TRIAL (*continued*)

THE first witness was the housekeeper at 101, Hatton Garden, who described how Silverman had an office on the third floor and used to arrive at nine or half-past nine in the morning until the beginning of June that year, when he started coming about eight o'clock, the time when the gate was opened. About that time the postman ceased to deliver letters for Silverman to him, the caretaker, but took them personally upstairs. He had seen Lockett at the building in Silverman's company about a dozen times, Grizard half a dozen times and Gutwirth frequently.

The next witness was from the office of the G.P.O. and produced the letter from Silverman, already mentioned, which asked for correspondence to be given to him personally by the postman. He was then shown a number of signatures upon receipts for registered packages, some to Silverman and some to Mr. Mayer, and all were in the postman Neville's handwriting, one of them being the receipt for the famous packet of pearls.

Mr. Curtis Bennett's opening question in cross-examination at once introduced a factor which was destined to provide considerable interest and excitement at a later stage of the trial.

Q. What is the name of the postman who signed those receipts?

A. W. E. Neville.

Q. How long had he been in the employ of the Post Office, in July of this year?

A. Between twenty and thirty years, I should think.

Q. Do you know where he is now?

A. At home I believe.

Q. What is his address, do you know?

A. Greville Street, Hatton Garden, off Leather Lane.

Q. Do you know the number?

A. I think it is 10.

Q. As far as you know, he is living there now?

A. Yes, I know for a fact he is.

The point of the cross-examination was this. Defending Counsel knew, of course, that Neville had not been called at the Bow Street hearing, and wanted to know at the earliest moment whether he was to be called at the trial. If not, his absence might provide a loophole of escape, or at least that longed-for commodity in such defences, a grievance to place before the Jury, in the hopes of thereby arousing their sympathy for the accused men in the dock. Counsel therefore established at once that the witness was available. There was a second point. From the point of view of Counsel a trial is a game, a grim, dramatic game, no doubt, but a game in the sense that the contest must be played according to recognised, traditional rules. For example, of the two, Prosecuting and Defending Counsel, one must address the Jury before the other, and clearly the second, having the " final word," has an advantage over his opponent in influencing their minds. Now the order in which Counsel speak depends on the witnesses they call, or do not call, for the defence. To call witnesses, other than one's client in the dock, deprives one of this "right of reply," and therefore it is vitally important to make the Prosecution call the witnesses whom one requires, if such is possible. Now it is the duty of the Prosecution, as we have seen when speaking of Sir Richard Muir, to place before the Court and Jury *all* the evidence which in their opinion has a bearing on the case, or else, and this is the recognised alternative, to provide a copy of the statements of such witnesses as they consider of no use to the Prosecution, but of potential value to the Defence, to someone representing the Defence to use or not at will. We shall see at a later stage what happened in this particular case. For the moment we will turn to other things. The next to step into the witness box was a gentleman already known to the readers of these pages, Mr. Peter Robertson Gordon, of King Street, Hammersmith, who was employed by a firm of engravers and had made the forged or copied seal for Silverman. This witness provided all unwittingly a badly needed element of humour by his two peculiarities. The first was a Scottish accent which to the Southern ear was almost unintelligible, and the second was his weakness, not unknown to possessors of the first, for a drink. When asked to state his movements from time to time he seemed unable to get further than a detailed description of his consumption of alcohol. He described, however, how he first met Silverman in the "Leather Bottle" at the corner of Leather Lane (which will be seen on the Plan of Hatton Garden and is still to

be found there), and while in the " L'thr Bo'le "
gave him his name and address. The copying of the
" double M " seal has already been described and
need not be repeated here, but the importance of his
evidence at the trial was, of course, his definite identification of Silverman as the man who had had Max
Mayer's seal deliberately copied a few weeks before
the robbery.

Mr. Gordon was followed by his employer, who
corroborated the identification of Silverman as a man
who had called at his premises and asked for Gordon.
He had sent him to where the latter was working
and knew no more of the nature of the deal. The
name of the next witness roused the attention of the
Court. Monsieur Henri Salomons was duly sworn
and described himself as a dealer in pearls and
precious stones and Mr. Mayer's representative in
Paris. He described the packing and posting of the
necklace and showed the round pearl and the drop
pearls to the Court but the Jury, on being invited
to examine them, exhibited no interest. Perhaps they
sensed that in a moment they were to see what all
in Court were waiting to see, the famous necklace
in its entirety. They had not long to wait. Mr.
Travers Humphreys, who was " calling " Mr.
Salomons, immediately asked:

Q. Now if you would look at the leather case
again for a moment. Do you see the necklace inside there?

A. Yes.

It consisted then of only fifty-seven pearls, three
being still detached and sealed with Brandstatter's
seal, while another had been lost by the finder, Mr.

The unbroken Seals at one end of the box.
Note the imprint of the double "M"

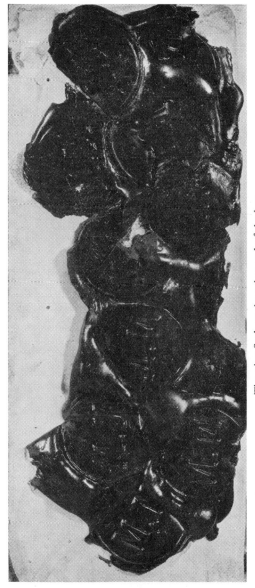

The nine Seals at the other end of the box.
The Seals are clever forgeries

Horne. But whether fifty-seven or sixty-one, it remained the necklace for which all Europe had been seeking and the theft of which had at last brought " Cammi " Grizard to the dock.

On Tuesday morning, the 18th, having proved the despatch of the parcel by Mr. Salomons, Mr. Muir proceeded to call the Post Office witnesses who handled the package in France. A great many names appear in the French Report already reproduced, but not all these were needed at the trial, and the number was reduced to four. All were examined by Mr. Muir through a French interpreter and all alike proved excellent witnesses. The first, Monsieur Henri Seince, a typical Parisian, said that he knew Mr. Salomons by sight and remembered him handing over the package on the 15th of July. He described what he did with the package and how other colleagues took it from him and, having checked the list, sent it to such and such a room where others handled it according to routine. His colleagues who were subsequently called, Messrs. Redinger and Peyrondet, between them filled in every gap and summarised the evidence of the French Report. Finally a Post Office Inspector at Paris, Jean Ducasse by name, who knew the routine of the Central Office thoroughly, was called and asked one general question to summarise the countless witnesses who appeared at the Inquiry held in France.

Q. Would it be possible in any stage of the French Post Office for that (the package) to be opened, its contents taken out and resealed, except in the presence of many persons?

A. It is impossible.

The finality of the reply brought Mr. Bennett to his feet.

Q. In spite of the care which is taken of postal packets in France do larcenies of packets take place?

A. Of course they occur sometimes, but never under these conditions.

Defending Counsel, apparently satisfied with this reply, sat down.

Having proved the handing over of the packet to the English representative at Calais, the Prosecution called Mr. Simpson, who received the mails from the boat at the Dover quay. It should be mentioned that someone places the mail on board at Calais and another official fetches it off at Dover, but no official crosses the Channel with the mail. No one seems to have commented on this fact at the trial, so presumably the bags are placed in such a position that tampering with them during the crossing is impossible. Mr. Simpson checked the bags and handed them over to the sorters on the train, who were the next witnesses called. As is generally known, there is a post office sorting van attached to the Continental mail train, and in this van the officials work in full view of each other all the time. The bags are opened and the contents checked with a list inside the mouth. Mr. Allen, the next witness, actually examined every packet and found the seals intact. He then handed them to Loades, a few feet away on his left, who sorted them into certain sections, among these one for the East Central Office in London, which would be the sorting office for Mr. Mayer's parcel. This

" Eastern " portion he would hand to Craymer, on his right, and therefore immediately on Allen's left. None of them could have opened the packet unobserved, still less could the packet have been resealed in a small compartment in which no wax was ever used, and therefore in which the smell of such would have been immediately observed. There were in this van no less than twelve men within what Counsel described as " smelling distance " of such wax. The witness Craymer was then called and corroborated Allen, after which both were asked in cross-examination, for reasons specified already, questions concerning the absence of the sorter Loades, hoping to force the Prosecution into calling him. Mr. Elliott's questions followed those which Mr. Bennett put to the witness from the Secretary's Office at the G.P.O. on the previous day.

Q. I understand Loades is still working with you?
A. He is still No. I Officer on the French night mail.
Q. When did you last see him?
A. Last Friday I believe.
Q. He is quite well and doing his work all right?
A. Doing his work as usual, yes, sir.

The next step was to trace the packet to the Eastern Central District Office in London. Mr. Southgate received this particular sack about 6.20 a.m., at the office, checked it and sent it to " 32 table " which deals with Hatton Garden. Here, as previously, the only additional question asked came from the Jury who, through their foreman, proved at intervals that they were following every detail of the evidence.

John George Sinclair was then called, and stated that he opened the bag and having checked its contents satisfied himself that every packet, Mr. Salomons' amongst them, was intact. He then made up a receipt, placed the number 587 on the parcel and on the receipt, and about 7.20 handed it over with several others to the postman on the Hatton Garden walk. He gave this postman, Neville, a duplicate of the receipt which it was the latter's duty to get signed and then return, so that Sinclair would have a record of the safe arrival of every registered letter or package which he gave to Neville for delivery. He was shown in the witness box a receipt for the Salomons parcel, signed by the name of Sawtell as receiving it from Neville, and similar receipts for packages delivered by Neville to Max Mayer's office and Silverman's on previous dates. In cross-examination he explained that about seven postmen would between them cover the Hatton Garden district on the first delivery. Neville would cover the part from No. 112, the bank at the corner of Holborn, to No. 85, beyond Mr. Mayer's office. (See plan, page 30).

This concluded the English Post Office officials, and the absence of the postman Neville in itself spoke volumes for the opinion of the Prosecution of his evidence.

When the members of Mr. Mayer's staff at 88, Hatton Garden, who had handled the packet had been called, the passage of the packet was accounted for from Paris to his office. The next step was to call the owner, and about 3 p.m. on the Tuesday afternoon Mr. Mayer entered the " box " and was duly sworn. His evidence has already been woven into

the story already told and need not be repeated here.
He placed the value of the three loose pearls at
about £1,600, and the necklace at a nominal
£135,000, though he hoped to sell it for more. In
fact he had actually given more than £10,000 for
the largest pearl in the necklace, needless to say in
the certainty that he could sell it for considerably
more. Mr. Mayer was not cross-examined, for indeed there was nothing which he could be asked,
and he was followed by Mr. Myer Cohen Quadratstein. He, too, said nothing which has not already
been incorporated in the story. When a witness is
first approached by the police to enquire what
evidence he can give, he makes a full and careful
statement of all he knows. Much of this is naturally
irrelevant, and still more is inadmissible in evidence
as being "hearsay" or in some other way repug-
nant to our rules of evidence. The relevant and
admissable material is extracted from him in the
witness box before the Magistrate, and the evidence
so given on oath taken down in writing by the Clerk
of the Court. This written statement, together with
any cross-examination, becomes, when signed, the
Deposition of the witnesses to be used at the trial.
From these Depositions Counsel calls his witnesses,
again discriminating as to what proportion of the
evidence is material to his case. This evidence in
turn is taken down in shorthand at the trial and filed
for future reference. If the prisoner appeals, a transcript of this evidence is made and sent with other
papers to the Court of Criminal Appeal, after which
the Statement, Deposition and Transcript are all filed
in the proper Government Department for the use

of—well, historians! It follows from this that it is very rare to find a witness stating at the trial anything of value which does not appear on his statement, and as much of the detail of this story has been drawn from such statements it is not surprising that the shorthand note reveals but little not already told.

Mr. Quadratstein was in the witness box for several hours, for both protagonists, the Prosecution and Defence, were fully aware that on the impression which his story made on the Jury depended to a large extent the outcome of the trial. His evidence appears upon the transcript as contained in over five hundred and fifty Questions and Answers, and his cross-examination covered over three hundred more. Mr. Bennett's first attack upon him was " to character," that is, he attempted to prove the witness so unreliable that the Jury could not with safety depend on anything he said. Much was made of the witness' cheerful admission that he was a brilliant liar, but as was pointed out at a later stage, it is one thing to lie to criminals in the course of catching them, another to do so on oath when proving the steps by which the capture was made. Mr. Bennett appeared for Lockett and was at pains to prove that Quadratstein only saw him twice for certain, in the café when he produced the pearls in a matchbox, and on the day of arrest. With this admission from the witness he resumed his seat and the Court adjourned for the second day.

On the Wednesday morning Mr. Elliott rose to cross-examine for the prisoner Grizard. After preliminary questioning to elicit the relationship be-

tween Brandstatter and Gutwirth, which resolved
itself into "the brother of the late husband of an
aunt," and being reprimanded by the Learned Judge
for wasting time, Mr. Elliott led up, again by
circuitous routes, to the fact that Quadratstein was
out for the reward and not to find a buyer for the
necklace at all. The reply was so frank and cheerful
that the point fell rather flat.

Q. When you first came to England, Messrs.
   Price and Gibbs had not been communicated
   with at all?

A. Quite so.

Q. Nor the Police?

A. Nor the Police.

Q. You were for the moment doing a little bit
   of amateur detective business on your own?

A. Quite so.

Q. To make use of it having regard to taking the
   reward?

A. Absolutely.

The interests of justice were a secondary consideration, and who shall blame the two young men for
that? Mr. Elliott then tried another line. Having
proved that the first transaction which Quadratstein
had had with Grizard years before had been quite
honest, he tried to lead him to admit that the conversation at Canonbury on the night he arrived in
England was on a similar level of ordinary business
intercourse. His failure was so pathetic that we reproduce a little of it here.

Q. Am I right—so far as the conversation went,
   it was a conversation which might take place

between any dealer and any broker or intermediary who had a buyer?

A. Not exactly. Do you speak of the stolen property?

This being the last thing which Mr. Elliott wanted to mention, he hurriedly tried to lead away from it.

Q. Never mind about stolen property at the moment.

A. But they told me it was stolen property!

(Metaphorical collapse of Mr. Elliott!)

He then attacked the witness for not trying to escape with the necklace from the bedroom when he had the chance, but as this point has been dealt with in a previous chapter it need not be repeated here.

Mr. Valetta's cross-examination was a model of brevity.

Q. I think at the Police Court you claimed the title of the perfect liar?

A. I did.

Q. You went on to say you could lie in so expert a manner that while you were in fact telling lies you could persuade people you were telling the truth?

A. Of course I had to play that part. If I told the truth they would never have believed me!

Q. You said " From the very first time I had an interview with Gutwirth of course I commenced to lie to him. I intended to lie so well to him that he should believe I was telling the truth."

A. It looked very much like it.

The Trial (*continued*)

Q. Do not be over shy.

A. I am not shy.

Q. After your estimate of yourself do you ask
the Jury to believe that everything you
have said the last two days in the witness
box is true?

A. Absolutely.

Mr. Frampton, for Gutwirth, was equally brief
after the failure of his predecessors, with no more
fortunate result. And so this cheerful little Jew left
the witness box, well satisfied with himself and all
the world, to be replaced by his cousin Brandstatter.
The latter spoke no English and had to be examined
through an interpreter. His evidence in no way
varied from his cousin's, but in cross-examination he
was asked if he could give a reason why Gutwirth
should have approached *him* of all people in
Antwerp to find a buyer for the stolen necklace. He
answered that he did not know, nor was it ever stated
what induced him to do so. Presumably having been
sent to Antwerp by the thieves to find a buyer he
approached the first man whom he knew. Mr.
Spanier was then called and told his story well. In
this case I have had the advantage of many personal
interviews with the witness, whose unusually retentive
memory has supplied innumerable details which between them help to make this story a living document instead of a mere recital of dry facts. It is
therefore not surprising that Mr. Spanier's evidence
told nothing which has not already been recorded
earlier in the book. In deference to what he no
doubt looks upon as the phlegmatic English temperament, he refrained from adding in the witness box

those touches of drama which made this story so out-standing, and contented himself with simple answers to the questions put. In cross-examination he was only asked his opportunities of escape from the hotel bed-room on the 25th, the replies to which we already know, and he was allowed to leave the witness box. Mr. Price then gave his evidence and was asked in cross-examination whether seals placed upon a stiff surface, such as paper stretched over a box, would be less likely to get cracked in the post than those on a limp surface, such as a letter, and agreed that this was so. In re-examination he was asked to compare the original and the altered seals, and described the former as of shiny appearance and the latter as being dull. Asked for the cause of difference, he explained that the former had been in contact with the flame and the latter had been boiled.

Q. Mr. Justice Lawrence. Have you tried the experiment yourself?

A. Yes, my Lord, lots of times. This is not the first case we have had of this description. We have experimented extensively with regard to it. We can write a book about sealing wax now!

Q. There is a different effect produced if you boil the wax in a ladle or burn it in a flame?

A. There is an absolute difference. With the wax you burn in a flame you get a black appearance on the surface, and you always find more or less the little black carbon pieces which have been burned in contact with the flame, but if you boil it you get a dead kind of surface, and you get an entire absence of those little black carbon bits which you see in the other.

This was the end of Mr. Price's evidence and therefore of the four men on whose story, as regards the identity of the criminals, the Prosecution rested. One might have been mistaken, or even lied; two might have exaggerated or spoken to the same thing by coincidence, but could four man say the self-same story and be quite mistaken or deliberately saying what they knew to be untrue? Nor were they cross-examined effectively, in the sense of diminishing in the eyes of the Jury the value of their evidence. But the Jury were not asked to convict upon their evidence alone. After one more witness, called in corroboration of the other evidence of conspiracy, the Prosecution were to produce that silent testimony which Mr. Price, in the wisdom of experience, had seen fit to prepare, the tracing of the notes.

The next witness was the last to be called that day and was the proprietor of the " flea pit," more politely known as the Vienna Restaurant in Charles Street, Hatton Garden. This restaurant still exists but under another name, and its position will be seen on the map of Hatton Garden to which reference has already been made. The witness was called to speak of seeing the prisoners together in his restaurant, so as to negative any subsequent attempt to prove that they were strangers to one another when the events narrated in this story first took place. In cross-examination, Mr. Frampton, for Gutwirth, made the witness agree that his restaurant was used by scores of diamond merchants, but he did not ask for what they used it besides the legitimate business of diamond dealing. So ended the third day of the hearing, and on the following morning the Prosecution turned to an entirely fresh type of evidence, the tracing of the notes.

It will now be appreciated how important it was for Mr. Price to keep a careful record of the numbers of the French notes which he gave to Mr. Spanier for the purchase of whatever pearls could be most readily identified. He trusted Mr. Spanier and the two young men whose efforts in fact had set him on the trail of the actual criminals, but he naturally wanted irrefutable corroboration of their evidence, if such could be obtained. By making use of the detailed organisation of the Force, and the fact that men can be detailed to follow patiently the course of every note which they desire to trace, it is remarkable how large a proportion of the notes which they are tracing can be finally produced, together with the witnesses who handled them. This is the case with notes of quite small value, but the tracing is very much easier when the note is foreign and of a large amount. A French note for a thousand francs was £40 in cash before the War, and it is not often that an Englishman will try to use in business such a large amount. It was therefore more than probable that within a few hours of the sale the four conspirators, having shared the proceeds, would attempt to change them into a less embarrassing form. But unless they asked for gold their only alternative in 1913 was the Bank of England note. If Grizard had been wiser, he would have sent an emissary to France to cash the large notes into smaller ones, away from the watchful eye of our Police. As it was, the efforts of all four men to turn their ill-gotten gains to practical advantage were almost as laborious as the effort of disposing of the pearls.

The Police began by notifying well-known changers of the notes whose history they sought to trace, and at the first of these, Thomas Cook's Head Office, as it then was, in Ludgate Circus, they were very fortunate. It would be tedious to set out in elaborate detail how each note was traced from hand to hand, to form upon completion an unanswerable mass of evidence involving all four men, and therefore it is only proposed to point out instances of how this evidence was obtained. The powers of the Police are as varied as remarkable, and their relation, for example, with a Bank is clearly defined. While an inquiry is being made they can always obtain from a Bank the details of notes paid in and out, and the dates which correspond to them, but until some person is arrested they have no power to examine the account of an individual unless his permission is obtained. Once take a man in custody, however, and they may search his property, with due permission from the Magistrate, and visit any Bank at which his private papers, such as a Pass Book, show that he has an account. From a duly certified copy of this they can obtain what information they will, and use it as the basis of further inquiry into the history of the notes which appear therein.

In this case the inquiry began at both ends of the story, for on the one hand, they had a list of the numbers of the French notes given to Grizard, and on the other, a corresponding list of the notes, both French and English, found on the men upon arrest.

Their task was to find some connection between the two, and such connection, barring the possibility of forgeries bearing identical numbers, would in itself provide conclusive evidence against which all the guns of cross-examination would boom in vain.

The French notes were exchanged with the pearls on Monday afternoon, the 25th of August, about 3 p.m. Within a few hours Silverman, his pockets filled with the first fruits of his felony, walked into Cook's in Ludgate Circus and thus sealed his doom. He there presented a note for a thousand francs at the Cashier's desk and asked for change. Amongst the Bank of England notes which he received in exchange were two £5 notes. But it was Silverman who gave to Quadratstein on the 29th two £5 notes, and, as the Police on receiving them from Quadratstein immediately verified, the numbers were the same. At the same time Lockett, possessed of the wherewithal to ransom the ring which he had pawned the day before the robbery, repaired forthwith to Leather Lane, and asked for his diamond ring. The sum which was owing amounted, with interest, to £25 12s. 6d., and (strangely enough!) by way of payment Lockett offered a French note for a thousand francs. The Police, having found the contract note in his possession, went to the pawnbroker's in Leather Lane and, armed with the list of numbers of the notes, compared the two. The number of one of them was the same.

Grizard, meanwhile, went to his Bank, the London and Provincial Bank in High Street, Kingsland, where he had an account, not in his own name, which might prove awkward at some later date, but in the

name of " J. Goldsmith," which was described by his
Counsel as his " business " name. An extract from
the books of the Bank, when examined by the Police
who found a note of it in Grizard's property, disclosed the fact that he had paid in on the 25th a
number of £5 notes, the numbers of which corresponded with a French note changed elsewhere.
Again, on the 29th of August, Grizard paid in a £10
note. But this note had been given by a cashier in
Cook's Office to the prisoner Lockett the preceding
day, when he had given three of the thousand franc
notes in exchange for Bank of England notes, which
included ten notes of £10. Two more of these were
traced to Grizard through a dozen hands, and seven
were found on Lockett on arrest. On this unfortunate visit Silverman apparently accompanied
him, but carefully went to another *guichet* at the
Exchange counter, and was served by a different
cashier.

Some of the notes found upon Lockett, notably
two for £50, were traced to a money-changer named
Hannam, who said that on the 28th he changed, for
a man he did not pretend to recognise, three notes for
a thousand francs, and gave him Bank of England
Notes in exchange. He did not keep a record of the
latter, but gave his Bank as the chief office of the
London Joint Stock Bank, from whom he had
obtained his notes for the purpose. The Police at
once went to this Bank and examined the books.
Sure enough, on the afternoon of the 28th they had
paid to this money-changer two notes of £50, which
were at once compared with those on Lockett. The
numbers were the same.

The Police went further afield. Mr. Bacon, of Cook's Branch at Southampton, changed a French note for " James Lockett," whom he knew because the latter actually offered him his card, and the note he got in exchange were found among his property.

Such evidence could be continued for many pages, but it would be wearisome. Enough has been given to show that the notes which Grizard took at the meeting of the 25th became, when traced from hand to hand, a type of evidence which nothing could, and nothing did, destroy.

So much for three of the four divisions into which the evidence was divided, the Post Office witnesses, the pseudo-purchasers and their assistants, and the tracing of the notes. There remained the evidence of the Police as to arrest and the articles found upon the prisoners or at their homes or offices.

In the course of their evidence it came out that a portion of the statement made by McCarthy when arrested was correct. Gutwirth's little girl *was* ill at the time, and it may be that he *was* about to give the father flowers to take home to her. In any event, he was, as we have seen, discharged at Bow Street, and therefore in the eyes of the law was innocent of complicity with those whom he had helped in changing the notes. As is usual on these occasions, little incidents were given in evidence which, but for the greater gravity of the offence at issue, might have been followed up and made the subject of a charge. Apparently, for example, there was found in a safe in Lockett's house a passport in the name of James Fitzpatrick. Why? Was Lockett kindly keeping a friend's passport for him, where the Police, for

226

instance, would not find it if they searched Fitzpatrick's premises, or was " Fitzpatrick " Lockett in another name, a name which would not be suspected at the barriers if this criminal with two identities desired to leave the country of his birth with unexpected speed? The English public will not readily forget the shock with which they learnt a few years ago, in the case of Hansen and McCartney, how the prisoners boasted in their correspondence that for £50 a passport could be obtained in any name desired. When search was made at the Passport Office, the letter said, it would be found that the " jacket " in which the forged forms had been filed away was empty, and on examination by the authorities it was found that the boast was true.

Strange happenings are sometimes brought to light from the underworld of London, and this was not the least of them.

However that may be, no further mention of the passport was ever made.

Then followed evidence by the Manager of a Southampton Hotel, who stated that the prisoner Lockett had arrived at his Hotel on August 18th with a party and stayed for several days. The point was, apparently, that Silverman and Grizard had visited him there during the week, and thus the witness could give independent evidence, if such was needed, that the men had been spending their time together in the intervals between the various meetings in London, of which Messrs. Quadratstein, Brandstatter and Spanier had already given evidence.

Two more witnesses alone remained, Mr. Horn, the lucky finder of the necklace, and the Station

Sergeant, to whom he handed it three-quarters of an hour later. When closely examined by the Learned Judge the former admitted that he could not recognise the people who he thought had put the pearls where they were found, but it was never suggested that he could. And so, on the afternoon of the fourth day of the hearing Mr. Muir, as solid and imperturbable as ever, rose to his feet and quietly announced to his Lordship: " That is the case for the Crown."

CHAPTER XII

THE CASE FOR THE DEFENCE

THE case for the Crown was ended, and it only remained for the four men in the Dock to produce such evidence or arguments, or both, as would convince the Jury that in spite of the case against them they were innocent of the offences with which they were charged.

To this, however, there was one possible preliminary step, a submission in law to the Learned Judge that on some ground or another the prisoners should not be called upon to answer the case for the Prosecution, or at least not in the form in which it then stood.

Without a moment's delay Mr. Curtis Bennett rose to take advantage of this opportunity, and once more pleaded, as was his right, the embarrassing nature of the Indictment as it stood. Having once more recapitulated the contents of the Indictment, he pointed out that Mr. Muir had all through the case for the Prosecution contended that the packet had been stolen in England, and that in his submission this contention was the only one in accordance with the evidence. In order that counts five and six of the Indictment, which charged the prisoners with receiving and having in their possession a necklace stolen outside the United Kingdom, might be allowed to stand, the Crown must produce at least some evidence that the preliminary averment to these counts, that the necklace had been stolen in France, was, in fact, true. " My Lord," Counsel continued, " I submit that there is no evidence at all to go to the Jury upon the 5th and 6th Counts. Unless it is proved that it was stolen in France, there can be no offence of receiving it under the 5th and 6th Counts." The argument then continued upon matters, which, having been since altered, have only a historic interest, and Counsel then concluded: " In my submission there is no such evidence to go to the Jury, and, as I have already pointed out, the Prosecution have gone to some pains here in proving, or attempting to prove, the opposite."

It will now be clear what was meant in an earlier portion of the book, when it was stated that the very thoroughness of the French inquiry, and its emphatic result, became a source of embarrassment to the Prosecution at the trial.

For a moment it seemed once more that the Judge was wavering in his opinion on the soundness of defending Counsel's argument, and it may have seemed that the golden figure of Justice overhead peered down through her bandaged eyes in horror lest her interests be again imperilled by the technicalities of the law. After a moment's pause, however, his Lordship's decision was made known. " I do not think," he said, " that I can say that the Jury are precluded from considering (the possibility) that the theft took place in France."

Gallantly recovering from this blow Mr. Curtis Bennett returned to the attack. " I was also going to submit," he said, " that on the 3rd and 4th Counts, which allege the general larceny committed in this country, my friend (Mr. Muir) said to the Jury that the only time when this could have been committed was between when the postman had the packet for delivery and when it was opened, and that on those two counts there is no evidence at all." On this point Mr. Muir was called upon to reply, and did so by contending that it was for the Jury to say which of the many witnesses they chose to believe, but he agreed that the Jury must find the prisoners guilty upon one or other of the conflicting pairs of Counts, not both. In brief, they must choose between England and France, but they must be allowed to choose. At this point Mr. Elliott and Mr. Valetta, for Grizard and Silverman respectively, rose to reinforce their spokesman's arguments, and the legal battle became, as it were, general, yet always conducted with that elaborate courtesy and patience which distinguishes this wordy warfare in our Courts of Law, though exceptions have been known. Slowly the issue worked round to the two men on whom the whole Defence was based. " Supposing," said the Learned Judge to Mr. Valetta, " Mr. Muir had called every person who came into the room or the same part where this parcel might be, from the time of placing it in the post office in Paris to the time it was opened in Mr. Mayer's presence, and they had all said it could not have been stolen while they were there, are the Jury bound to say it was not stolen?"

Mr. Valetta: " Now see how far that can be relied upon. He has not called two people who, as he opened to the Jury, had possession of the parcel—Loades and Neville (the Southern Railway sorter and the postman). Why has he not called them? I propose to call those witnesses, and your Lordship will hear them. . . . Here you have two gaps left in order that my friend can say to the Jury: " Here are these two people whom we have not thought fit to call—we invite you to say *that* is where the trouble arose." But I submit there was no evidence on which the Jury could find the larceny was committed there (in those gaps). My friend cannot say on the first two counts, firstly: " Believe my witnesses because the opportunity (for someone else to do it) existed "; and secondly: " Do not believe my witnesses because no opportunity existed."

All this was extremely clever, and may seem to the lay reader unanswerable, but the Learned Judge was more than equal to this clever sophistry. " Supposing the Prosecution had called every witness upon all the counts, if your argument is good it would enable you to say there is no count upon which there is evidence!"

Mr. Valetta (taken off his guard, but deciding that the boldest policy was the best): " I should not have hesitated to do so!"

The Learned Judge (firmly): " I am afraid I must overrule that."

After this the massed forces of the Defence sat down in silence, to be recalled to the urgency of the moment by His Lordship's mild inquiry: " Now what are you going to do? Are you going to call evidence?"

Mr. Valetta: " I am going to call Neville and I am going to call Loades."

As the hour was then late the Court adjourned

until the following morning, and so, with this dramatic statement, ended the fourth day of the trial.

This seems a convenient opportunity for explaining the procedure for the Defence at a criminal trial. Before the year 1898 no prisoner was allowed to give evidence on his own behalf, and although this limitation hampered the efforts of an innocent man to impress his innocence upon the Jury by his demeanour in the witness box, the advocate who appeared for a guilty man had a splendid argument, which subsequent legislation has swept away, for use in the final speech for the Defence. However hopeless the case against his client, Counsel could always plead in his most moving tones: " If only my unfortunate and innocent client were allowed to give evidence on his own behalf, with what ease and celerity he would prove to you the spotless purity of his life . . ." etc., etc., until, so the younger generation are informed, the tears came to the eyes of all in Court.

With the passing of the Criminal Evidence Act of 1898, however, prisoners were permitted to give evidence on oath on their own behalf, subject, of course, to being cross-examined like any other witness. This was a great advantage to the innocent man, but a source of danger to the security of the guilty. For although it was enacted that Counsel for the Crown was not to comment upon the Prisoner's absence from the witness box, no such restriction was imposed upon the Learned Judge. The decision which defending Counsel now have to make in cases such as murder trials is a great responsibility, and causes grave anxiety to every conscientious barrister who is called upon to advise his client on the best course to pursue. If he gives evidence, he lays himself open to ruthless cross-examination by a brain far better trained than his. If, on the other hand, he refuses to give evidence, and remains in the comparative security of the Dock where none can question him, he may hear the Learned Judge asking the jury in his Summing Up to consider why, if a man be innocent, he should be unwilling to give his explanation upon oath. The latter argument is almost unanswerable in the great majority of cases, and, though I speak subject to correction, I think I am right in saying that only very rarely has a man who refused to enter the witness box been found not guilty—upon an issue of fact alone. The success of a submission in law is, of course, quite another matter.

The average member of a jury is no fool, and a defence which clearly relies upon a submission in law thereby tacitly admits in many cases that on the naked issue of fact the prisoner will have but little to say. In this case the fierceness of Defending Counsel's legal argument at the commencement of the trial, and again at the close of the case for the Prosecution, betrayed the fact that if this method of defence should fail they would have but little else on which to rely. Especially was this the case of the four men who not only did not themselves go into the witness box, but called no evidence at all. Their only defence was a speech, delivered no doubt with considerable skill, but only a speech with which to demolish the mountain of accumulated fact which the deliberate, untiring energy of Richard Muir had prepared and produced in evidence against them.

Mr. Valetta, however, felt that he ought to do something more for his client Silverman, and on the morning of the fifth day of the trial attempted to make a grievance of necessity by calling the missing witnesses. He adopted the attitude that *someone* had to call them, and that if the Prosecution failed to do their duty he must do it for them. His Lordship, however, saw to it that the point fell somewhat flat. Having elicited that copies of the " proofs," or statements of the witnesses, had been supplied by the Prosecution to the Defence, he pointed out that this was their sole duty according to established precedent, and that the supposed grievance was non-existent. After this Mr. Valetta had no option but to call his first witness, the postman Neville, without delay.

The position of this man was, and is, very difficult. He was addicted to drink, and at some time subsequent to this trial was dismissed from the service of the Post Office on account of his intemperate habits. As he thereby forfeited his pension, the Post Office authorities lost sight of him, and it is not definitely known whether or not he is still alive. In case he is still living it is only fair to say of him at once that he was never charged with complicity in the robbery, and that he was ultimately dismissed from the service of the Post Office for intemperance, and not for dishonesty. On the other hand, in attempting to analyse the way in which the larceny was committed, it may be that the evidence as given upon oath at the trial, and apparently accepted by the Jury, will be found to point to a conclusion incompatible with his innocence. If so, I can only plead the privilege that is accorded to an accurate report of a trial and fair comment thereon.

W. E. Neville was the postman whose duty it was to take the early morning mail from the Eastern Central District Office in Newgate Street to the corner of Hatton Garden, and there deliver the contents of his bag from No. 112, a Bank (see map on page 30) to No. 84, a house some way beyond Mr. Mayer's Office. At the time of the trial he had been thirty-two years in the employ of the Post Office, and nothing was recorded against his honesty. On the other hand, he was of intemperate habits and had forfeited three of his good conduct stripes for this incurable weakness. He lived off Leather Lane, a street into which Charles Street runs from Hatton Garden, and was therefore known in the locality. Many of those who knew him as a frequenter of the local public-houses have expressed surprise that such a wretched specimen should have been given this particular " walk," on which the value of the packets delivered was only rivalled by those which included West End jewellers. However that may be, this was the man who on the 18th of July, two days after the robbery, was interviewed by two officials in the Investigation Department of the Post Office, and made a statement, of which the following is a summary:

" About 7.20 a.m. on the 16th I signed for three or four registered letters, including a large one addressed: ' Max Mayer, 88, Hatton Garden,' No. 587. This is the receipt I gave to Mr. Sinclair, the sorter, in respect of it. I first heard about there being something wrong with one of Mr. Mayer's registered packets when I came on duty at 4 a.m. on Thursday morning (the 17th). About 5 a.m. I was shown a newspaper with headlines about the robbery. One of the men said: ' You are going to cop it. One of the parcels you delivered has been tampered with." . . . I treated the matter with contempt. I read the paper about 6 or 7 and endeavoured to recall to mind the packets I had delivered to Mayer on the 16th. I seemed to remember three for Mayer, and one for Keller in the same building, and that two of Mayer's were small and one large.

" I left the Office at 7.50 a.m. and proceeded to No. 112, Hatton Garden. A bag-carrier was with me. I forget his name. The correspondence for firms from 112 to 94 I put in my bag to be carried by the bag-carrier. The remainder I put in my own. The packet for Mayer was in my bag carried by the carrier. . . . At Simon and Co., No. 101, the lift-man signs for registered packets. There I have to go about twenty yards along the corridor. I can't re-member how long I had to wait on Wednesday, probably not more than three minutes. During that time the bag-carrier was waiting just inside the door. . . .

" When I had delivered as far as 94, Hatton Garden I took my bag from the bag-carrier and dis-missed him—about 8.20 a.m."

From there he went on alone to the corner of Charles Street, turned down Charles Street past " The Globe " Public House at the corner, so to the Vienna Café (the " flea-pit," to which reference has already been made), thence to " The Old Leather Bottle " at the corner of Leather Lane, across to what was then " The Pewter Platter," and so back along the other side to Hatton Garden and from there to No. 88.

" I reached Mayer's about 8.30 a.m. All the letters for 88 were tied up in a bundle before I left the Office. I opened the bundle in the presence of Mr. Sawtell, the housekeeper, who checked and signed for them. I think he examined the registered packets. . . . He made no comment about them."

On July 21st the bag-carrier, by name Hollands, was interviewed. The first important point to notice is that these bag-carriers are volunteers, men who, to earn extra money, volunteer to act as carriers for those whose load exceeds the weight which any individual is expected to carry. They line up with empty sacks and are told off, in the order in which they stand, to accompany the next man who applies for a carrier. It is therefore impossible for any carrier to know beforehand whom he will accompany, much less to arrange that he shall accompany on any given date a given man. As the very essence of this robbery was elaborate pre-arrangement, the likelihood of Hollands' complicity is reduced to a minimum, and in fact it has never been suggested that he behaved in any way at variance with his duty.

In his statement he said that it was only on the Saturday after the robbery that he realised that the stolen packet was one of those delivered by Neville. At the time when he was told off to accompany Neville, whom he had never assisted before, the latter had already enclosed the whole of the correspondence in his own bag. On being given a carrier he, Neville, transferred about six bundles of correspondence to Hollands' bag, including those addressed to Nos. 112 to 98, Hatton Garden inclusive. This did not therefore include the Mayer packet, which was for No. 88.

At 112, Hatton Garden, Neville took his, Hollands', bag and began to deliver from it while he, Hollands, carried Neville's bag with letters for No. 98 and beyond. They never left each other's sight until they reached No. 101.

" There he said to me: ' Deliver this bundle to the lift-man, and tell him there is one registered to sign for, while I go upstairs.' He then took a small bundle of correspondence and went upstairs, and I delivered Simon's correspondence to the lift-man. I am quite sure he did not have Mayer's large registered packet in his possession when he went upstairs. He was away only about two minutes, and during that time both bags were in my custody. From 101 to 98 Neville continued to carry my bag and I his. At 98 he had finished my bag, and at 94 he dismissed me. The time was then close upon 8.30 a.m. I did not see him take out of either bag any packet as large as the one from which the pearls were stolen. I am certain that during the time I was with him he did not have such a registered packet in his hands. It would have been impossible for him to have concealed such a packet about his person without my noticing it."

Four days later, on the 22nd, Neville was faced with Hollands' statement, and invited to comment on the discrepancies. There are two points of difference, one unimportant and the other vital. On July 22nd Neville, having read through Hollands' statement,

239

said that the latter's description of the division of the correspondence between the two bags was the more correct, and then concluded with a most significant remark: " I remember now that I did have to go upstairs at 101, Hatton Garden. There is one firm at 101 who insist on letters being placed in their letterbox. I forget the name."

In this way the matter was left until the following October, by which time further evidence had come to light. During the inquiries which followed the arrest of the four men in September it was discovered that Silverman was in possession of a forged seal with a double M, and a crucible in which wax might be melted in the way in which the seals on the opened end of the packet had been made. His curious request of the previous June to have his first mail delivered to him personally had also assumed a criminal significance. The Officers in the Investigation Department of the Post Office therefore sent for Neville and again questioned him.

The interview is recorded in the form of Question and Answer and is enlightening. The following is a resumé of the more important parts.

Q. Since I last saw you in respect of the theft of Mr. Mayer's necklace, further facts have come to light, and it is considered that you as the postman who delivered the packet should be given opportunity of making any comment you wish about them.

A. I quite understand what you say.

As Neville was then under grave suspicion he was cautioned.

The examination then continued:

Q. Have you ever spoken to Silverman?

A. I have spoken to him in Hatton Garden once or twice before the liftman opened the gate.

Q. Had Silverman very much correspondence?

A. No, only one about every other day. . . . When I got one I used to take it up, and I left the other stuff with the bag-carrier.

Q. Was the lift working at 8 a.m.?

A. The lift was working, but the attendant had other things to do. I didn't bother him. I went up the stairs.

He was then taxed with remembering on July 18th a great deal of detail, yet curiously enough forgetting the vital matter of going upstairs at No. 101.

A. Is that what I said? Well, it's a mistake, of course. If that man had a letter I'd have to go up with it. Perhaps I did not have a letter on that particular morning.

As further discrepancies were pointed out to him, Neville's memory began to get more muddled still.

Q. On the 24th July I told you the bag-carrier said you had gone upstairs at 101, and you said:." Now I hear Mr. Hollands' statement I remember I did go upstairs at 101, Hatton Garden. There is one firm at 101 who insist on letters being placed in their letter-box. I forget the name of the firm." How is it you forget the name, having delivered letters up there and signed the paper (authorising personal delivery)?

A. I believe I told you it was Solomon Silverman. Perhaps I said Simon and Co.

Q. I am quite certain that you did not. How is it
that you forgot the name? You deny you
said you had forgotten the name?

A. Well, you say so.

Q. Have you spoken to Silverman at any time
about his letters?

A. He has asked me on one or two occasions
whether I had any letters for him—before
the gates have been open in the morning.

Q. Hollands says you took a bundle upstairs at
101 on the 16th July.

A. No, I don't think so. I might have taken a
bundle for the next two or three doors.

Q. Did you take any registered packet upstairs?

A. No, certainly not.

Q. Do you know Gutwirth?

A. I have known him for several years and spoken
to him.

Q. Do you know Grizard?

A. No, never spoken to him.

The interrogating official then very fairly put to
him the evidence then known which seemed to concern him as the delivering postman.

Q. Silverman had a seal made with the initials
M.M. exactly like Mr. Mayer's seal.

He commenced to come to his office at 8 a.m.
instead of 9.30 or 10 just before the theft, and
Gutwirth was often with him. He reached his office
a few minutes before you would get there. He said
he wanted the seal for the purpose of sealing packets.
He made a request about his letters which would
cause you to go upstairs every morning to his office
instead of leaving all letters downstairs. These facts

suggest that he may have taken the necklace out of the packet in his office.

You had the packet in your custody from 7.25 a.m. until 8.30 a.m.

How do you suggest that Silverman got hold of the packet?

A. Goodness knows. No packet left my hands to nobody. I always put that registered stuff to the bottom of my bag, which I left with the bag-carrier. Mr. Mayer's packet was in the bottom of my bag with the bag-carrier.

Q. Gutwirth said they got it from the postman and gave them £100 each.

A. It's a lot of rot.

Neville began to get more and more truculent in his answers, and as nothing more could be elicited, the interview was brought to a close.

So unsatisfactory was this examination thought to be, or rather the answers which Neville gave in the course of it, that it was decided that although there was not sufficient evidence upon which he could be placed beside the others in the Dock, he was not such a witness as could usefully be put forward to give evidence against his possible confederates. But if Neville were not to be called there was no point in calling Hollands. Copies of the statements made by the two men to the Police were therefore forwarded to the Defence, as is the custom in such circumstances, and the matter was there left.

On November 21st, the fifth day of the Trial, however, Mr. Valetta, for the prisoner Silverman, decided, as already explained, to place the absentees before the Jury, in the hopes that they might thereby have their minds prepared for the type of argument which he hoped to use effectively in his final speech.

On the Friday morning, then, the postman Neville entered the witness box. It is not proposed to give his evidence in detail, but his cross-examination by Mr. Richard Muir will be to some extent reproduced in order to provide material for the conclusions which we wish to draw.

Mr. Valetta began by eliciting that Neville was still employed by the Post Office, in the hopes of convincing the Jury that his employers at least did not think him guilty of dishonesty.

The witness then told his story as already given. He remembered delivering at No. 88 a parcel like the one which was later rifled, but noticed nothing peculiar about it. He knew Gutwirth and Silverman, but did not speak to either that morning. He did not know Lockett or Grizard. Counsel then approached more vital matters.

Q. Did you deliver (that morning) any parcel to Silverman's office in No. 101?

A. There was a letter, I think, for him which I put in his letter-box, but I did not speak to him.

He was then asked formally if he had ever received a bribe in connection with the case, and, of course, denied such a charge, whereupon Mr. Valetta sat down.

Mr. Muir rose to his feet and the two men looked at one another. Muir knew of the result of Neville's previous cross-examination, and Neville knew that he knew of it, and probably knew as well that it had been seriously considered whether or not he should be prosecuted. However, he now had no option but to face the ordeal to the best of his ability.

Counsel began by bringing out the postman's drunken habits, and then asked to what extent he knew Gutwirth. Neville began by saying that he only knew him as a man to whom he delivered letters, but ended by admitting that Gutwirth had stood him drinks in neighbouring public-houses. He then made his first slip. Asked about his knowledge of Silverman, he said he had known him by sight for a few months, but then admitted that he knew that previous to his taking an office in No. 101 he had rented an office at No. 60, Hatton Garden. Asked how he came to know this, if his first answer were true, he had no satisfactory reply.

He was then pressed as to the peculiar nature of Silverman's request to have his first delivery handed to him personally. Neville agreed that the usual course in such an event was to have the first mail held back until the second delivery, but he vaguely announced that he had heard of requests similar to Silverman's " on other walks."

Then came a far more vital topic.

Q. Which floor is Silverman on?

A. On the third.

Q. There is a lift there, is there not?

A. Quite so.

Q. And a liftman in attendance?

A. Yes.

Q. When you delivered Silverman's letters, did you go up in the lift or not?

A. No, I walked up the stairs. I do not think the

lift is always working at that time of the
morning.

Q. So this change necessitated your walking up
three flights of stairs to Silverman every
morning, if there was a letter for him?

A. Yes. I *have* been up in the lift. It was not
often I had a letter for him—three perhaps
a week.

Neville was then made to admit that he sometimes
met Silverman outside the gate in the early morning,
before eight o'clock, on which occasions he would give
him then and there any letters which there might be
for him.

Q. Did you ever see him there before eight o'clock
earlier than June this year?

A. No, I do not think I have.

He was then more closely pressed as to what
happened at No. 101 that morning. He admitted
that he had a registered letter for someone else in the
same building, and a letter for Silverman.

Q. Why did not you send the bag-carrier with the
letter up to Silverman?

A. It is not his duty. I am in charge of the
delivery.

Q. But you gave him the whole correspondence to
deliver, and you went upstairs to Silverman?

A. I said: " You look after my bag while I go upstairs and down again." I also said: " You
can take this receipt when they've signed for
it, while I slip up with Silverman's letter."

Having lured him into the impasse Mr. Muir
then put the position to him. If he was not allowed
to let Hollands do any of the delivering, why did

he give him the registered packet to deliver? If Hollands *was* allowed to do part of the delivering, why not send *him* upstairs? In any event, why not give the liftman the registered packet and take the lift up to Silverman, leaving Hollands with the bags downstairs? His reply was so muddled and contradictory as to be no answer at all.

He was then taxed with the statement which he made on July 18th, in which he never mentioned Silverman's name or the vital fact that he had been upstairs at No. 101. Neville seemed to see nothing remarkable in having forgotten two days after the robbery that he had been upstairs that morning, but remembering it at once when faced with the statement made by Hollands.

Finally he was asked a few questions on the extreme placidity with which he apparently received the news that a valuable parcel for which he was responsible had been rifled in the post. He admitted that he made no inquiries. " I did not really trouble. I thought I had done my duty. That is all."

He was followed in the witness box by Hollands. After describing the division of the correspondence between the two bags, the carrier was asked what happened at No. 101. He said that Neville gave some correspondence to the liftman and told him, Hollands, to wait for the receipt while he, Neville, took some letters upstairs. He was only away about a minute, by which time Hollands had got the receipt from the lift attendant. They then continued the delivery together until Hollands was discharged at No. 94. Until that time the No. 88 correspondence was, as far as he knew, in the bag which he had carried

247

from No. 112 to No. 94, and he never saw the Max Mayer packet in Neville's hands. It was the first time that he had ever acted as his carrier.

Cross-examined, he said that there were eight or nine registered packets for the lift attendant at No. 101. He then admitted that he had got this item muddled up with a later delivery, and amended his statement to " one." The mistake is of no importance except as showing that his memory was unreliable. There was practically no further cross-examination, which proves that in Mr. Muir's mind no blame attached to Hollands at all. His account of the procedure at No. 101 was the same as that which he gave on the 21st of July to the Post Office officials.

In re-examination he was pressed to say whether Neville or he actually handed the packets to the liftman. Though none too certain, he inclined to the view that he, Hollands, gave the letters to the liftman and waited for the receipt while Neville went upstairs.

With this he was allowed to leave the witness box, and was replaced by the witness Loades. We have already spoken of this man's curious and dangerous mistake. It was he who, having seen photographs and read the descriptions of the rifled packet, was convinced that he had seen it in his sorting office on the mail train up from Dover, and was prepared to swear on oath that he had so seen it. His evidence, had it been reliable, would have fundamentally altered the case for the prosecution, for it would have proved that the substitution had taken place on French soil. As it was, Mr. Muir, in a masterly

analysis of the man's mentality, proved all but conclusively that it was a case of auto-suggestion, and so
removed the value of his evidence. The story, however, told by a man who certainly believed it, was so
embellished with corroborative detail that its danger
cannot be exaggerated.

Such was the whole of the evidence in this famous
trial, and the moment seems a suitable one for a brief
examination of the way in which the crime was
probably committed.

To say that Grizard was its organiser is to say that
every detail was elaborately worked out.

Now the previous June Silverman had done two
peculiar things. He had made a request to the Post
Office that his first delivery of letters should be
brought to him in person at his Office on the third
floor. Note that this only applied to the first delivery,
which was Neville's round. From that time he began
to arrive at his Office a little before eight o'clock
each morning instead of at half-past nine or ten as
previously.

Secondly, he had had made for him a seal on which
was engraved a double capital M. This seal, so reproduced, was a passable imitation of a seal used by
a famous pearl and diamond merchant who lived but
a few doors up the road—on the same " walk." He
had in his Office, maybe by chance, but none the less
available, a lamp for melting wax in a crucible. It
will be remembered that the seals on the damaged
end of the parcel were so made, and not with wax
which has been melted in a flame, such as Mr.
Salomons always used.

These preparations were curious in themselves, and

never explained, but they were not enough. No postman in the due performance of his duty would allow a registered packet addressed to another firm to come into the possession of a man who had no legitimate interest in handling it. Yet, miracles apart, there can be not the slightest doubt that the packet was rifled by someone who not only sealed it up again with a seal the double of that which Silverman possessed, but melted the necessary wax in his unusual way. The evidence is all but conclusive that the packet was not touched between the Rue de Provence and the Eastern Central District Office in Newgate Street. It was therefore opened by someone having a seal all ready and who lived between No. 112 and No. 88, Hatton Garden. Now, as we have already shown, the likelihood of Hollands being a party to anything so obviously criminal may be with safety put aside. There remains the necessity of finding at what moment there was the opportunity for someone to make the lightning substitution of sugar for pearls when Hollands' eyes were turned away. What opportunity of such a kind existed save at No. 101.

It is true that according to both Neville's and Hollands' evidence, Hollands carried the bag which held the Mayer parcel from No. 112 to No. 94, but *did* the bag which he was carrying contain the parcel, which he says he never saw? It will be remembered that when Hollands first saw Neville at the Post Office, it was Neville who transferred into his open bag such packets as he chose, and he certainly had the opportunity of keeping in his own bag, or far more probably concealed about his person, one which should have been transferred to the carrier's bag. It may be said that at any point upon the journey, whether at the Post Office or in No. 101, such sleight of hand would have been difficult, but the only remaining theory, that Silverman's elaborate preparations were never used, is far more difficult.

It was suggested during the trial that the fuddled Neville might easily have been beguiled into parting temporarily with the possession of a packet in his charge, and of delivering it later, in its sadly altered state, in perfect innocence. This would make him a useful tool in the hands of the gang without his realising that he was thereby taking part in a criminal conspiracy. Such is a charitable view to take, but whether or not it is compatible with the evidence given at the trial is a matter which must ever remain in the province of personal opinion.

Such, at any rate, was the evidence as proved on oath, and further comment is as speculative as it is unprofitable. Just what happened in that office on the morning of the 16th of July will probably never be made known, but this at least is clear, that when Silverman or some other member of the gang extracted Mr. Mayer's necklace from the swiftly opened parcel, he was stealing something of little greater value to a thief than a handful of those pretty marbles which Mr. Horn announced that he had taken them to be. Had the packet contained a consignment of diamonds, or even pearls of less international renown, how different would have been the famous story which by now is all but told.

To return to the closing stages of the trial, after a short adjournment Mr. Valetta addressed the Jury on behalf of the prisoner Silverman. As there is no record extant of the wording or even substance of this speech it cannot be reproduced, but it may be taken that Mr. Valetta made every point on behalf of his client which could be made. In face of the evidence before them, however, it would have been an impressionable Jury who would have been persuaded by any speech, however skilful, into ignoring the accumulated evidence before them, especially when Silverman had failed to repeat on oath the statement that he was not guilty, much less give an explanation, upon which he could be cross-examined, of the evidence against him.

Having said all there was to be said, Mr. Valetta resumed his seat to make way for the representative of the master criminal, the organising genius of the robbery, Cammi Grizard.

Unfortunately, it often happens in a trial of such considerable length that Counsel have more than one case to attend at once, and leave to their Juniors the task of handling the unimportant part of the Defence and of taking a note of all that occurs while the Leader is away. Now it happened that Mr. Elliott, " Genial George," as he was known to his intimates, was busy on a " long firm fraud " case in another Court, where he was defending one of a number of Parisians who were charged with conspiracy to defraud. His client in this case was, in fact, an Englishman of French extraction, and although his name was Lambert he was always known, and was referred to throughout the case, as Monsieur Lambert, pronouncing his name as though it were French. His full name was so beautiful to hear that Mr. Elliott never lost an opportunity of pronouncing it in full, while Travers Humphreys, as he then was, who was Junior in this case to the man who was his opponent in the Grizard trial, was all but constrained to plunge into a poem which could be opened with such a glorious line as " Aurèle de Labat de Lambert "! However that may be, George Elliott, in the intervals of attending to the Grizard trial, had been airing his French accent for days on end, and wedding it to his accustomed grace of gesture and manner. When, therefore, he was suddenly told that he was wanted in the First Court to make his speech on behalf of Grizard, he could not divest himself of his new-found Continental manner. To the consternation of his client he rose majestically to his feet and announced to all and sundry that he appeared (with a graceful gesture to the Dock) for Monsieur Georges Grizard, pronouncing the name in French! The point of the *faux pas* will be realised when it is understood that Grizard's attitude all through had been that of the typical Englishman who understood no word of any other language, and was quite unable to understand the bargaining which Quadratstein had said took place between himself and the other polylingual Continental Jews!

The speech was, however, duly made, and no doubt made with the persuasive ease which characterised George Elliott, after which the hearing was adjourned to the following Monday at 11 o'clock.

On Monday, November 24th, the sixth and last day of the trial was opened by the speeches on behalf of the remaining prisoners, Lockett and Gutwirth, but as no record remains of the points which were raised therein, there is little use in speculating what they may have been.

And so the last of the defending Counsel took his seat and left the arena vacant for that mighty advocate, the late Sir Richard Muir, to demolish such poor argument as had been raised to check the advancing wall of evidence. In a few well-chosen and deliberate words he tabulated to the listening Jurymen the damning evidence against all four of the prisoners. In the absence of all evidence on their behalf save that of men who for one reason or another were already discredited by the Prosecution, and above all in the absence of the men themselves from the witness-box in which their true defence, if any, might have been revealed, to labour any more the case against them was but thrashing a defeated man. The defence was one of law, and that having failed there was nothing left but to await the law's reward. But hope dies hard, and hope, in a criminal trial, is never dead until the verdict has been given and the sentence passed, for none can say with certainty what verdict will in a given case be found. It was therefore with considerable interest that the four men settled back into their seats to listen to the summary of the evidence which, in his usual quiet way, Mr. Justice Lawrence proceeded to address to the waiting Jurymen.

CHAPTER XIII

SUMMING UP AND VERDICT

MR. JUSTICE LAWRENCE: " Gentlemen of the Jury, the four prisoners in this case are charged with the crimes of larceny and receiving stolen goods knowing them to have been stolen. There are six counts in the Indictment, and a great deal has been made of them in the addresses of learned counsel for the defence. It is not a usual subject for discussion with the jury who, as a rule, are addressed upon the facts, but in this case we have had elaborate arguments addressed to the Judge and, when the Judge had given the ruling which seemed to him to be the right one, with all the privileges now lying in the hands of counsel of going to the Court of Criminal Appeal they have, instead of abiding by that, addressed you upon the proper joinder of these counts. They have not addressed you at all upon the facts of the case. They have treated you as though they were absolutely ignorant of the existence of the doctrine of recent possession of stolen goods, which is not a matter of law, but a matter merely of sense; it is an inference of fact, and it is of this nature. The man who steals and carries away the property of another has necessarily to come into possession of it, either by himself or his agent. He might have it in his hand, or he might have it in the hand of his agent, but he must, at the moment of stealing, and until he has the opportunity of disposing of it, be in possession of it.

255

So it has been the practice for many hundreds of years to say that you may draw the inference from the possession of goods recently stolen, that the man who is in possession of those goods is the person who stole them. In some classes of goods the inference remains for a very long time, depending on the nature of the goods and how soon you can get rid of them.

" It is a perfectly simple thing, if you come by goods—even though they are as valuable as these pearls—honestly and innocently, to show how you are led into having them—to call the people who can prove it—but here there is not one word. The learned counsel have ignored that altogether, and introduced an entirely new proposition into the law of this country. They say quite correctly that the prosecution must prove their case. Of course they must, but then the learned counsel go on to say the prosecution must prove the time and the place at which the property is stolen—a doctrine which is entirely new. As long ago as the time of Lord Hale, goods might be put on to the stage-coach in London and stolen somewhere between London and Exeter, and the person found in possession of them might be at Weston-super-Mare the morning after they are stolen; then if he could not give a good explanation of how he came by them, juries would say: 'Very well, we are not going to inquire at which particular stage of the 30 stages or so between London and Exeter the things were stolen, but if you do not give us some explanation of how you came by this property we shall hold that you are the thief.' In the particular circumstances of this Indictment you have got to carry the matter a little further. It is not the ordinary doctrines of the criminal law or any principal of justice which they have been declaiming about. It is simply because in this particular case the goods were stolen from the Post Office either of France or of England, or after they had left the Post Office, and it happens that the Statute Law which deals with these offences empowers the Court to give certain punishment for them, different punishment in the case of goods stolen in the Post Office from goods stolen otherwise than through the Post, and so it becomes important for the purposes of this case that you should have regard to the question of whether this was stolen from the French Post or from the English Post or after it left the Post. Now let me deal first of all with the French Post. Learned Counsel for Lockett quite properly submitted in the first instance that I ought to put the Prosecution to its election whether they would proceed upon the one count or upon the other. I had to consider the matter and remember what this Statute of 1896 was passed to deal with, and according to my recollection it was cases of this sort. There were large robberies of bonds payable to bearer, and in the case of those bonds it became sometimes very difficult to show where the larceny occurred. If the Prisoners were able to raise sufficient doubt to induce the Juries to find that the goods were stolen abroad, then they could not be convicted upon the indictment for stealing and receiving in England, because the offence of receiving involves there having been a crime of stealing. So this Statute of 1896 became necessary, and it enacted that in any indictment for stealing you might also put a count for receiving the goods stolen abroad, and it is enacted that the new Statute of 1896 should be read with and construed as part of the Larceny Act of 1861, which authorised the joining of counts for receiving with counts of larceny. Now, as I read that Statute, it was intended to apply to this very class of case, in order that prisoners might not have a loop-hole for escape by calling witnesses to say that they did receive the goods and did not know they were stolen, and that they were stolen in France, and therefore you cannot convict. Then Mr. Curtis Bennett ingeniously asked me to say: ' Very well, now it has been proved those things left France safely, according to the case for the Prosecution; therefore I ask you now to rule that there is no evidence to go to the Jury upon that count.' I was bound to consider that again. It was a very ingenious contention, and for a moment I thought there might be something in it. But then Mr. Muir pointed out that there *is* evidence, there is the recent possession of those goods, and that is consistent with the Jury's finding that the larceny occurred at any place, either in the Post Office or in France or in the steam-boat crossing from Calais to Dover or in the train from Dover to London or in the delivery at Hatton Garden, or even from Mr. Mayer himself. Well, that seemed to me to be the proper contention, and it seemed to me to be my duty to say that I must not strike this out, and so open a door by which Prisoners may call a number of witnesses to say that this *did* occur in France, for once that count with regard to France were gone it would have opened the door for escape. Now, Gentlemen, English law is perfectly fair, and indeed partial, to Prisoners. It gives them

11th November 1913.

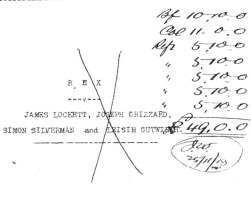

R E X

--- v ---

JAMES LOCKETT, JOSEPH GRIZZARD,

SIMON SILVERMAN and LEISIR GUTWIRTH.

Bf 10.10.0
Coe 11. 0.0
Rep 5.10.0
" 5.10.0
" 5.10.0
" 5.10.0
" 5.10.0
£49.0.0

B R I E F   F O R   T H E   P R O S E C U T I O N

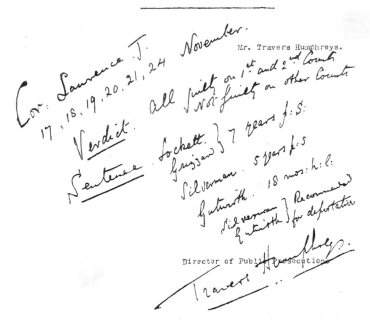

Cor: Lawrence J.
17, 18, 19, 20, 21, 24 November.

Mr. Travers Humphreys.

Verdict. All guilty on 1st and 2nd Counts
Not guilty on other Counts

Sentence. Lockett.
Grizzard. } 7 years p.S:

Silverman. 5 years p.S

Gutwirth. 18 mos: h.l:

Silverman } Recommended
Gutwirth } for deportation

Director of Public Prosecution.

Travers Humphreys.

The " back-sheet " of Mr. Justice Humphreys' Brief at the Trial,
as endorsed at the time. The figures in the top right hand corner
are an office addition and do not represent Counsel's fees.

every chance, a ' sporting ' chance. It is not, as Mr.
Muir says, quite such an ass as to open doors for
Prisoners to walk out of the dock. So it comes about
that I thought it my duty to say: ' No, I cannot have
that count struck out. You must go to the Jury and
deal with this as a matter of substance and fact and
see what explanation you can give.' Then what do
they do? They do not give any explanation at all;
they leave all this evidence of the prosecution untouched and only try to dissect the place at which this
larceny occurred. Gentlemen, you know that the
moral guilt of receiving goods is the same whether
they are stolen in France or in England, and the loss
to the owner is precisely the same. It is purely a
question of legal technicality. Still, you must give
your best attention to it because, as I have told you,
it is necessary that you should determine where,
according to your judgment, the goods were stolen,
that is to say, in which of these main divisions, the
French or the English Post Office. Now let us
see what is the evidence about it. As to France,
those goods were put into the Post by Mr. Henri
Salomons at Post Office 22 in Paris, and there received
by a gentleman who was called before you, who said:
' I remember the occasion; they were in my custody
and under my eyes from that time until they were
put into the bag and sent to the *cabine chargement* ';
from there they were taken by the Postal Authorities
in a sealed bag to the Central Post Office in Paris;
there they were re-sorted and re-packed, all the time
in the presence of a number of officials, and then they
were put into a bag in a sealed sack which was never
opened, according to the evidence, until it reached

259

Dover. Now there was not a question asked to suggest to either of those witnesses that anything had happened to the bag, or that they were open to mistake in their evidence. Now you have to consider what had to be done to get these pearls out of this sealed box. It was not an operation that could be done in seconds. It must have taken a very considerable period of time, because it was not done roughly and clumsily by tearing the paper or anything of that sort, but the seals were in some way, which I have not entirely grasped, removed so that the paper could be taken off. It was apparently done in some hurry because the lid of the box was broken, and the paper was put on in the wrong way; that is to say, what had been the top of the box had got the bottom of the paper on it, and what had been the bottom of the box had got the top of the paper on it.

" Now, to do all that, and to take out the pearls, put in the sugar, put in the newspaper and put the box back again, was an operation that could not be performed in the presence of five or six or a dozen people without their knowing something about it. So is goes to Calais and gets to Dover in that condition in this sack with the seals untouched. It is difficult to see how it could have been tampered with during that transit from Paris to Calais. From Calais to Mr. Mayer's office is the English Post, and that is the point of time which Mr. Muir, for the prosecution, says you should find these pearls were stolen. It is quite true that Mr. Muir submits to you the view that they were stolen in the delivery at Hatton Garden by the Postman, but it is quite open to you if you think, for instance, that the evidence of Loades

is so overwhelming that you must come to the conclusion that this box was pilfered before he saw it,
to come to the conclusion that it was done between
Calais and Dover, because from the evidence put
before you it was in the hold of the ship for whatever time the boat took to cross at night. It may be
you think it might have been done then. Loades says
that he noticed that the box had a continuous line of
seals. A great attack has been made upon Mr. Muir
in this case for not having called Loades, but it is a
mistake to suppose that if you think a man is not
correct, you are bound to put him in the witness box;
your duty is to try to put every witness who you
believe has got knowledge on the subject, and that
knowledge true knowledge, before the jury, so that
they shall have the opportunity of hearing it. The
prosecution are under no duty to confuse and make
difficulties, but are doing everything that is right and
fair in saying to the other side: ' There is this man's
testimony; if you want him, call him; we do not
accept his statement at all.' That is what the
prosecution have done in this case, and in my experience, which is upward of forty years, I have never
before heard Counsel attacked who have pursued that
course of conduct. I think there is no justification
for the attack which has been made on Mr. Muir for
not calling Loades. Then it is said he has not called
Neville or Hollands. There, Gentlemen, the attack
is not only unfounded, it is multiplied. Counsel for
the prosecution in opening said: ' That is the point
I fixed upon as the place where this larceny occurred.'
Yet they are asked: ' Why do you not call the people
that you say were either by negligence or breach of

duty the means of it being stolen?' You might as well say: 'Why do you not call the Prisoner himself, and ask him whether he will admit he stole the goods?' Of course, you do not call a witness for the prosecution who you say is himself a wrong-doer in the matter. What is the good of calling a man to say: 'Although it was my duty not to let this out of my hand I committed a breach of that duty?' It is no good at all, and in this case there was this additional ground for not doing it, that one of the prisoners, Gutwirth, has said that as one of the expenses of getting these pearls, 'We had to pay a £100 apiece to two postmen and promised them another £100 apiece.' No names were mentioned, and no identity of the postmen. It may be utterly untrue that such a thing happened, but certainly it was not a statement which would induce Counsel for the prosecution to put them into the witness box.

" Then how does the matter stand? Somewhere or another those pearls were stolen. It is not disputed that these men had possession of them. You must ask yourselves whether they were all acting in concert. If they were all four acting in concert in the matter, it is not necessary that you should find each one in possession of the pearls at any particular moment. If you are satisfied that they were in possession of stolen pearls knowing them to be stolen, and were acting together in the matter of disposing of them, they would be guilty of the crime of receiving, knowing the property to be stolen, and if you think the time sufficiently proximate to raise the inference that they were the persons who stole these pearls, and you think they were acting together, then you are entitled to find them guilty of the crime of stealing those pearls. Now you must ask yourself: Did they steal them, and did they steal them from the Post Office?

" I have disposed of France and now will deal with the other end of the line. Upon that subject they must have been stolen after they were received by Sawtell. Sawtell was a sergeant in the Corps of Commissionaires, a man who had been ten years at 88, Hatton Garden, a trusted man, who gave his evidence very clearly and apparently truthfully. He said: ' I received the box; I signed for it; I put it in the safe, and kept it in the safe until Mr. Smith came. I handed it to Smith when he came; I took his receipt from him,' and Smith says: ' I put it in the inner room. I was in the outer office until Mr. Mayer came, and nobody could have got into that office while that box was there, until it was received by Mr. Mayer and opened in his presence by his two clerks.' If you believe their evidence it is clear there was a larceny and receipt of these goods which did not take place after they were delivered to Mr. Mayer. That leaves the only possible conclusion that they were stolen from the Post Office somewhere between Calais and 88, Hatton Garden, and though you have got to find that matter of fact you have not got to say at which particular point of transit the larceny took place. You have got to be satisfied there was larceny, and that these men knew that the things were stolen. Now, how does the matter stand upon that subject? On the 4th August Gutwirth is at Antwerp, meets that young man Brandstatter. He began by asking whether he was open to buy a large purchase.

Brandstatter said he was, up to one hundred thousand or two hundred thousand francs or something of that sort. ' Oh,' he said, ' much more than that; see me to-morrow." He saw him the next day and told him they were Mr. Mayer's pearls; he might go to a million or a million and a half francs. Brandstatter goes back to Paris and *then* sees the reward which Mr. Price with great dash and boldness had caused to be advertised in London and Paris, a reward of £10,000. Brandstatter has a conversation with that intelligent and cool-headed young man Quadratstein and thinks he may get some of the reward. Quadratstein takes the same view. That is the very object of offering the reward, to get somebody to come forward and try to get it. After talking it over together, Brandstatter writes that letter that we have not got—Gutwirth seems to have destroyed it—of the 12th August, but we have got Gutwirth's reply. The substance of it is that he wants him to come over with ' one and a half,' which is, of course, the one and a half million francs mentioned in Antwerp, and if he could not get his buyer to entrust him with the money he might bring his buyer with him, but he was to be sure that he was a person that could be trusted and was all right. Quadratstein says he did not believe at this time that they had actually got the pearls, and he thought this was a dodge to get Brandstatter over there with a million and a half francs upon him in order to rob him. That is still a little eccentric in this country, but when one hears, as one does, about these motor bandits that have terrorised Paris, it is perhaps not so extraordinary to the mind of the Parisian. However, Quadratstein proposed they should come over, and they took care to arm themselves with revolvers and came. At Charing Cross Station, in accordance with that letter, there is Gutwirth to meet them. . . . Then they go off to Gutwirth's house. There they see outside the man with the white neck-cloth. They evidently think it is Lockett, and they ask you to think so because when Lockett appears the next day at the tea-room he is also dressed in a similar way, with a white scarf, and at that meeting there Lockett is the person who throws down the match-box at the request of Silverman. Now, say the prosecution, Lockett is the person who either had personal charge or had personal control over these pearls during the period of these negotiations, which lasted from the 16th August to the 2nd September. On the 16th August that match-box is thrown on to the table, and, according to the literature of criminal acts, it was a very clever ruse to adopt.

" ' There is nothing like being absolutely open and bold if you want to escape detection,' is what Edgar Allan Poe and other writers upon the subject have said. ' If you want to provoke attention, try and do a thing secretly, and you will have everybody looking at you and trying to make out what you are at. If you want to do it without anyone detecting, do it perfectly openly.' Whether Lockett is a reader of Edgar Allan Poe I do not know, but they appeared according to the evidence to have acted under that principle. The match-box contained what appeared to be real pearls, and Grizard says: ' A pretty piece of work, eh? ' really taking a pride in this robbery. Lockett gets up, leans over the table, and says: ' It is all right, isn't it? ' or some words to that effect.

265

The young men say: ' They are certainly pearls, but we cannot tell whether they are Mr. Max Mayer's pearls until we have examined them and weighed them '; so they go off. Then there is another question. The case is full of incidents. If you believe the evidence, it shows these people knew these things were stolen, and they make no concealment on the subject. They make one of these young men carry the pearls, so that they knew, perhaps very much better than learned Counsel, the danger of recent possession of stolen property. Quadratstein said the possession of the things was always in the hands of somebody who was not really taking part in the negotiation, as far as it was humanly possible to observe that rule. They were bound by the reason of the trust, and the circumstances, to produce the pearls upon one occasion; namely, when the so-called buyer, Mr. Spanier, a gentleman of high position in this trade in Paris, was got over by Mr. Price and Mr. Mayer to try and assist them to unravel this very curious robbery. He came. He, unlike the other two, was not coming to gain the reward, but he was coming with an indemnity against personal injury, and with the statement that his expenses would be paid, and a fee. Not a word has been suggested against his evidence here. With regard to the other two witnesses, there have been suggestions made, not that they have been guilty of any misconduct before, but that you ought not to believe them, because they admit they told lies in the course of the negotiations. Gentlemen, I am not going to advocate the telling of lies, but you cannot cook an omelette without cracking eggs, and you cannot receive a parcel that has been stolen, and try to dispose of it by telling them the circumstances under which you are there. Therefore when Quadratstein says, ' Of course I was telling them lies; that is what I was there to do,' the question is not whether he was wrong in telling lies. He was acting a part, and in acting that part he was telling all the fairy stories that he could think of about having a buyer and a Rajah and all the rest of it . . . Then you have Mr. Spanier going into Room 197, and there Mr. Spanier with the pearls and the reward bill weighs the pearls and checks them with the weights on the bill, and it is suggested—or rather I do not know that *is* suggested—I think that is the beauty of that part of this defence, that it never has been suggested that they did not know these pearls were stolen. Really the whole defence has been a criticism of Mr. Muir telling you Gentlemen that you have not got the manhood to say that these pearls were stolen in any particular place; they seem to think you are such a wobble-minded body of men that you will not be able to agree as to where this evidence points that the pearls were stolen. They are quite entitled to run that line of defence if they like, but it is for you to make up your minds, looking honestly at the evidence. What the prosecution say about it is this; if a body of men wanted to commit a larceny of this sort, what they do is to fix upon the weak link in the chain and at once attempt to attack that link. They knew that this man Neville was a man who was very fond of his glass, being found drunk on duty on one occasion and reprimanded for injuring his health, rendering himself liable to be absent from duty by constant intemperance. They

say that that is just the sort of man that clever people
would pitch upon as likely, while muddled or con-
fused by drink, to commit some breach of duty, which
need not have been in his eyes a very grievous
one . . . There may have been any sort of tarra-
diddle told him which would lead him to believe
he could do it without doing any grave injustice.
However, that is what the prosecution say; that is
the sort of man you have to consider. Whether they
are right in saying that this is the spot at which this
robbery was committed, is for you to say. You have
in support of that view the curious facts that Silverman, who has this office at 101, had written on the
27th June, just before this larceny is committed, to
the Post Office to have his letters and things delivered personally. There has never been any explanation given either to Dickson, the housekeeper
there, or to you, of why that letter was sent to the
Post Office. You have it further that Silverman is
at that very time arranging to have a seal made, and
he goes to another man whom he meets in one of
the public houses that seem to abound in Hatton
Garden, and there he finds Gordon, and gets him to
make a seal ' M.M.' No explanation why Silverman should have wanted the seal ' M.M.' made,
and done at once. If Silverman was arranging this,
there may have been other heads as able scheming
this thing, to have a seal, to arrange that the postman should be a little careless or a little drunk, and
that things could be taken out of his hands for a time
and put back again at a later time. At all events you
have it, that the thing brought to Gordon to copy
was an indented seal. It was therefore not from a

die but taken from an impression. The prosecution suggest it was copied from one of Mr. Max Mayer's own packages. Silverman must have got possession of one of Mr. Mayer's packages before this, taken a cast in wax of his seal, taken it to Gordon and got it copied, and then had it in his possession on the 16th July so that he could whip these off and put on the other seals, and hand it back to Neville in time to have it delivered at Mr. Mayer's office. Now then, was Gordon telling you the truth? His evidence is corroborated in the most remarkable way . . . He came down there on the second occasion to have a seal and locket done, and there in Silverman's office are the seal and locket too. Now that is important for this reason, that at the times Gordon makes that statement to the authorities there had been no notification whatever of there being any seal or locket found in Silverman's office . . . So there you have Gordon corroborated in a most remarkable manner. Then you have got at the office of the same man two things, one a piece of modelling wax and further, the sealing wax in a ladle or pot so that you melt the wax in the pot instead of burning it in the flame of a lamp, candle, or taper, as the case may be. Now Mr. Price may be looked upon as an expert in these matters, and he says that this produces a different appearance in the seal from that which the wax does when it is lit in the flame. In one case it has a sheen or polish upon it; in the other case it has a dull look, and he gave you a more or less scientific explanation why that is so. So that really the theory of the prosecution is that the pearls were changed and the sealing done by someone who

used a ladle or a pot to melt his wax, that is to say
by someone who had a seal ' M.M.,' a copy of Mr.
Max Mayer's seal, and at the place where Silverman arranged to meet the postman to deliver the
parcels to him. On all those facts, you are asked
whether it is possible to believe all those things could
have occurred, and yet Silverman be perfectly guilt-
less in the matter. If you think there is anything in
the criticism which Mr. Valetta has passed upon this
matter, or upon the evidence of Neville or Hollands,
you must give due weight to it. What Mr. Valetta asks
you to believe, is that those two men cannot be telling
you either what is untrue or be mistaken in what they
say. What Mr. Muir on the other hand asks you to
say is that either one or the other is certain; that there
is no reasonable doubt, that either the man was taking
part in this for reward or he was guilty of such
negligence as enabled these people to do it. With
regard to the bag carrier, he says that his memory is
not to be trusted in the matter, and certain it is that
whichever of those two arguments you are going to
adopt, those two men do contradict one another in
the statements they make at one time and another in
a remarkable degree. Neville first says he never
went upstairs at all. When the bag-carrier gives his
statement, he says the letters were given him to
deliver to the liftman and that Neville went upstairs.
Then Neville says: Oh, yes, he did go upstairs, but
even then, when he is reminded of this, he professes
not to remember the name of the firm to whom he
has to go upstairs. So that you have this peculiarity.
You have the statement that two postmen were being
bribed; you have further that Neville, when he is

first asked, says he never went upstairs; secondly, he says he did go upstairs, and he says: ' I do not know the name of the persons to whose address I went.' Yet we have it that he had gone upstairs from the 27th June regularly to this man's office.

" So far you have the case as it is against Silverman. Then you have got to consider whether they are not all tied together in one compact body of either thieves or receivers by this transaction with regard to the notes. It is not necessary to take you through the whole of the tracings of the notes, because you have got this meeting when 100,000 francs are handed over to Grizard for two pearls on the 25th August; they are handed by Grizard to Silverman to be counted; he counts them; they are handed back to Grizard and Grizard walks away. Before that time the prisoners have been pawning things. Lockett had been pawning a diamond ring. Silverman had raised a considerable sum of money, £80, Gutwirth had raised £50 and Lockett £25, all recently in the summer when they were wanting money for whatever they were doing. If that is true, this robbery was costing money, and for bribing postmen or anybody else they wanted funds. You find them pawning things and obtaining funds, and you have on the 25th August 100,000 francs in French notes handed over. You will not forget they insisted on the notes being French, and they gave as a reason, that they were not so easily traced. Directly after those notes were handed over, you get them changed in a variety of directions, and either the notes or the proceeds of them are traced to every one of these prisoners. They are all found dealing with the notes . . . As

T

for Gutwirth, according to the statement of Quadratstein and Brandstatter, he was trying to best his
partners in this transaction; he was trying to get his
share of the profits and to get commission out of
Spanier, the buyer, of 5 per cent in addition, and his
partners were not to know anything about it. That
only shows that he was a dishonest man, that he was
guilty either of this larceny, or of receiving it knowing it to be stolen; so that it is impossible to see how
it can be said that Gutwirth was not just as much in
this transaction as the others . . . So it is that on
the 2nd September they are all arrested.

" Those, gentlemen, are the material facts. You
must ask yourselves whether those prisoners are not
guilty of being the persons who arranged to steal,
and stole those pearls. Secondly, if you have any
doubt about it you must ask yourselves whether they
are not the persons who received them knowing
them to be stolen; and finally you must ask yourselves whether they were not so received having been
stolen while in transit in the English post. Of course
you have the other possibilities before you, but the
prosecution do not ask you to find that they were
either stolen in France or that they were stolen from
Mr. Mayer, and I myself do not see any ground for
suggesting to you that that is the inference which
sensible men should draw. It seems to me that if you
look at this boldly and fairly you will come to the
conclusion that these pearls were stolen whilst in
transit through the English post. You have not got
to determine whether Neville or his bag carrier were
concerned in the theft. It may have been that they
were stolen in some other way. Our knowledge does

not go far enough to indicate safely; but that they were stolen in transit through the English post is that which the prosecution ask you to find here. It is for you to say whether you can have any reasonable doubt upon the matter. Of course if you have, you must give the prisoners the benefit of any reasonable doubt, but it should be a reasonable doubt and not one created by what appears to me to be foolish hair splitting, or such arguments as Mr. George Elliott addressed to you that if it was true, what these people were telling, they would have seized the pearls and got in their first shot in that room 197. It seems to me almost grotesque to suggest that two young men should go firing shots into these people in that room. It is not as though you were going to launch a rocket or were in a shooting saloon—therefore it seems to me an idle suggestion to make in the City of London. Mr. Price tells you that he impressed upon them that they were not to do anything foolish; he was not going to be responsible to his underwriters for keeping their families for the rest of their lives, and of course he did not want anything of this sort committed. He wanted detection, evidence, means of laying the case before a Jury of twelve Gentlemen who could come to a reasonable conclusion upon it. And that is what the prosecution ask you to do in the case. As I said, if you can find any ground for reasonable doubt upon it, give the prisoners the benefit of it, but let it be a reasonable doubt. Do not give way to any foolish or any quixotic doubt. Look at the matter broadly here and come to a conclusion and say what you find."

The fact that the Learned Judge in this Direction

273

to the Jury only touched upon certain aspects of the evidence and omitted others shows that in his opinion the Jury's verdict was already in their minds, and it is doubtful if any one in Court expected the twelve men to be absent from the Jury box for long.

Nevertheless the speed of their return speaks volumes for the crushing weight of evidence adduced by the untiring Scotsman, who so ably represented the interests of the public in his position as Counsel for the Crown.

In the laconic wording of the shorthand note: " The Jury retired at 4.36 and returned into Court at 4.47."

In anticipation of a somewhat longer wait the four men had been taken below in the interval, but when the summons was called down for them to return they must have known the verdict they were going to hear. All four of them walked to the rail of the dock while the Clerk of the Court pronounced in immemorial form:

Clerk of the Court: Gentlemen of the Jury, have you agreed upon your verdict?

The Foreman: We have.

Clerk of the Court: Do you find James Lockett Guilty or Not Guilty upon this indictment?

The Foreman: On which count?

A murmur ran through the ranks of Defending Counsel. Apparently their eloquence had at least had *some* effect. But their victory was of little worth.

Clerk of the Court: Do you find him Guilty or Not Guilty of stealing a pearl necklace, the property of the Postmaster General, it then being a postal packet in course of transmission by post?

The Foreman: Guilty.

Clerk of the Court: Do you find him Guilty or Not Guilty of receiving that pearl necklace well knowing the same to have been stolen while in course of transmission by post?

The Foreman: Guilty.

Clerk of the Court: Do you find him Guilty or Not Guilty on the rest of the indictment?

The Foreman: Not Guilty on the other Counts.

The same verdict was given in respect of the other prisoners and was summarised in the following way.

Clerk of the Court: You say all the prisoners are Guilty on the first and second counts of the indictment, and Not Guilty on the third, fourth, fifth, and sixth counts?

The Foreman: Precisely.

Clerk of the Court: And that is the verdict of you all?

The Foreman: The verdict of us all.

In addition Lockett and Grizard formally pleaded guilty to previous convictions of felony, at Liverpool in 1906 and in London in 1910 respectively, and the Clerk of the Court sat down.

The rest of the proceedings were, as always in such cases, somewhat of an anti-climax. Whatever the sentence given, " Cammi " Grizard, the uncrowned " King of the Receivers " and the brains of countless West End robberies, was at last dethroned and reduced to the level of a convicted criminal. The police, however, bear no grudge against the men who openly defy them, and when Inspector Ward was called into the witness box to tell His Lordship something of the men he was about to sentence, no trace of the inward exultation which he felt at such a victory betrayed itself in the dry recital of the prisoners' antecedents which he gave the Court. All which he told the Court has been incorporated in a previous chapter of this volume and need not be here repeated, but one question put to the officer by Mr. Jones who, in the absence of his leader, represented Grizard spoke of a factor which was already beginning to affect the receiver's life and was in a few years to bring that life to an end.

Q. I do not know if you can tell me. I think he has been in very bad health for some time, suffering from diabetes?

A. I understand that that is so.

Apparently no speeches in mitigation of severity of sentence were advanced for any of the men, and, at a murmured request from the Bench, the Clerk of the Court proceeded to "call upon" the waiting prisoners.

Clerk of the Court: Prisoners at the Bar, you stand convicted of felony. Have you or either of you anything to say why the Court should not give you Judgment according to law?

There was silence for a moment in Court, and then the Learned Judge leant forward to administer the law's reward.

"Now Lockett, you have been convicted of this crime upon the clearest evidence. Indeed, the one thing I think can be said in your favour is that you did not attempt to deny the facts of this case, but merely, through your Counsel, attacked the law, which is certainly more open to attack than individuals. I commend you for that, but your previous record and the position that you occupied in this case, in which I have no doubt you were a leading mind, is a very serious one. You have attacked one of the most important branches of the public service in a particularly bold and skilful manner. You have directed your attack to property of exceptional value, and no doubt you are aware that you exposed yourself to penal servitude for life. You have been convicted before and you do not seem to be amenable to the logic of punishment. I must remove you, as a danger to the community, for a considerable period of time.

" And you, Grizard, you seem to have shared with Lockett the leadership and headwork of this robbery. I am sorry to hear that you are ill, but I have no doubt you will be looked after under the sentence I am going to give you as well as you would be in your own home. You must both be sent to penal servitude for seven years."

Seven years! For an unsuccessful attempt to get away with the proceeds of a brilliant robbery. How Grizard must have cursed the moment when he realised that his confederates had stolen such a useless and incriminating article. Nor was he flattered at being sentenced as the assistant of the burglar Lockett who was never, it would seem, the brains of the enterprise. Seven years in penal servitude for a quarter share for one week of £4,000! Dimly he heard the sentence on the other men.

" Silverman," the Judge was saying, " perhaps I have done you an injustice in saying that the others were the brains of the plot; still it does seem to me that you were to some extent the ingenious tool rather than the originator of this scheme. You were too ingenious. You must be sent to penal servitude for five years, and there must be a recommendation at the end of your term that you be by the Home Secretary's Order expelled from this country.

" You, Gutwirth are said to be the less implicated party, but you took a very active part in it."

Gutwirth, ever ready, and as the others thought, too ready with his tongue, broke in with voluble excuse.

" I was dragged into it. I have been eighteen years in Hatton Garden, my Lord, always straight-forward. I do not know what made me do it. I was a broker. I ought never to have done a thing like that. It is not my business. Mine is a straightfor-ward business."

The Judge was waiting patiently, while the passionate plea was made. " I do not think," he then continued, " that you are as bad as the others, but you seem to have been a very willing tool. You must be imprisoned and kept to hard labour for 18 calendar months, and similar recommendation must be made in your case."

Mr. Frampton rose to plead the recission of this final item in the sentence, on the ground that Gut-wirth had been twenty-five years in the country and was a married man.

Mr. Justice Lawrence: " That may be, but he is an alien and we do not want such aliens here."

And so, after six days' hearing, ended the famous trial which finally disbanded this notorious and dangerous partnership.

CHAPTER XIV

APPEAL AND EPILOGUE

FROM this decision and sentence all four prisoners appealed. The appellate Court for cases from Assize, and it will be remembered that the Central Criminal Court is the Assize Court of London, is the Court of Criminal Appeal, created by Statute in 1907 to replace the Court of Crown Cases Reserved. This Court consists of not less than three, but always an odd number of Judges of the King's Bench Division, and is usually presided over by the Lord Chief Justice. According to the Statute, the decision " shall be according to the majority of the members of the court hearing the case," and this decision is pronounced by the President of the Court as representing the members forming it. The importance of the Court from the public point of view is that, save in exceptional circumstances when appeal is allowed to the House of Lords, it is the final arbiter of life and death in cases of appeal from the verdict at a murder trial.

Section 3 of the Act, " the Criminal Appeal Act 1907," enacts that " a person convicted on indictment may appeal under this Act to the Court of Criminal Appeal—

> (a) against his conviction on any ground of appeal which involves a question of law alone; and

279

    (*b*) with the leave of the Court of Criminal Appeal, or upon the certificate of the judge who tried him that it is a fit case for appeal, against his conviction on any ground of appeal which involves a question of fact alone, or a question of mixed law and fact, or any other ground which appears to the court to be a sufficient ground of appeal; and

    (*c*) with the leave of the Court of Criminal Appeal against the sentence passed on his conviction, unless the sentence is one fixed by law.

The last few words refer to murder or high treason, in which the sentence is not in the discretion of the Court but is fixed by law, namely, death. The Home Secretary alone, as adviser to His Majesty, can modify or remit such sentence, and this, as the public know, is often done. Only one more section needs attention.

Section 4 provides that the Court shall allow the appeal if they think that the verdict should be set aside as being unreasonable, or contrary to the weight of evidence, or that the Judge was guilty of a wrong decision in law, or that on any ground there was a miscarriage of justice, and in other cases shall dismiss the appeal, provided that, and this is the rock on which so many hopes have been forever shattered,

"Provided that the Court may, notwithstanding that they are of opinion that the point raised in the appeal might be decided in favour of the appellant, dismiss the appeal if they consider that no substantial miscarriage of justice has actually occurred."

These final words are of great importance to the effective administration of justice. It is not enough for a convicted criminal to prove some minor mistake of law or a slight mishandling of the facts. If this were so he might escape on a puerile technicality. He must, in addition, prove that by reason of such error " a substantial miscarriage of justice " has occurred, and that he is thereby the sufferer.

Each of the men sent in, as is required, a Notice of Appeal. Needless to say these notices are filled in by the persons representing the accused and merely signed in prison by the convicted man. It is not surprising, therefore, to find that Lockett's and Grizard's, being drafted by the same solicitors, are identical, but the two unfortunate Austrians, who had in addition to imprisonment been ordered to be sent back to Austria upon the expiration of their sentences, had spent all the money which they could raise on their defence at the trial. It is, however, obvious that legal help was given them. The grounds of appeal as signed by Grizard and Lockett were:

1. That the Indictment was bad on the ground of duplicity.
2. That the Indictment was bad owing to the fact that the prisoners were embarrassed by being charged therein with three offences, and the learned Judge ought either to have quashed the Indictment or put the prosecution to their election.
3. That there was no evidence to go to the Jury upon Counts 3, 4, 5, and 6.
4. That the learned Judge misdirected the Jury.

The grounds of appeal of Silverman and Gutwirth were slightly more.

1. Misdirection.
2. That the Indictment was bad on the ground of duplicity.
3. That the Indictment was embarrassing.
4. That there was no evidence for the Judge to properly leave the questions to the Jury.
5. That there was no evidence upon which the Jury could properly find a verdict of guilty.
6. That there was no evidence that the necklace, the subject of the charge of theft, was stolen in England or within the jurisdiction of this Honourable Court.
7. (Further, by Gutwirth only), that the order for expulsion should not have been granted, on the ground that I have lived in England for 25 years. I have always borne a good character. My children have been born in Antwerp, but my home and domicile is England, and no conviction has been recorded against me.

There are two reports of the case, in Criminal Appeal Reports, Volume 9 page 268, and in 1914 2 King's Bench Division at page 720. The hearing took place on the 19th and 20th of December, 1913, before the then Lord Chief Justice, Sir Rufus Isaacs, afterwards Lord Reading, and Bray and Lush J.J.

The following pages are compiled from the two official reports.

For the benefit of those who are interested from the legal point of view, the headnote to the K.B.D. report, which summarises the decision, is here set out.

" There is no rule in law that separate and distinct felonies cannot be tried together in one indictment. As a matter of practice and procedure the judge presiding at the trial can, in the exercise of his discretion, quash the indictment or call upon the prosecution to elect upon which of the counts for felony they will proceed, in order to safeguard the interests of the prisoner and to prevent him from being embarrassed by being put upon his trial upon an indictment in which there are several counts for distinct felonies. In exercising his discretion as to putting the prosecution to their election, the material element to which the judge should direct his attention is whether the overt acts relied on as proving the different offences charged are in substance the same."

The following Counsel appeared, being slightly different from those who appeared at the trial.

" Vachell, K.C., and Curtis Bennett for the prisoner Lockett.

" G. W. H. Jones and A. Crew for Grizard.

" Valetta and D. W. Corrie for Silverman.

" W. Frampton for Gutwirth.

" R. D. Muir and Travers Humphreys for the prosecution."

The reports then set out an abstract of the Indictment and a brief outline of the main facts which appeared in evidence at the trial, and the K.B.D. report concludes:

" The inference which the prosecution asked the jury to draw from the facts was that the packet containing the necklace was stolen between its leaving the East Central District Office in London and its reaching 88, Hatton Garden, about half an hour before Mr. Mayer saw the packet—in other words, that it was stolen while it ought to have been in the possession of the postman who had it to deliver."

All four men were present in Court on both days, and sat huddled together in the little dock in the corner, surrounded by warders, no longer merely accused men who defied the prosecution to prove their guilt to the satisfaction of a jury, but convicted felons, sentenced to long terms of imprisonment, appearing as a last and final hope to plead that the penalty of crime might be withheld. At the trial the presumption was that they were innocent until their guilt was proved. Now, the presumption was that the conduct of the Learned Judge was right in all particulars until it could be proved to three of his equals that his conduct was not only open to their criticism but that " a substantial miscarriage of justice had actually occurred."

Mr. Vachell, K.C., by arrangement with his fellows, spoke on behalf of all the prisoners. Having outlined the facts and the counts in the Indictment he continued:

" My submission is that this was misjoinder of an embarrassing character which entitles the appellants to have the Indictment quashed. The last two counts relate to a charge which is quite separate from the other four, and which was not an offence at all before 1896; the maximum sentence under these counts is seven years' penal servitude, whereas under the first two counts it is penal servitude for life . . .

" It is not necessary for the defence to show how the appellants were embarrassed; it is sufficient if they are likely to be embarrassed. The judge said that the embarrassment to be guarded against was that which would affect an innocent man; here an innocent man would have been seriously hampered in having to meet at the same time charges of crime in England and France. The case for the prosecution was that the theft was committed while the parcel was in the English post, and the judge ought to have held, as was submitted, that there was no evidence to go to the jury on the last four counts. The jury found the appellants guilty on the first two counts only, but counsel in their speeches had to deal with the question where the theft was committed, and the appellants were prejudiced by this.

"Further, the judge misdirected the jury on various points. He suggested that Neville, the postman, was just the sort of man who might be got hold of by clever criminals and induced to leave the bag in the passage for a few minutes. There was no evidence at all to support this suggestion. He also suggested that the postman had been bribed; there was only one piece of evidence as to bribery, and that was only evidence against Gutwirth. The judge ought to have pointed out to the jury that it was not evidence against the other three prisoners."

Such was his speech, and there was nothing more to say.

Mr. Jones, for Grizard, put one point of Mr. Vachell's argument in a different way, but that was all.

"I adopt," he said, "Mr. Vachell's arguments. As to misjoinder, the real test as to whether the felonies are the same or not, is to see whether the facts which prove one also prove the other. Here, proof of an offence under the Post Office Act disproved the other offences. Section 92 of the Larceny Act, 1861, does not make the joinder right, for it only justifies joining a count for receiving to a count which charges the theft. Beyond this it does not justify the joining of two or more different or inconsistent offences. In meeting a charge of felonious receiving it can be shown that there was no theft; such a defence must be embarrassed by this Indictment owing to the necessity of meeting two different and inconsistent sets of facts."

Counsel for Silverman and Gutwirth associated themselves with the arguments already put forward, and withdrew their appeals against the order of recommendation of expulsion, having realised that such an order was merely a recommendation to the Home Secretary upon which he might act or not in his discretion, and that it was not a matter which came into the province of the Court of Criminal Appeal.

The case for the appellants was finished. The final word had been said on their behalf, and the waiting prisoners could but listen to the reply for the Prosecution and the Judgment of the Court.

At least they were spared the ignominy of that phrase which often appears in newspaper and other reports of such appeals—" the Prosecution were not called upon." It will be appreciated that in an appeal it is for the appellant to prove such a *prima facie* case for dismissing the appeal that the Court will wish to hear Counsel for the Prosecution defend the judgment or sentence of the Court below, and prove that it was right. If, therefore, in the opinion of the

Court, the appeal is of such little worth that, even as it stands, the Court can see no ground for quashing the appeal, that phrase, so painfully clear in its meaning to the waiting prisoner, is murmured to Counsel as he rises to his feet—" We need not trouble you, Mr. So and So," and the Court proceeds in a brief and final judgment to dismiss the appeal.

In this case the appeal at least possessed such merits that the Court was in need of arguments from the other side of that narrow gangway which divides the court in two, to refute the legal submission of the appellants on the question of " misjoinder," that is, of including in one indictment more than one distinct and separate felony.

Mr. Muir, in replying for the Crown, quoted from various cases in which indictments such as that which he had drawn had been held by an appellate Court to be sound in law. In his usual clear, succinct and heavy style he summarised his reply by saying, " there is in law no objection to the joinder of various felonies in different counts of the same indictment, but the Judge in his discretion may put the Prosecution to election. There is no appeal from the exercise of this discretion . . ."

The Lord Chief Justice: " We need not trouble you further on that point. But can the verdict be justified, by which, on the first two counts, all four appellants were found guilty of both stealing and receiving?"

The four men strained to hear Mr. Muir's reply. Here was hope indeed, and at the eleventh hour.

Mr. Muir: " The verdict can only be justified by

U

taking these two counts as one indictment; where an indictment charges in different accounts larceny and receiving, a general verdict may be returned."

He resumed his seat, and Mr. Vachell rose to say one final word. " In all the cases cited," he said, " the ground for decision was that the facts in each charge were the same, although the charge varied. Here the facts were different."

It is hoped that from the above summary the legal point at issue is made clear, and hence the Judgment or decision of the court, as delivered by one whose greatness had already brought him to this great office and who was destined to become more famous still, will be of equal interest, not only to lawyers, who can read the reports themselves, but to general readers, as an example of the care with which each point submitted by an appellant is considered by the tribunal in whose hands his future lies. Nor are the points discussed therein of purely academic value, for the basis of our criminal procedure is the Indictment against the prisoner, in which are set out brief particulars of the crime alleged. It follows that the nature of such indictment is a matter of the gravest interest to all who take an interest in the cause of justice in our land.

As Mr. Vachell resumed his seat the warders nudged the prisoners to stand up to receive the decision of the Court, and so they stood, the master criminal well knowing that at last his hour was come, yet with a hope that once again he would escape through a loophole in the law; Lockett, to whom the gates of penal servitude were only too well known; Silverman, the " little Jew," and Gutwirth, Austrians,

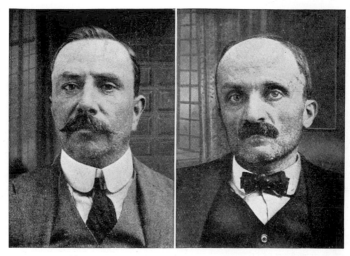

"Jim" Lockett   Simon Silverman

Leisir Gutwirth

aliens to the land whose laws they had defied, and tools, though willing ones, in the hands of a man far greater than themselves; each in his own way waited with that pathetic patience usually shown by prisoners in the dock, while the solemn, red-robed figures on the bench deliberated on their fate.

Finally, the Lord Chief Justice cleared his throat, and quietly and deliberately began to speak. His judgment was, compared with the great majority of appeals, of unusual length, but the prisoners who waited on his judgment and the points on which decision had to be made were of unusual importance, and no one can, with justice, say that either time or trouble is spared in the fair yet accurate administration of our law.

For the benefit of those interested, a somewhat abbreviated report of the Judgment is reproduced below.

THE LORD CHIEF JUSTICE: This is an appeal by four persons, who were convicted on an indictment which charges them with stealing and receiving a pearl necklace and three loose pearls. They were found guilty on two of the six counts of the indictment, and the two counts on which they were found guilty were framed under the Post Office Act, 1908, that as to stealing under s. 50, and that as to receiving under s. 52. The maximum punishment for offences of that character, either stealing or receiving, is penal servitude for life. It is for the court to determine whether the offence was proved against the appellants, whether a proper direction was given to the jury by the judge, and whether the indictment was good in law and ought to have been put to the jury in the form in which it was put by the judge. There were four other counts in the indictment; under the third, the appellants were charged with stealing, and under the fourth with receiving the property of Max Mayer, these counts being framed under the Larceny Act, 1861; and under them it was necessary to prove that the property had been stolen in this country. The fifth count was under the Larceny Act, 1896; s.1, which makes it an offence to receive goods stolen outside the United Kingdom, the taking of which would have constituted larceny if it had happened in the United Kingdom; and the sixth count, under the same statute, charged them with being in unlawful possession in this country of goods stolen outside the United Kingdom. In both the fifth and sixth counts it was part of the necessary averment that the appellants knew that the property had been stolen.

It is unnecessary to recapitulate the facts; they have been stated shortly and clearly by Mr. Vachell. The facts proved at the trial disclosed as plainly as possible that the offence was, in fact, committed by the four prisoners. It would be waste of time to go through the evidence, for it was manifest that on the facts alone, apart from the question of law, no defence could be made. Mr. Vachell relies on the only points that can be urged—namely, arguments based on the legal aspect of the case, and upon the practice and procedure adopted, as distinguished from the merits. That renders it obligatory on the court to examine with care the legal propositions and arguments which have been put forward.

The first point taken was that this indictment is

bad for misjoinder; and I think I am doing no injustice to the admirable and concise argument which
he addressed to us if I say that this was the most
substantial point upon which he based his contentions.
It is said that the judge ought to have quashed the
indictment upon motion made to him before plea, and
that, if he did not do that, he ought to have put the
prosecution to election upon which of the various
counts they would proceed; and, further, that, even
if he did not adopt that course, he ought to have ruled
at the end of the case for the Crown that there was no
evidence upon any of the counts other than the first
and second. Then it is said, further, that, even if he
did not take that view at the end of the case for the
Crown, he ought to have directed the jury to that
effect at the end of the evidence and before the case
was summed up.

The main proposition involved in these contentions is that there were in this case three distinct and
separate felonies alleged in the counts. In substance
it amounts to this, that there were in the journey three
sections in the course of which the larceny of these
pearls may have been committed; either in France,
or while in transmission by post in England, or after
delivery by the postal officials in England. In the
first case the offence of stealing would not be committed in this country, although under the Larceny
Act of 1896 the offence of receiving or being in unlawful possession of the pearls, knowing that they
were stolen, could still be committed.

Now, apart altogether from the Larceny Act, 1861,
and the Larceny Act, 1896, and simply from the point
of view of common law practice and procedure, it is

said that these offences could not be charged together in one indictment. No doubt, as a matter of practice and procedure, subject to certain exceptions upon which I shall have something to say later, the practice is well known and well established that if there are more offences than one charged in an indictment for felony, the judge can, if he thinks right, call upon the prosecution to elect upon which count they intend to proceed. But it is said in this case that he is bound in law to do so. We must consider the various authorities, and see what principle is to be deduced from them.

His Lordship then proceeded to do so, but it is not proposed to weary the general public with the details of this citation. The judgment continues:

It is apparent, on examination of the authorities, that this rule is one of practice and procedure devised by the judges who have presided in the past at criminal trials for the purpose of protecting prisoners from embarrassment and oppression, and that these opinions expressed by the judges are not laid down as rules of law, and are not rules of law, but are guides to the course which the presiding judge should, in his wisdom and discretion, adopt at the trial.

Then it is said that in such a case, although it may be a matter of discretion, the judge must exercise his discretion judicially, and in this case, if he refused to quash the indictment, he should have put the prosecution to election. That involves consideration of the overt acts relied upon by the prosecution. In our view that is the material element to which the judge's

attention should be directed in determining what
course he should adopt. He must consider whether
the prisoner will be embarrassed in his defence, and
in determining that he must examine whether the
overt acts relied upon in support of the offences
charged in the counts of the indictment are in
substance the same for each offence. Now, once we
have arrived at that conclusion it becomes apparent
that if in substance the facts are the same, the overt
acts relied upon are the same, and if so, then there is
no repugnance in these counts, and the consequence
would be that they might be charged together in one
indictment, and there would be no ground upon which
we could say that the judge should have put the
prosecution to election. In this connection it is right
that we should note the argument of Mr. Vachell
that the overt acts are not the same, and in support
of it he says: " You have here to consider that the
offence may have been committed in France, which
is not the same as saying that it was committed in
England, and it may have been committed in transmission in the post; nobody knows where it was committed." That may be true, and no doubt it is true
in a great many cases, that you may not be able to
locate the exact spot at which the particular offence
charged was committed; you may not be able to prove
the exact point of time at which it was committed, but
what the court has to consider is whether in substance
the acts charged are the same. Here there was a theft
of these pearls at some point of what I may describe
as the one transaction of the sending of the pearls.
We think the judge was quite right in the view he
took, and that in these circumstances there was nothing

which made it incumbent upon him to exercise his discretion in the way suggested; therefore these points fail.

It is further contended that the judge ought to have directed the jury that there was no evidence on the last four counts. That involves the consideration of the summing up, and of the criticisms made upon it. They may be put quite shortly; as I understand, there are two points made. One was that the judge ought to have ruled that there was no evidence on the last four counts, and the other put forward by Mr. Jones, and not substantially different from the first, that although there was evidence upon the first two counts, yet it was wrong to submit to the jury the evidence given with regard to the other four, notwithstanding that the jury only convicted on the first two counts, and acquitted on the other four. It was said that the defence was embarrassed because the jury had all the facts put together on the six counts; they may have thought that, once the pearls were stolen, they could come to a conclusion that they were stolen whilst in transit of post, and could, therefore, convict under the statute of 1908, which is the one which gives the right to impose the heaviest sentence; and that it was never clearly brought home to their minds that they must find where the pearls were stolen, and not merely that they were, in fact, stolen. Once the summing up is looked at it seems to us that it is not open to the appellants to make out any grievance with regard to this. At the end of the summing up the judge, having dealt with the facts, puts it perfectly plainly to the jury, and in a way which leaves it beyond any doubt. He says: " You must ask your-

selves whether these prisoners are not guilty of being
the persons who arranged to steal and stole those
pearls. Secondly, if you have any doubt about it, you
must ask yourselves whether they are not the persons
who received them, knowing them to have been
stolen; and finally, you must ask yourselves whether
they were not so received, having been stolen whilst
in transit in the English post. Of course, you have
the other possibilities before you, but the prosecution
do not ask you to find that they were either stolen in
France or that they were stolen from Mr. Mayer,
and I myself do not see any ground for suggesting
to you that that is the inference which sensible men
should draw. It seems to me that if you want to
look at this case boldly and fairly, you would come to
the conclusion that these pearls were stolen whilst in
transit through the English post." The jury had
the various theories before them, and they came to
the conclusion that the offences were proved under
the first and second counts. We think there was a
right direction, and that no complaint can be made
with reference to it.

There was a further grievance made with reference
to the summing up, the complaint being that the
judge put the suggestion of the prosecution how the
theft happened. It was argued that although the
Crown may do that through their counsel, the judge
ought not to have taken that course. It is enough to
say that it was very proper for the judge to point out
to the jury: " Certain facts are proved; it is open to
you if you come to that conclusion to draw certain
inferences of fact which it is suggested by the Crown
you should draw." The complaint in the main was

that the judge had suggested that the postmen were bribed, and that the theft was committed by that means. There was the evidence of Quadratstein and Brandstatter with regard to the postmen, and if the jury accepted it there was undoubtedly evidence of statements made by one or other of the appellants that the postmen had been bribed. Upon that point, therefore, we see no ground of complaint.

Upon the whole, and taking into account all the points raised, we think that, on the facts, it was quite impossible to come to any other conclusion, and upon the various aspects of the law to which our attention has been directed, there is no ground of complaint open to the appellants.

I may add that in our view it is not possible to convict these four defendants both of stealing and receiving. It was, of course, open to the jury to find that one or other of the prisoners had stolen the pearls, and that one or other had received them, but they have found a verdict against the four prisoners on the two counts. It has no practical value in this case, because we are dealing with exactly the same facts with regard to which, on any finding, whether one prisoner is regarded as guilty on the first count, and another as guilty on the second, both would certainly receive the same sentence. No doubt Mr. Muir is right in saying that in substance what was intended was to find them guilty on the indictment. In form—I only call attention to it so that it may not be thought that the point has been overlooked—the conviction of all the four prisoners on the two counts is not right, but for the reasons which we have already given that has no value, and does not affect the sentences which have been pronounced upon these prisoners.

Therefore the conclusion to which we have come is that this appeal must be dismissed. As no leave to appeal was given, the sentences will run from the present date.

The report continues, and concludes, with the ominous and final words " Appeal Dismissed," and the four men were removed from court.

There is little more to add. Silverman and Gutwirth duly served their sentences, and were then deported from the country, never to return.

Lockett served his sentence, and was released in 1919. Shortly after his release he married again and took up the business of a bookmaker. He has never since been arrested for any crime, and it is to be hoped that the second " stretch " of penal servitude has damped his ardour for running counter to the law. Burglary at the age of sixty-seven is hardly becoming to one's years!

Grizard was not so fortunate. He was a sick man when he came out of prison, and the photographs taken at the time of his subsequent offence present a haggard mockery of the plump and cheerful " Cammi " of the days of yore. He received a great welcome from his cronies in the " Garden," and the more respectable of his friends urged him again to quit the paths of crime for something more in keeping with his great ability. But all in vain. The love of the game for its own sake claimed the ailing man, and three years later the prison gates were once more closed on him, only to open that he might come forth to die.

The facts of the crime were a sordid anti-climax to the famous robbery which earned him a niche in the gallery of crime. From his comfortable house in Dalston he planned with a certain Major Harrison to obtain a quantity of jewellery from a City jeweller and " smash " it on the Continent. To this end he " advanced " him money to the extent of £3,000, which the gallant but, in fact, ex-major, paid into an account in Barclay's bank. Having an excellent—that is to say, confidence-inspiring presence—he was then deputed to visit the jeweller's, Messrs. Bedford and Co., in Aldersgate Street, and purchase certain jewellery. He did so, and bought several diamonds on approval " to show them," he said, " to a Colonel friend of his who was shortly returning to India and would probably buy many more." Cheques were given against certain purchases and duly met. Confidence thus established, further diamonds were chosen and bought and cheques presented to the unsuspecting jeweller. The further consignment was worth £10,000, and included a diamond worth a thousand pounds in itself. On the day that Harrison received the diamond, and before the cheque could be dishonoured by the bank, another tool of Grizard's, Michael Spellman, tried to sell it in Hatton Garden, but in vain. Later he crossed to Antwerp with Harrison, and the two of them there sold it for £900. Unfortunately for his future freedom, Spellman returned to England, and when later arrested was found with a further consignment of the stolen jewellery. Cammi's carefulness was failing with his health, and the evidence of " receiving " the greater part of the property, so carefully concealed in the

hey-day of his genius, was this time found and subsequently proved. In August, 1922, the dying man
was arrested, and in October brought to trial at the
Central Criminal Court, this time before the Common
Serjeant, then, as now, Sir Henry Dickens, K.C.
Once more the great Sir Richard Muir, with himself
but two more years of life to run, appeared for the
prosecution, while Sir Henry Curtis-Bennett appeared
again for the defence, this time for Grizard. Spellman was defended by Cecil Whiteley, K.C., who had
previously himself been one of the Treasury Counsel
of which mention has been made in Chapter VIII.
The trial took four days, but the verdict was inevitable. " Cammi " had lost his nerve and skill, and
the verdict was his end. Both prisoners received a
sentence of twelve months' imprisonment, Grizard's
being made the lighter for his obviously broken
health. He made no attempt to appeal, and in prison
was taken straight to hospital. Before the expiration
of his sentence he was allowed to go, and was taken
home to die. He died on September 11th, 1923, and
was buried in the Jewish cemetery at Barking. Born
in 1867, he was 57 when he died, a broken, tired and
disappointed man. Two of the great protagonists in
the pearl case had preceded him to death, George
Elliott and Chief Inspector Ward, who was blown
to pieces by a bomb in an air-raid in the War. Mr.
Mayer, the owner of the necklace, Mr. Salomons, his
agent, and Sir Richard Muir, who came to be his
friend, died shortly afterwards. Yet the Learned
Judge, now Lord Trevethin, who had already
reached " the allotted span " at the time of the
famous trial, is still, at eighty-six, not only alive,

but as ardent a fisherman as twenty years ago.

And the pearls? That priceless handful of " coloured marbles " around which all the excitement once revolved? Mr. Mayer's son explained that it was broken up into three articles of jewellery a few years later and subsequently sold, a third of it in Bond Street, a third in Paris, and the remainder in New York.

So ends the story of the world's most famous necklace and of those who stole it, only to find their larceny in vain. But when the reader puts down a work of fiction, having finished it, and seeks to compare it with the story which has here been told, let him remember that the first was fiction, but that this, with all its human interest and passion, with its failures and successes and triumphant end, is true.

THE END